Expository
Parenting

Josh Niemi

DEDICATION

From the outset, this book was written
primarily for those nearest and dearest to me:
my wonderful wife Jill, my older son Carter,
my daughter Lucia, and my younger son Knox.

I am so thankful that Jesus made each of you.

CONTENTS

ACKNOWLEDGMENTS

I owe a great deal of gratitude to those whom God used in bringing about this book. My sincere thanks goes to:

My wife, Jill, who has been a source of encouragement, patience, and love not only for this book, but for all of my endeavors in life.

My friend and mentor, Pete Sammons, who has invested in me so much over the years, answering my never-ending theological questions with precision.

My friend and father-in-law, Craig Swanson, who gave me the greatest gift he could: his own daughter, discipled so well throughout childhood.

My friend and disciple, Logan Ruder, who has provided me with both a teaching outlet and a sounding board for my ideas.

My friends and editors, Greg Elsasser, who graciously worked through this book in its rawest form, Pastor Tom Zobrist, who provided thought-provoking questions to help clarify my thoughts, and Pastor Mark Dever, who generously dedicated his time and his staff to strengthen my manuscript.

You are all dearly loved and appreciated. This book is exceedingly better than it otherwise would have been thanks to your efforts.

Josh Niemi
July 2017

INTRODUCTION

Many parents remember the feelings they had immediately after the birth of their first child. They remember the joy of finally seeing the face of their new baby. They remember the excitement of showing off their new son or daughter to friends and family. They remember anticipating what the following years would bring. But many Christian parents probably remember one other feeling they had: the fear of facing the monumental task of raising their child to know the Lord.

Perhaps this fear stems from a lack of direction. Does the Bible provide us with a comprehensive plan to carry out this task? Consider, for example, that the entire book of Ephesians contains only one verse directed towards parents, which states, "Fathers, do not provoke your children to anger, but bring them up in the discipline and instruction of the Lord" (Eph. 6:4). Similarly, examine the book of Colossians and only a single passage will be found, stating, "Fathers, do not exasperate your children, so that they will not lose heart" (Col. 3:21). Some books contain brief passages of parental wisdom, but only by way of implication (for example, Hebrews 12:7-11 indirectly provides principles for discipline). Other passages, such as the book of Proverbs, are loaded with parental wisdom, but not with a specific plan for imparting it to children. Yet for such an important responsibility, one would think that entire sections of Scripture would be dedicated to the precise ins and outs of bringing a child to saving faith in Jesus Christ and spiritual maturity as a believer.

So where are these sections? Which chapter gives a detailed outline of how this is to be done? Where is the "Parenting 101" portion of the Bible? The answer is—it's not there. Why not? Because the task of parenting is actually the task of shepherding. Thus, in order to parent, you need only to know how to shepherd. And thankfully, when it comes to the task of shepherding, the Bible gives us all the principles we need.

When Jesus appeared to His disciples after His resurrection, we read of His encounter with Peter, the disciple who just days prior had denied knowing Him. Even before this denial happened, Peter was told by Jesus that it would come to pass but boldly declared that he would never do such a thing (cf. Matt. 26:34-35). Thus, when it occurred, Peter instantly remembered what he had heard from Jesus, which undoubtedly increased the shame and guilt he felt for lying about his association. Yet during the time after the resurrection, Peter found himself restored by Christ in a most memorable way. Just as Peter denied knowing Jesus three times, Jesus gave him the opportunity to repent by professing allegiance to Him three times.

John 21:15-17 tells us of the account. Jesus asked, "Simon, son of John, do you love Me more than these?" (the word *these* referring to the other disciples). Peter responded, "Yes, Lord; You know that I love You." Jesus responded by saying, "Tend My lambs." Again, Jesus asked, "Simon, son of John, do you love Me?" Again, Peter responded, "Yes Lord; You know that I love You." Jesus replied with, "Shepherd My sheep." A third time, Jesus issued the question and, for the third time, Peter responded in the affirmative. Jesus finished with a final command: "Tend My sheep." Hence, what we see is that Peter's restoration put him under the divine command to take care of God's sheep—disciples of the Lord Jesus Christ who would need to be fed and cared for under the careful watch of a shepherd.

Fast forward several decades and we see the profound impact that this personal encounter had on the Apostle Peter. Just as he was commanded by Christ to care for the flock, Peter likewise commanded church leaders to "shepherd the flock of God among you" (1 Pet. 5:2). He understood that the same charge given to him was to be carried on by others as well. The Greek verb for "shepherd" is *poimainó*, which means "to guard and direct a flock," and comes from the noun *poimén*, which means "a herdsman or shepherd." Although we don't often use the term "shepherd" to describe a church leader, we do use the Latin translation of this word — *pastor.* Thus, we understand that a pastor is ultimately one who cares for a "flock" of people. He has been entrusted with a local group of believers that he is under obligation to spiritually nurture and protect, just as a shepherd physically nurtures and protects a group of sheep.

If you are a parent, you have also been entrusted with a flock and commanded to tend the sheep. Perhaps your flock consists of only one child. Or, maybe you have been blessed with a much larger number of sheep. Regardless, the parallels between parent and pastor are numerous.

As a parent, you want to bring your child to saving faith in Christ. Likewise, a pastor's ministry is fulfilled by bringing people to saving faith in Christ (cf. 2 Tim. 4:5). As a parent, you desire to raise your child to spiritual maturity in Christ. A pastor's ministry is also intended to mature and equip the saints (cf. Eph. 4:11-12). As a parent, you want to protect your children from influences that would negatively impact them. So, too, is the job of a pastor to protect his flock from wolves (cf. Acts 20:28-29).

In fact, the two roles have so much overlap that even to be qualified for the office of pastor, a potential candidate must first demonstrate that he can faithfully manage his own household (cf. 1 Tim. 3:4, Titus 1:6). Is a man to be entrusted with much? He must first demonstrate his trustworthiness with little. Thus, the home is a school of sanctification from which a man must graduate if he is to be considered for the pastorate.

In many ways, the only difference between the pastor's flock and the parent's flock is that of quantity. Therefore, to know how to raise our children we ought to determine how to care for a flock; and to know how to care for a flock, we need to think like a pastor.

The Apostle Paul wrote letters to Timothy and Titus, teaching them how to carry out their ministry, and for that reason these are commonly referred to as the "pastoral epistles." But the worst thing we could do would be to write off these portions of Scripture as only relevant for church leaders. Instead, as parents we must also begin to view these as *parental* epistles. A better understanding of biblical pastoring gives us a better understanding of biblical parenting; know how to lead a church and you will know how to lead a family.

One epistle in particular provides us with a comprehensive overview of shepherding a flock: Second Timothy. This incredible letter was written by the Apostle Paul in order to bolster his disciple Timothy's confidence in the Word of God and it continues to bolster the confidence of faithful believers throughout the generations. It stands as Paul's final marching orders to his young disciple, just prior to his death. It was written to prepare Timothy for pastoral ministry in Paul's absence, and the overarching message is clear: carry on the faith by devoting yourself entirely to the ministry of the Word of God—*feed Christ's sheep.*

While this message was written to Pastor Timothy, the reality is that pastors are to serve as examples—making their ministries the template that we all must follow in whatever capacity we minister (cf. 1 Tim. 4:12, Phil. 3:17, Titus 2:7). Thus, as a parent, you must devote yourself to the ministry of the Word in the lives of your children as a pastor would his congregation. Much ink has been spilled to remind parents of their responsibility to raise up their children in the fear and admonition of the Lord. But how? How exactly is this discipleship to be carried out? We must first examine the Bible's instructions for pastors, and then use that wisdom in the home. Unpacking the book of Second Timothy equips us in tremendous ways for this task.

1

FOOD FOR THE FLOCK

"The most important doctrine that you will ever hold is your conviction that the Bible is the Word of God. If you don't believe that, you'll never be able to motivate yourself to the discipline of exacting out of that Scripture what it teaches."[1]

–John MacArthur

Focus Text: *All Scripture is inspired by God and profitable for teaching, for reproof, for correction, for training in righteousness; so that the man of God may be adequate, equipped for every good work. (2 Timothy 3:16-17)*

As the Apostle Paul sat in the dungeon of the Mamertine Prison in Rome, he wrote a second letter to his disciple Timothy. Years prior, Timothy had traveled with Paul around much of the first-century Roman Empire, learning the teachings of the New Covenant, preaching the Gospel, and establishing churches alongside his mentor. But by the time of this particular letter, Paul's life was coming to a close.

Paul understood that the Christian life was one of persecution, even going so far as to teach that the Kingdom of God was entered through "many tribulations" (cf. Acts 14:22). He was experiencing that

---

[1] John MacArthur, "Consequences of Non-Expository Preaching, Part I," *PM 501: Fundamentals of Expository Preaching*, The Master's Seminary Theological Resource Center, accessed August 19, 2016, http://www.theologicalresources.org/the-masters-seminary/24-fundamentals-of-expository-preaching.

reality for the final time. Imprisoned as an enemy of Rome, he knew that his life was coming to a close and determined to use his final moments to reach out to his son in the faith, Timothy, who had become a pastor of a local church.

Like Paul, Timothy was well acquainted with the difficulties of the Christian life, experiencing them from outside the church (in the form of Roman persecution) and inside the church (in the form of spiritual opposition). As a pastor, the stress of his Christian life only compounded his natural instinct to shrink back from his duties, cave in to the pressures of life, and abandon the proverbial ship of the ministry in order to avoid conflict with others. By the time of Paul's letter, the fear of man had begun to make inroads into Timothy's heart and mind, and if left unaddressed, could lead to spiritual compromise.

And can we blame him? As Christians, we know that the Gospel is foolishness to the world (cf. 1 Cor. 1:18). We know that scoffers mock the reality of coming judgment (cf. 2 Pet. 3:3). And we know that the message of the cross is offensive to unbelievers (cf. Gal. 5:11). Thus, to live in a world that hates Christ, and speak the truth of the Bible with clarity and courage, will inevitably bring heartache and discomfort to our lives. Conversely, to downplay the teachings of Scripture and ignore the aspects of the Bible that others (including those within the church) deem offensive will inevitably make our lives here easier and more pleasant.

Each day, we are faced with a decision: will we stand and speak on the claims of the Bible, or will we deviate as it becomes expedient for our own well-being? That same dilemma faced Timothy. Thus, to encourage and strengthen Timothy, the Apostle Paul authored the highly motivating letter we know as Second Timothy.

However, with Timothy soon to be left on his own, Paul also knew that he needed more than just motivation; he needed instruction.

Timothy needed his mind re-focused on the duties necessary for fulfilling The Great Commission. Sure, Timothy knew that his job as a believer, and even more so as a pastor, was to make disciples. But pursuing that task according to his own contrived methodology (or worse, abandoning his duties altogether) would spell disaster for the spiritual health of those under his care. That same danger faces us in the way we raise our kids. In anticipation of this, Paul's letter represents divine wisdom for the biblical approach to ministry, providing us with insight not only for pastors and their congregations, but also for parents and their children.

The climax of the letter appears in the final chapter, in which the Apostle Paul issued a string of commands in order to make Timothy's duties crystal-clear. He told Timothy to "preach the Word," "endure hardship," and "fulfill your ministry," among other instructions (cf. 2 Tim. 4:2-5). But just prior to reaching this climactic catalogue of imperatives, he provided Timothy with a critically important description of Scripture. Why did he do this? Because he knew that Timothy's perspective of God's Word would be the driving force dictating whether or not Timothy faithfully carried out his duties.

The same holds true today. When a pastor has the right view of Scripture, he will deliver it accordingly. Likewise, when parents understand the true nature of God's Word, they will have a singular devotion to discipling their children accordingly. Thus, in order to understand how to lead our children, we need the same reminder that Timothy needed. Our approach to discipleship is a product of our view of the Bible. Thus, we consider Paul's testimony of Scripture:

All Scripture is inspired by God and profitable for teaching, for reproof, for correction, for training in righteousness; so that the man of God may be adequate, equipped for every good work. (2 Timothy 3:16-17)

Although there are a seemingly infinite number of characteristics that could be extracted from this passage, five in particular can be highlighted to demonstrate the Bible's perfection as the only necessary food for your flock: the Word of God is *authoritative, trustworthy, effective, clear, and sufficient.*

God's Word Is Authoritative

The first detail provided in this passage is that all Scripture is "inspired by God." It's significant that Paul highlighted this from the outset because it is the source of Scripture that lends itself to the authority of Scripture, and the authority of Scripture must be the first thing that we as parents affirm.

Consider this: the authority of words comes from the authority of the one who spoke them. For example, if my neighbor said to me, "Put your hands behind your head," I'd likely not comply with his command. But if an on-duty police officer said, "Put your hands behind your head," I would submit immediately. Same command, different response. Why? Because the source of each command carries a different level of authority. I would recognize that words spoken by an officer carry a greater degree of force than words spoken by my neighbor. The officer's words carry with them the weight of local, state, or federal law.

When Paul told Timothy that all Scripture is "inspired by God" he used the Greek word *theopneustos,* which is a compound adjective formed from the words *theos* (meaning "God") and *pnéō* (meaning "to breathe out").[2] Paul's point was that all of Scripture, whether written by the prophets of the Old Testament or the apostles of the New

---

[2] Frederick W. Danker, Walter Bauer, and William F. Arndt, *A Greek-English Lexicon of the New Testament and Other Early Christian Literature, 3rd ed.* (Chicago: University of Chicago Press, 2000), 449.

Testament, is actually "breathed out by God" (coming from His innermost being). Why is this important? Because this means that rather than carrying the authority of the men who wrote the words, Scripture actually carries the authority of God Himself.

No, God did not drop a 66-book Bible straight out of the sky. No, God did not cause words to miraculously appear on the pages of scrolls. No, God did not induce men into mystical trances to record His words. God used the personalities, temperaments, and backgrounds of each of the human authors in order to deliver His Word as He intended. Yet, the words themselves are not of human origin (cf. 2 Pet. 1:21). If they were, they'd simply carry the same level of authority as any other human—just like my neighbor trying to arrest me. Instead, these words are inspired by God Himself, which means they carry *His* authority.

The first letter to the Thessalonians provides us with an excellent example of this. When Paul ministered to these believers, not only did they receive his message with joy, but they also grew in their faith so much that their godly example became an influence on believers in other cities (cf. 1 Thess. 1:6-7). Yet, Paul admitted that his preaching to them was not performed with words of eloquent speech or flattery; his ministry was not flashy or impressive (cf. 1 Thess. 2:5). How then were the Thessalonians influenced to such an extent that they turned "to God from idols to serve a living and true God" (1 Thess. 1:9)? What was so compelling about Paul's preaching that they submitted to his message, abandoned the very idols which were a part of their cultural identity, and radically changed the direction of their lives? It was because, as Paul explained, they did not accept his testimony as the word of man, but instead received it for what it actually was—*the Word of God* (cf. 1 Thess. 2:13).

The Thessalonians understood that the message they heard from

Paul was a divine command to which they needed to submit. Had the message consisted of Paul's own ideas, there would have been little reason for the Thessalonians to take interest. A message of human origin would have been inconsequential at best. But, by God's grace, the believers in Thessalonica recognized that what they heard was from their Creator in Heaven. The Word of God, preached by Paul, exercised God's authority in their hearts and minds.

Consider this reality when it comes to modern preaching. It seems there is no shortage of personal opinions that come from the pulpit in many churches. Setting aside the Bible, many pastors are happy to serve up their own philosophical insight into theological issues, current events, and cultural discussions. Some have no qualms with developing their own "How-to" and "Top Ten" instructions for the life of their hearers. But just like my neighbor attempting to arrest me, there is an inherent problem—this kind of instruction lacks authority.

Certainly, pastors are leaders of their congregations; they are the ones who hold others accountable, lead in the administration of discipline when necessary, and safeguard the church (cf. Heb. 13:17, 1 Pet. 5:2). But in terms of binding the consciences of their hearers, pastors have no authority outside of the Word of God. Their spiritual jurisdiction begins and ends where Scripture's begins and ends. Thus, they wield a greater amount of legitimate influence to the degree that their instructions conform to God's.

What does this mean for you as a parent? One of the most common questions asked by children, especially at a young age, is, "Why do I have to obey you?" Likewise, whether stated or merely implied, one of the most common answers is, "My house, my rules. Once you are an adult and live on your own you can do whatever you want." While there is a slight hint of truth to that answer, the reality is that it is an insufficient and unbiblical answer overall. Why? Because once your kids become adults they *can't* do whatever they want—they will always be under the authority of God. Thus, your goal as a parent ultimately isn't to bind your children to your own rules; your job is to teach them to be under the authority of God's rules. Commands that come by your own authority are transient and passing, but commands that come by the authority of God are fixed and eternal.

Sure, while your kids live with you they are, in a sense, serving God by proxy. Their submission to God is rendered to Him via their submission to you. Colossians 3:20 states, "Children, be obedient to your parents in all things, for this is well-pleasing *to the Lord*." This passage reminds us that your children glorify God through their obedience to you as a parent. But once they grow up, move out, and have families of their own this is no longer the case (cf. Gen. 2:24). Therefore, if the only authority they have ever known is the authority that you as a parent possess, that sends the message that once they are no longer under your authority, they are without authority altogether.

Sure, you ought to give them counsel and insight to prepare for adulthood. Yes, you are an authoritative figure in their lives. Of course, they must submit to your commands. But the most important authority you can convey to your children is not your own authority over their lives, but *God's* authority over their lives. Therefore, it is essential that you direct their attention to the Bible such that they receive it like the Thessalonians: not as the word of man, but as it really is—the authoritative Word of God.

God's Word Is Trustworthy

A second characteristic inherent to the Bible is its trustworthiness. Again, because the Bible is the very "breath" of God, inspired by Him, it reflects His nature.[3] God is immutable, meaning He does not change (cf. Mal. 3:6, Heb. 13:8); His nature and attributes are eternal. Since God was sovereign yesterday, you can know that He is still sovereign today—Psalm 66:7 says, "He rules by His might *forever*." If God chooses to set His redemptive love upon a man, that man can know that God will always love him—Psalm 136:1 says, "Give thanks to the Lord, for He is good, for His lovingkindness is *everlasting*." Since God was righteous in eternity past, then He will be righteous in eternity future—Psalm 111:3 says, "Splendid and majestic is His work, And His righteousness endures *forever*." This ought to be of great comfort to us because it means He is *always* dependable (which is a redundant way of putting it!). God's immutability provides us with confidence that we can always rely on Him to be who He has always been.

When it comes to God's Word, we must affirm that same level of reliability—Psalm 119:89 says, "Forever, O Lord, Your word is *settled* in heaven." Unlike the word of a politician which morphs based on public opinion, or that of a salesman which may advertise unfulfillable promises, God's Word is a product of His divine character which means it is established, consistent, and ultimately more trustworthy than anything else in the world.

The Apostle Peter attested to this reliability in one of the most profound ways recorded in the Bible. In his second letter, he set out to warn believers of false teachers who would try to deceive them (cf. 2 Pet. 1:12-15). These false teachers would try to convince believers that Christ was not going to return to judge the world, meaning that no one needed to worry about living in holiness—such was their warped rationale. In response to this, Peter reminded his hearers that he had

---

[3] John MacArthur and Richard Mayhue, eds., *Biblical Doctrine: A Systematic Summary of Bible Truth* (Wheaton, IL: Crossway 2017), 70.

already been given a vision of Christ in His coming glory (cf. Matt. 16:27-17:2). He knew the Second Coming was certain because he saw its future reality with his own eyes.

But the Apostle Peter didn't rely on his own eyewitness account as his defense of Christ's second coming. Instead, right after referring to the Transfiguration experience that he had with Jesus, Peter went on to say, "So we have the prophetic word made more sure, to which you do well to pay attention to" (cf. 2 Pet. 1:19). The "prophetic word" is a reference to the Old Testament Scriptures, which Peter cited as a reminder that even the Old Testament taught about the Second Coming. In other words, Peter was telling his hearers that they had something that was even *more sure* than the supernatural experience he had. Although Peter's firsthand account of the Transfiguration was a reliable testimony that Jesus would indeed return again, he actually said that the Old Testament Scriptures were more reliable than his own experience!

Today, we have that exact same source of reliable information. And with a similar abundance of false teachers, false prophets, false gospels, false brothers, false churches, false teachings, and false movements, we need it. After all, whom can we trust? How can we separate truth from error?

Like Peter, we must confess that our own experiences don't hold the highest level of trustworthiness. The fact that we are created beings means that our experiences are subject to creaturely limitations. Let's face it: God does not sleep (cf. Psa. 121:4), need food (cf. Psa. 50:12-13), nor find anything too difficult (cf. Jer. 32:27). Yet for us, all it takes is a bad night's sleep, a poor diet, or a trial in life, and suddenly our own human wisdom is negatively impacted. Our energy level, emotions, and experiences in life have the ability to radically alter how we think and feel. As a consequence, then, our words are not always dependable. But God has no such restrictions (cf. Psa. 147:5). Therefore, neither does His Word.

Do we parent our children with this understanding? Often not. One of the common temptations we face is to rely on our own human wisdom and experiences in raising our children. Those who grew up in a fairly good home may simply parent their children the same way because that's how they were raised and after all, they "turned out ok." On the other hand, those who grew up in a bad home environment may be so fixated on past hurts that their sole parenting goal is to avoid repeating those same mistakes. Whatever the case may be, the common element is that parenting philosophies are often based on past experiences.

But the testimony of the Apostle Peter indicates that even if we experience something that may prove to be helpful, there is something better upon which we ought to rely—God's Word. Try as we might, we do not always offer the right advice to our children. We may possess a certain amount of earthly wisdom by virtue of our age, but as fallen people, our knowledge has limitations. Human wisdom is unpredictable. Parental advice may be subject to change. But we have a book that is unimpaired; a book that is *more sure*. God's Word is trustworthy and we would do well to pay attention to it.

God's Word Is Effective

In Isaiah 55:10-11, the prophet compared God's Word to rain which falls from the sky and waters the ground before evaporating back up into the clouds. Isaiah went on to say that just as rain accomplishes its purposes before returning to the sky, so too does God's Word accomplish all that God intends; it does not return to Him void. When God exhales His Word, He inhales results.

And what exactly does God's Word accomplish? The Apostle Paul provided the answer in 2 Timothy 3:16 as he described Scripture's purpose: "...for teaching, for reproof, for correction, for training in righteousness." Although these four concepts refer to distinct acts, they are intricately related. "Teaching" refers to communicating biblical truth, which includes defining right and wrong thoughts and behaviors. "Reproof" refers to exposing sinful thoughts and behaviors based on biblical truth. "Correction" refers to providing the biblical solution to particular sins. And "training in righteousness" carries the idea of general instruction for a lifestyle of holiness.

In considering these functions of Scripture, we immediately ought to recognize that the Apostle Paul gave no caveats or contingencies. He did not say that Scripture could perform these tasks *if a certain condition was met*. There was nothing Timothy had to contribute in order to somehow "activate" the power of the Word. Instead, it was fully capable on its own. The Scriptures, in and of themselves, are able to reach the depths of a man and perform the necessary conviction and correction.

Just how adequate is Scripture though? Is it truly able to accomplish these things on its own? After all, many modern perspectives would tell us that in order for the Bible to be effective in the life of a person, it needs to be supplemented with something such as a personal relationship or a good deed. A common refrain is that "people don't care what you know until they know that you care." Others would go so far as to say the Bible needs to be made "relevant" to people's lives—as if to say it is irrelevant until it has been adapted to a particular demographic.

But Hebrews 4:12 stands in contrast to those perspectives, stating, "For the word of God is alive and active. Sharper than any double-edged sword, it penetrates even to dividing soul and spirit, joints and marrow; it judges the thoughts and attitudes of the heart." By this passage, we know that God's Word has life in itself. It is active (based on the Greek word *energés,* which means "powerful" and "capable").[4] It effectively cuts deep within a person to the point that it can distinguish between the indistinguishable (soul and spirit).

In fact, as a two-sided blade, the Word does not need to be turned over or reoriented in order to make additional cuts. It has no dull side. Swing the Bible in one direction and Genesis will make an incision in the hearer's conscience; swing it back the other direction and Revelation will slice open the hidden thought life of a man. The Bible has no blunt edges and makes no bad cuts. In short, it absolutely does accomplish its intended purpose. Timothy simply needed the reminder from Paul that God's Word would do the work for him.

On the other hand, those who try to augment the power of God's Word functionally deny the Bible's inherent capability. Strobe lights, dunk tanks, and confetti make for a great birthday party, but they contribute nothing to the effectiveness of God's Word in convicting a youth group of sin. Child psychology may be able to probe the thought patterns of a troubled soul, but a thousand years in the therapist's chair cannot accomplish what God's Word does in a moment. Bribes and incentives may outwardly motivate your daughter's conduct, but only God's Word can conform her inner self to genuine Christlikeness. Like Timothy, it's vitally important that we understand the inherent effectiveness of Scripture in performing the work of teaching, reproof, correction, and training our flocks in righteousness.

God's Word Is Clear

Unfortunately, another perspective that seems to plague many

---

[4] Frederick W. Danker, Walter Bauer, and William F. Arndt, *A Greek-English Lexicon of the New Testament and Other Early Christian Literature, 3rd ed.* (Chicago: University of Chicago Press, 2000), 335.

within the church is that some parts of the Bible are actually unknowable and therefore subject to each individual's interpretation. A common misunderstanding, whether intentionally or unintentionally, is that there is an underlying "mystery" associated with God's Word that renders the exact truths of some passages undiscernible. But that idea runs contrary to the very nature of the Bible itself. The Bible is God's revelation to mankind, and revelation is (by definition) that which is revealed or disclosed. Thus, to say that God's revelation is unknowable is a self-contradiction.

Instead, Paul told Timothy that all Scripture is "profitable," meaning that it is beneficial, advantageous, and useful. This necessarily means that Scripture must also be knowable—after all, you can't use what you don't know. Thus, another conviction that we must hold to is that God's Word truly is clear in what it means.

The biblical authors affirm the clarity of Scripture as well. Consider, for example, the words of the Apostle John at the end of his first epistle: "These things I have written to you who believe in the name of the Son of God, so that you may *know* that you have eternal life" (1 John 5:13). John believed that what he had written was clear enough to be used in evaluating whether or not someone is genuinely saved. Or, consider the words of the Psalmist: "Your word is a lamp to my feet and a light to my path" (Psalm 119:105). In this well-known verse, he affirmed that God's Word sheds illuminating insight into the darkened situations we face, giving us clarity to walk in a God-honoring way. To claim that some passages of the Bible are hopelessly unknowable is to assault the clarity of Scripture. It is to portray the high-beam spotlight of God's Word as little more than a broken flashlight.

Of course this is not to say that understanding the Bible is effortless. Sure, certain parts of Scripture are more difficult for us to comprehend (cf. 2 Pet. 3:16). Some passages inevitably require a greater amount of work in order to interpret properly. Yet, any difficulty that we have in grasping the Bible is due to the frailty of our own minds, not the clarity of God's Word. The New Testament authors intended for us to know what they were writing and the Old Testament saints rejoiced in the clarity of what had been written. Rest assured that the Bible is clear enough for you to understand and explain to your disciples (cf. Psa. 78:1-6).

God's Word Is Sufficient

Last, but by no means least, the Apostle Paul told Timothy that Scripture makes the man of God "adequate, equipped for every good work." The significance of this simply cannot be overstated. As believers, we understand that God's plan for us not only includes our salvation, but also the carrying out of good works He has planned for us (cf. Eph. 2:10). Since we have been purchased by the precious blood of Christ, our lives are not our own. Instead, our lives must be offered back to God in thankful service, and one of the primary means of this is through our faith-based good works (cf. Titus 2:14).

But how do we know what constitutes a "good work?" After all, if it were left up to every individual believer to decide how to glorify God that would be a recipe for disaster. Rather than leaving Timothy to do what seemed right in his own eyes, Paul reminded him that God's answers to all of life's difficulties are comprehensively given in the Bible. Through knowledge of Scripture, we can identify how to carry out *every* good work in life.

This necessarily implies that Scripture will first assist us in identifying what those good works are. At times, the Bible explicitly states what is expected of every believer. At other times, the Bible provides the principles by which we can come to conclusions. Either way, we have not been left alone to determine what good works look like in the life of a Christian.

Once we identify these good works, where can we learn how to carry them out? Paul stated that Scripture *equips* the man of God. The more we study the Word, the more we not only understand what God-honoring works are, but the more we also learn how to accomplish them. Again, in some cases the Bible explicitly lays out steps for us to follow in order to carry out a particular task. The four-step plan for church discipline found in Matthew 18:15-17 serves as a fine example of this. Such a direct command requires only our humble obedience.

In other cases, the Bible's plan for our lives may require a more systematic combination of principles. Either way, God's Word does the equipping. And this point must also be highlighted—the Greek verb Paul used for "equipped" in 2 Timothy 3:17 is in the passive voice, indicating that the Bible does the equipping and the believer is simply the recipient of this incredible work![5] Paul wanted Timothy to be reminded full well that as a man of God, the Scriptures would do the work of guiding his hands and feet.

With that in mind, imagine if you came across a superfood that contained a comprehensive array of nutritional content that met every one of your body's health needs. Imagine this food possessed all of the protein, carbohydrates, fats, fiber, vitamins, and minerals that you needed—in the exact amounts and proportions perfect for your health. Upon consuming it, your hunger was satiated, your energy levels were elevated, and your general well-being was improved. Such is the Word of God for the spiritual health of His people!

Make no mistake about it: God's Word truly can equip your child

---

[5] George W. Knight, III, *The Pastoral Epistles: A Commentary on the Greek Text,* The New International Greek Commentary (Grand Rapids, MI: W.B. Eerdmans, 1992), 450.

for *every* good work. Finding a spouse, serving in a local church, handling finances, looking for a job, showing hospitality, interacting with the government, counseling a friend, evangelizing the lost, educating children, praying for others, choosing recreational endeavors, handling persecution, and most importantly, being saved from sin and reconciled to God through Jesus Christ, are all areas of life for which the Bible has a comprehensive set of principles. Let that sink in for a moment.

When God's Word is implanted in the hearts and minds of His people, Paul said they become "adequate" to carry out good works. Don't let this English word soften the true meaning—the Greek word is *artios*, translated in some versions as "perfect" or "complete." Coming from the root word *arti* which means "now," the word *artios* carries the idea of making a person ready to perform a task *now*.[6]

The one who submits to Scripture will find that it immediately prepares him for life. That is not to say that long-term study is unnecessary, or that a surface-level reading instantly makes for a mature believer, but it is to say that once a biblical principle is properly and thoroughly understood, there is no further spiritual enlightenment or advancement needed. We can rest assured that if God has planned good works for us to perform in this lifetime (which He has), then we wouldn't have to come to the end of our lives before possessing the spiritual ability to perform them—at that point it would be too late. Instead, the believer who invests himself in God's Word becomes adequate, ready to live a God-glorifying life *now*.

Paul wanted Timothy to be committed to the reality that everything he would need to know for godly living and ministry could

---

[6] Warren C. Trenchard, *Complete Vocabulary Guide to the Greek New Testament* (Grand Rapids, MI: Zondervan Publishing House, 1998), 16.

be derived from Scripture. With Paul's death imminent, Timothy needed to understand that he would lack nothing once his mentor was gone.

The same is true today. Everything a pastor needs for life and godliness is found in Scripture. By extension, everything *anyone* needs for life and godliness is found in Scripture. When it comes to us as parents, our greatest desire is to prepare our children for the life they will lead once they leave our homes. We want our kids to be equipped for life without us, just as Paul wanted Timothy to be equipped for life without him. In preparation, many parents exhaust themselves trying to implement every latest parenting trick in an effort to provide their children with what they think will be needed. Others fret and worry that they may have overlooked something in the raising of their children. But the wise parent finds rest in a single source, a sufficient "superfood" that has it all—the Bible. It has everything your child needs for life and godliness, now and into adulthood.

Jesus, Paul, Timothy, and You

In order for Timothy to carry out a biblical ministry, the Apostle Paul had to make sure that his disciple had a firm understanding of these characteristics of God's Word. It was vitally important for his spiritual health as well as the spiritual health of those to whom he would minister. But where did *Paul* get such a perspective of the Word? Surely he was not born with it. Nor was he raised with it. On the contrary, growing up as a zealous Pharisee, Paul actually had a *wrong* perspective of the Word—misusing it, supplementing it, and even setting it aside in favor of rabbinic tradition (cf. Gal. 1:14, Mark 7:8-9).

Ultimately, he was taught the supremacy of the Scriptures by the one who discipled him—none other than the Lord Jesus Christ (cf. Gal.

1:16). While Paul was traveling on the road to Damascus, intending to persecute Christians, he was accosted by Christ and taught the Gospel message directly from Him. In a moment, Paul was converted and his heart was reoriented to properly understand the inspired Word of God—the same understanding of Scripture that Jesus had.

During His earthly ministry, Jesus demonstrated a firm commitment to the authority of Scripture. Surely, as the Son of God, Jesus could have spent His entire time preaching by His own authority. And at times He certainly did invoke His own divine authority while teaching the crowds (cf. Matt. 5:21-22). He had no problem telling the crowds, "I say to you..." and then issuing a non-negotiable command.

Yet at other times, He would say, "It is written..." and then reiterate an equally-binding command from the Old Testament. In fact, the Bible records twenty occasions in which He deferred to the Scriptures this way.[7] In doing so, not only did Christ affirm the authority of God's Word, but the trustworthiness of what had been written centuries prior.

It can also be seen that Jesus affirmed the clarity of Scripture. During a conversation with the Pharisee Nicodemus, Jesus explained the need to be born again in order to see the Kingdom of Heaven (cf. John 3:3). Nicodemus, clearly puzzled by what he thought meant re-entering his mother's womb, said to Jesus, "How can these things be?" Consider the implications of Jesus' response: "Are you the teacher of Israel and do not understand these things?" Rather than comforting Nicodemus at a time of confusion, Jesus indicted him for not understanding what should have been plain as day (especially to someone in a position of teaching authority). He exposed the fact that

---

[7] Mike Abendroth, *Jesus Christ: The Prince of Preachers: Learning from the Teaching Ministry of Jesus* (Leominster, England: Day One Publications, 2008), 38.

Nicodemus should have already understood Scripture's teaching concerning the new birth. But such a charge would have been unwarranted if the Old Testament Scriptures were vague and undiscernible. How could Nicodemus have understood the concept of being born again if the Old Testament was cryptic and veiled?

Finally, Jesus put the effectiveness and sufficiency of Scripture on display during His time of trial with Satan in the wilderness (cf. Matt. 4:1-11). Three times Satan tried to tempt Jesus and three times Jesus appealed to the Scriptures. Knowing the physical state Jesus was in, the first thing Satan did was try to capitalize on Jesus' malnourishment by tempting Him to work a miracle for food. After this, Satan tried to convince Him to test God. Finally, he tried to convince Christ to worship him. Each time, Jesus rebuked Satan with Scripture, and in the end, Satan fled. Jesus didn't need a clever strategy for withstanding Satan. He didn't seek out a pragmatic approach for enduring His trial. And He didn't need to utilize His own supernatural ability to provide for His hunger. He simply unleashed the Word of God—and *only* the Word of God. It was effective and it was sufficient.

In fact, if you were to ask Jesus about His view of God's Word, here's what He would tell you: it is the strongest medicine (cf. Psa. 119:25), greatest comfort (cf. Psa. 119:52), highest delight (cf. Psa. 119:70), richest treasure (cf. Psa. 119:72), timeliest message (cf. Psa. 119:89), wisest counsel (cf. Psa. 119:100), sweetest food (cf. Psa. 119:103), brightest light (cf. Psa. 119:105), safest refuge (cf. Psa. 119:114), healthiest nourishment (cf. Psa. 119:116), fiercest warning (cf. Psa. 119:120), purest instruction (cf. Psa. 119:140), truest statement (cf. Psa. 119:142), surest promise (cf. Psa. 119:147), and kindest aid (cf. Psa. 119:173)!

Jesus knew that man lives by *every word* that proceeds out of the mouth of God, and He taught Paul this perspective (cf. Matt. 4:4, John

8:28). Paul knew that *all* Scripture is inspired by God to equip us for good works, and he taught Timothy this perspective (cf. 2 Tim. 3:16, Acts 20:20). Ultimately, Timothy's job was to pass on this same perspective to his disciples.

So what about you? Do you view Scripture like these men? The evidence of your conviction must be more than a head nodded in agreement; it must be a life lived out in action. Recognizing these characteristics of the Bible is absolutely foundational to your role as a Christian parent. You must have this high view of Scripture if you are to shepherd your children biblically.

On the other hand, if you reject these characteristics of the Bible, your journey unfortunately ends here. If you do not believe the Bible is truly authoritative, then you can find a myriad of other non-authoritative books from which to teach your children. If you do not believe the Bible is trustworthy, then the options of equally untrustworthy texts are endless. If you do not believe the Bible is effective, there are plenty of other ineffective resources to implement. If you do not believe the Bible is clear, you have the opportunity to rely on many other unclear sources. And if you do not believe the Bible is sufficient, your local bookstore would be happy to help you select another insufficient title.

Ultimately, Paul made such a theologically-loaded statement because he knew that a proper perspective of God's Word would lead to a proper ministry of God's Word. Once a shepherd is aware of the best food for his flock, he will do everything in his power to provide it. A lofty view of the Bible must precede the lofty task of discipleship.

At this point, simply think through the implications: *all* Scripture is inspired by God and bears authority over your child's life, *all* Scripture is profitable for your child's instruction, and *all* of Scripture will prepare him or her for everything in life. So how much of the Bible does your child need to learn? *All of it.* Not just *parts* of God's Word. Not just *some* of God's Word. Not even *most* of God's Word. Christian discipleship requires *all* Scripture—no verse left behind, no passage neglected. But before the implications of this fall on us as parents, we must first consider what this means for pastors. Thus, after such an exalted statement of God's Word, what was the very next thing that Paul commanded Timothy to do? Preach it.

2

THE DIVINE MANDATE

"At its core, discipling is teaching. We teach with words. We teach all the words that Jesus taught his disciples, and all the words of the Bible. Corporately, this is why my own church preaches expositionally and consecutively through books of the Bible, alternating between the Old and New Testaments, as well as between big chunks of Scripture and little ones."[8]

–Mark Dever

Focus Text: *I solemnly charge you in the presence of God and of Christ Jesus, who is to judge the living and the dead, and by His appearing and His kingdom: preach the word; be ready in season and out of season; reprove, rebuke, exhort, with great patience and instruction. (2 Timothy 4:1-2)*

Imagine if you took the time to draft an important letter to someone you cared for dearly, giving attention to every detail, phrase, and word to make sure the letter represented your thoughts with absolute precision. Then imagine that you entrusted the letter to a messenger to deliver it to the recipient on your behalf, but before the letter arrived at its destination the messenger decided that he would adjust, rephrase, modify, edit, shorten, lengthen, and summarize parts of your letter in order to present it the way he thinks it ought to be presented. How would you feel? What would your response be?

---

[8] Mark Dever, *Discipling: How to Help Others Follow Jesus* (Wheaton, IL: Crossway, 2016), 38.

Even if the messenger had the best of intentions, you would probably not appreciate him taking such liberties with your personal note, nor would you likely ever trust such a person with future letters. You would recognize that the messenger overstepped his bounds, made a judgment call on something for which he was not authorized, and, in effect, determined that the content and structure of your letter were inadequate and needed improvement.

Does a scenario like this ever happen in real life? It sure does—every Sunday morning. Rather than simply delivering the message of the Bible in the manner that God wrote it to His people (line by line and book by book), many pastors unilaterally decide to repackage various parts of the Bible according to their choosing. Even with the best of intentions, this type of preaching (most often what we would call *topical preaching,* among other forms) does not accurately deliver the message as it was constructed by the biblical authors; it uses a verse or selection of verses to say what the preacher wants to say, rather than leaving the verses in their original context to say what the original author wanted to say. This would be the equivalent of a messenger opening up your letter, cutting out various parts of it, and delivering it to your loved ones in an altered form.

On the other hand, pastors who preach through books of the Bible verse by verse, simply reading the text in context, explaining the meaning of the author's words, and urging the hearers to respond to what has been written, are performing what would be called *expository preaching.* This would be the equivalent of a messenger delivering your letter intact and unmodified. Why do we as parents need to consider these distinctions for preaching methodology? Because as we determine how to shepherd our flocks in the home it is critical that we first recognize how a faithful pastor shepherds his flock in the church.

What Is Expository Preaching?

To begin with, we need a more robust definition of "expository preaching." Like almost anything, if you were to ask ten different people for an exact definition, you are likely to get ten different answers. But despite the various nuances that each person might include, the one central theme you would find is this: *expository preaching sets forth the content and meaning of the Bible according to the manner and purpose with which the authors originally wrote it.*

The root of the word expository is "expose," thus expository preaching is preaching that *exposes* the meaning of Scripture. Expository preaching respects the original wording, context, and sequence of an author's writing and simply looks to shed light on (expose) a passage's meaning based on its context. Simply put, if you were to explain what a verse means by what it says, applying the implications of the verse to your hearers, you would be performing the task of expository preaching (also known as *biblical exposition*). The one who performs the task of expository preaching would therefore be called an *expositor*. The hallmark characteristic of any expositor is that he endeavors to act only as a mouthpiece for God, a mailman who delivers the mail precisely as he received it, saying what God has said in the way God has said it. [9]

Fundamentally, expository preaching on a given Sunday would simply entail teaching through a single passage of Scripture, ranging from just one verse to perhaps paragraphs of verses. Over the course of multiple Sundays, then, an expositor leads his congregation through successive sets of verses in the particular book of the Bible that is being taught. Each Sunday, the expositor picks up where he left off the

---

[9] John MacArthur, "Messengers or Manipulators?, " *GTY Resources: Questions*, Grace to You, accessed August 19, 2016, https://www.gty.org/library/questions/QA192/messengers-or-manipulators.

previous Sunday. This practice of preaching in consecutive order would therefore be called *consecutive expository preaching* (also known as *sequential exposition*). Once a book of the Bible has been taught sequentially in its entirety, the expositor then simply begins the following Sunday in the first verse of another book of the Bible.

When it comes to sequential exposition, the distinguishing factor that makes it stand out from any other kind of preaching is that the Bible, not the preacher, determines what is taught each Sunday; the Scripture passage used for each sermon is simply a continuation of the passage that preceded it (just as the Holy Spirit wrote it).

It's also helpful to define expository preaching by contrasting it with forms of non-expository preaching, such as topical preaching (in which a passage of Scripture is used to support a topic or principle of the preacher's choice). Rather than simply explaining what the text means by what it says, non-expository preaching often *imposes* meaning onto the text. In topical preaching, for example, a preacher pre-determines what he would like to teach and then searches through the Bible to piece together passages in order to bolster his selected topic. Thus, like an overly-ambitious messenger, he has taken unauthorized and unwarranted liberty in repackaging the message.

To demonstrate the differences in these two forms of preaching, consider the preaching ministries of two hypothetical churches. The first church decides to do a topical sermon series entitled "How To Have a Better Marriage" and offers principles for establishing joy and peace in marriage based on various passages such as Colossians 3:18-19, 1 Peter 3:1-7, and 1 Corinthians 13:1-3. Meanwhile, the second church begins a sermon series entitled "Ephesians," starting at Ephesians 1:1 the first week. Sunday after Sunday, the series for the first church jumps around to various passages selected by the pastor and ends whenever the pastor has decided that he has taught enough about having a better marriage. The series for the second church continues verse by verse each Sunday, explaining what Paul wrote to the Ephesians, and simply ends at the conclusion of the letter.

Which of these churches has been taught the Bible in context? Which of these pastors has acted as a faithful messenger, delivering the original message from the sender? The first church may have been teaching *about* the Bible and perhaps offering helpful principles *from* the Bible, but it was the second church that was actually teaching *the* Bible. The second church understands that biblical preaching is not about communicating *a* message; it's about transmitting *the* message. It's not about determining *what to say*; it's about delivering *what has already been said.*

This is not to say that the Bible can never be used to address topics that come up in life. On the contrary, the Bible *must* be used to respond to all of the unforeseeable situations that we each uniquely face. In fact, the Bereans in Acts 17:11 were commended for searching the Scriptures, and it is still commendable today. But an individual's private study of Scripture is a categorically different exercise than a pastor's public proclamation of Scripture. There are a number of legitimate outlets in which topical studies are appropriate, such as during personal study, counseling sessions, classroom lectures, or annual conferences—but not as the pastor's primary preaching ministry during the official assembly of the congregation.

When the people of God gather together on the Lord's Day, it is because they have been summoned by the King to hear His message announced, not abbreviated—proclaimed, not partitioned. Other teaching ministries (such as doctrinal surveys or topical studies) can be beneficial for believers at other times of the week, but the most important ministry in a church's life is the verse-by-verse exposition of God's Word each Sunday morning. This is the necessary work of expository preaching.

But is expository preaching really the only legitimate method for a Sunday morning preaching ministry? The answer is a resounding "Yes!" Not only does any given sermon need to be rooted and grounded firmly in the text, but the overall pattern of any year-round, Sunday-by-Sunday preaching ministry must be sequential exposition.

Unfortunately, even posing the question of expository preaching as a "method" undermines the essence of what it is. A great deal of confusion is caused when it comes to the discussion of expository preaching because it is presented as one method among many from which a pastor may choose. Thus, to portray it as a *method* unnecessarily confuses the issue. In truth, expository preaching is the only form of *biblical* preaching. It is not one way among many, but stands alone as the sole means that God has ordained for pastoral preaching ministry.

Dr. Al Mohler, president of The Southern Baptist Theological Seminary, asserts this as well, saying,

> I am convinced that we add to the confusion by discussing expository preaching as merely one *kind* of preaching—or even the *best* kind. When we fall into that pattern, we do serious injury to the scriptural vision of preaching. Let's be clear. According to the Bible, exposition is preaching. And preaching is exposition.[10]

As a parent, it is so vitally important that you become convinced that pastors are to preach the Word verse by verse, because the biblical pattern set for pastors also functions as the biblical pattern for all who are in ministry—including the ministry of parenting. There is no way

---

[10] R. Albert Mohler, *He Is Not Silent: Preaching in a Postmodern World* (Chicago: Moody, 2008), 50.

around this; we must take the time to settle in our minds what the Bible says about this issue. A closer look at the concept of sequential exposition confirms that it is *divinely mandated, theologically motivated, biblically demonstrated, historically validated, logically required, and authorially intended*—indeed, expository preaching is God's pattern for ministry.

Expository Preaching Is Divinely Mandated

> *I solemnly charge you in the presence of God and of Christ Jesus, who is to judge the living and the dead, and by His appearing and His kingdom: preach the word; be ready in season and out of season; reprove, rebuke, exhort, with great patience and instruction. (2 Timothy 4:1-2)*

As we continue to examine Paul's second letter to Timothy, we come across the most definitive command in the Bible for expository preaching. Because Paul recognized that his death was imminent, the message he had for Timothy was intensely personal, urgent, and sobering. It is as if Paul summoned Timothy to his bedside to whisper parting words into his disciple's ear. But Paul's message was more than a final request of a dying man; it was a divine mandate from the living God. In three short words, Timothy's number one priority was given to him: "preach the Word" (cf. 2 Tim. 4:2). And to emphasize just how critical this was, Paul preceded this command with a solemn oath.

He began with the phrase, "I solemnly charge you in the presence of God and of Christ Jesus." Just as with other instructions to Timothy, this phrase reflects the legal vernacular of the first-century culture in which a person would be formally summoned to court to appear before an official (cf. 1 Tim. 5:21, 2 Tim. 2:14). With this aspect of the oath, Paul emphasized the reality that Timothy's ministry would be under the scrutiny of God, the One to whom all things are laid bare (cf. Heb. 4:13).

Paul then went on to speak of Christ Jesus as the one "who is to judge," emphasizing that Timothy was accountable to Christ Himself. Like every believer, Timothy would stand before the judgment seat of Christ to be evaluated for his faithfulness to this work (cf. 2 Cor. 5:10).

Next, Paul explained that judgment will be for "the living and the dead," which highlights the reality that no one will escape judgment. The Bible states that once a man dies he will enter into judgment (cf. Heb. 9:27). In other words, death is not a means to avoid the judgment of God but, on the contrary, is precisely what ushers every man straight into God's courtroom.

From there, Paul issued the phrase "by His appearing," which pointed Timothy's thoughts toward the imminent return of Christ. Just as the planned visit of an Emperor to a Roman city would motivate that city to quickly clean up its streets and buildings to prepare, so too did Timothy need to be faithful in ministry so that he would be ready at a moment's notice for Christ's appearing. Every child who has ever been assigned the task of cleaning his or her room can easily associate with Paul's sentiment. Knowing that mom or dad will be checking in to see that the work has been completed is enough motivation to get the job done right. Similarly, every pastor has been assigned a task and ought to prepare for a divine audit at any given moment.

Finally, Paul finished the oath by referring to "His Kingdom," the eternal reign of King Jesus. Paul invoked this to remind Timothy that he was not accountable to a momentary monarch, a passing prince, or a short-term sovereign. No, Timothy was a servant of the One whose government will have no end (cf. Isa. 9:7). Paul wanted Timothy to be able to enter God's Kingdom having faithfully completed his task.

Thus, with those five components, Paul constructed the most

explicitly authoritative charge given in the entire Bible.[11] He then issued the landmark command for expository preaching: "preach the word."

The Greek word for "preach" in this passage is *kerusso* which means "to make an official announcement," used in first-century times to describe a messenger bringing the news of a king or emperor.[12] Such a messenger was always under the authority of a sovereign ruler, given the task of announcing the decree with which he was entrusted. Serving as a herald meant that he had absolutely no liberty of his own to deviate from the content of his message or negotiate with his hearers, but instead held the sacred duty of announcing official orders from start to finish.[13] The herald's job was straightforward: stand in the town square and cry out, "Hear ye! Hear ye!" followed by an announcement of the exact message of his king. A magistrate would provide him with a message, and he would be commissioned to assemble, organize, and broadcast it to crowds in a city.[14]

On that basis, an imperial messenger would never consider himself to be at liberty to modify the king's message. He wouldn't dare think about turning the royal decree into topics of his choosing. The announcement would be far too lofty and serious to alter. Instead, the herald would simply act as a conduit to transmit the message intact.

Therefore, to "preach" according to Paul's command follows this

---

[11] John Piper, *Brothers, We Are Not Professionals* (Nashville, TN: B&H Publishing Group, 2013), 89.

[12] Frederick W. Danker, Walter Bauer, and William F. Arndt, *A Greek-English Lexicon of the New Testament and Other Early Christian Literature, 3rd ed.* (Chicago: University of Chicago Press, 2000), 543.

[13] Verlyn D. Verbrugge, *The NIV Theological Dictionary of New Testament Words: An Abridgment of New International Dictionary of New Testament Theology* (Grand Rapids, MI: Zondervan Publishing House), 2000.

[14] Sarah E. Bond, *Trade and Taboo: Disreputable Professions in the Roman Mediterranean* (Ann Arbor, MI: Univ. of Michigan Press, 2016), 36.

exact same idea of delivering an official message. Just as the herald would not think to deviate from the message he was given to announce, so too must the pastor not think to deviate from the message he has been given to announce.

With that in mind, what constitutes or defines what Timothy was to herald? What message was he given? Paul provided the answer: *the Word.* Like elsewhere in Scripture, such as Psalm 119:105 and Hebrews 4:12, "the Word" refers to all of divine revelation that has been given—the entire testimony of Scripture—not just selected parts and pieces. With the completion of the canon, this represents all sixty-six books of the Old and New Testaments.

Since it is the Word itself which is to be preached, we must understand that Paul wasn't telling Timothy to preach *about* the Word, *from* the Word, *with* the Word, or even *based on* the Word (as noble as those intentions may be). Rather, the Word itself was to be the heralded message—preach *the Word.*[15] It is not as if Scripture were simply a blank canvas upon which Timothy could make his own artistic contributions. Timothy was to deliver what he had received—nothing more and nothing less.[16]

Like Timothy, every preacher today is under the same solemn oath and stands under the watchful eye of God. There are a number of reasons why pastors must commit to expository preaching, but the number one reason is that they are under divine orders to do so. Towards the end of the first century, persecution was beginning to rise. Fear of man and a desire for self-preservation were very real temptations for Timothy to abandon preaching certain parts, or

---

[15] Martyn Lloyd-Jones, *Preaching and Preachers,* (London: Hodder and Stoughton, 1971), 67.
[16] Steven J. Cole, *Preaching and Hearing God's Word* (Flagstaff, AZ: Flagstaff Christian Fellowship, 2007), 4.

perhaps all, of what he had learned. Thus, Paul had to make it clear that Timothy was accountable to a higher authority if he dared to willfully neglect parts of God's Word. With Heaven as his witness, Paul ordered Timothy to preach the whole message.

In the present day, there are a variety of reasons why many pastors have abandoned expository preaching: inconvenience, political correctness, laziness, apathy, "relevance," innovation, and other man-centered purposes. But Paul's authoritative oath and divine mandate to Timothy also go out to every man who stands behind the pulpit today: God is presently observing your ministry, one day you will give an account of your work, neither death nor life can avert judgment, Christ is coming quickly, and He will reign forever. By that authority, you are under orders to herald the entire written Word of God.

Expository Preaching Is Theologically Motivated

Why would Paul use such a solemn oath in commanding Timothy to preach the Word? Why couldn't Timothy try different approaches to Christian ministry? Because Paul understood the theology of the Word—it accomplishes all that God intends when it is properly heralded (cf. Isa. 55:11, 2 Pet. 3:16). As previously stated, expository preaching is much more than a methodology. Instead, it is a theologically-motivated practice that recognizes the *authority* of the Word to dictate the content of the preacher's sermon, the *perfection* of the Word to effectively accomplish its work, and the *necessity* of the Word in order to fully equip believers.

The first theological distinctive of expository preaching is that it represents a submission to the authority of the Word of God. Consider this: when a pastor engages in topical preaching (or other non-expository alternatives), who ultimately makes the decision about the content of the sermon? Who decides which passages will be taught?

The answer: the pastor. He selects the topics as well as the passages used to bolster his selection. Contrast that with sequential exposition, in which verses are taught one after another in the sequence they were written. Who has decided which passages are to be taught in this case? The Holy Spirit. He is the one who inspired the words in the particular sequence they were written, using the human author's flow of thought (cf. 2 Pet. 1:21).

Truth be told, every pastor's preaching ministry is inherently sequential by virtue of the fact that he preaches Sunday after Sunday. Over the course of a given year there will be an identifiable sequence of passages that the congregation has been taught. Thus, to preach verse by verse is to align with the Holy Spirit's intended sequence and, as a result, submits to the authority of the Word of God in deciding the content of each Sunday's sermon. Instead of a preacher exalting himself over the Bible, selecting from it the passages that he'd like to preach, the proper posture is to humble himself under the Bible, allowing it to dictate his agenda. One of the most important characteristics of expository preaching is its submission to God's authority.

The second theological distinctive of expository preaching is that it recognizes the perfection of the written Word of God. Psalm 19:7 says, "The law of the Lord is perfect, restoring the soul." By this, we understand that we cannot improve on the message God has written, nor should we try—it cannot be enhanced. God has perfectly prepared His Word in such a way that it "restores the soul."

In a very real sense, no pastor should be spending his time each week crafting a message. Why? Because the message has already been crafted, having been completed and perfected over two thousand years ago by Christ and His apostles (cf. Heb. 1:1-2). Thus, rather than spending time getting a message ready, the pastor's job is actually to spend time getting *himself* ready—gaining doctrinal knowledge, diagramming sentences, preparing his outline, consulting commentaries, and honing his homiletical skills in order to accurately and effectively preach God's message. A pastor should certainly offer illustrations and other comments, but only insofar as they help to explain the message he has been entrusted to deliver.

After all, when it really comes down to it, what other message is there? What more could someone possibly bring to the table that God has not already provided in Scripture? How could anyone ever improve on an inerrant and infallible book? Expository preaching triumphantly declares, "God's Word is perfect as it stands!"

The final theological distinctive of expository preaching is that it recognizes the necessity of the entire written Word of God. As 2 Timothy 3:16-17 states, not only is all Scripture authoritative and perfect for accomplishing its task, but it is also absolutely necessary in the lives of believers because it makes them "adequate, equipped for every good work." If *all* Scripture is needed to equip us for good works, then it is necessary to teach *all* of it.

To the extent that a pastor willfully neglects any part of God's Word, he handicaps his flock for the situations they will face in life. In order to carry out God-glorifying good works, we as believers need to pursue a comprehensive knowledge of the Bible. Thus, when the Word is properly preached, God speaks to us through the man in the pulpit, fully preparing us for life. By necessity, every verse must be preached to ensure that every believer is prepared for every good work.

Expository Preaching Is Biblically Demonstrated

Does the Bible actually demonstrate how to herald the Word with these kinds of theological commitments? Most definitely. When it comes to the act of expository preaching itself, one of the most profound accounts is found in the book of Nehemiah.

Continuing the narrative found in Ezra, the book of Nehemiah describes the return of the Jews back to their land after decades of exile. Because of their spiritual unfaithfulness, God judged the nation of Judah, which included the burning of Jerusalem, destruction of the temple, and seventy years of captivity in Babylon. But, by God's grace and according to His promise, the Jews were allowed to return to their land (cf. Ezra 1:3), rebuild their temple (cf. Ezra 6:13-15), and fortify Jerusalem with new walls (cf. Neh. 6:6).

Everything seemed to be back in order for the Jews, but there was just one problem—as a result of national apostasy and years of spiritual deterioration, the generation of Israelites who returned did not know the Law of Moses. They rightly desired to return to their land and have a temple in which to worship the one true God, but they did not have a functional knowledge of the covenant that God had made centuries ago with their forefathers.

Yet, despite being spiritually uneducated, they were also spiritually thirsty. They had a renewed commitment to the things of God and a desire to serve Him properly. Thus, under Ezra the scribe's leadership, the nation was instructed in God's Word.

Nehemiah 8:1 says, "And all the people gathered as one man at the square which was in front of the Water Gate, and they asked Ezra the scribe to bring the book of the law of Moses which the Lord had given to Israel." In order to understand their place in redemptive history and what God required of them as His people, they assembled together, built a wooden podium for Ezra, and stood to hear God's Word preached to them.

This moment was a critical juncture in the life of the Jews, because it represented a return to proper worship of Yahweh in the temple and a correct understanding of how they were to live as His covenant people. Their spiritual well-being was wholly contingent on re-learning the things Moses had taught. Thus, this community was not interested in a topical sermon from Ezra. They weren't looking for a fanciful message replete with comedic relief. Their gathering was not for the purpose of superficial, self-help instruction. No, they were desperate for God's Word, not man's word—"Bring the book!" was their cry. Consequently, Ezra stood before the people, opened the book, and began explaining the Law of God to them.

Nehemiah 8:8 says, "They read from the book, from the law of God, translating to give the sense so that they understood the reading." This is a clear statement of how they carried out instructing God's people. Not only did Ezra's assistants translate the Hebrew Scriptures into Aramaic so that this congregation could understand (since, growing up in Babylon, many did not know Hebrew), but Ezra and the other priests also "gave the sense so that they understood."[17] This "giving of the sense" is the heart of expository preaching—Ezra publicly read and explained the text line after line so that the people had a correct understanding of God's Word.[18]

Quite simply, Ezra performed the noble work of expository preaching, and it clearly left an impression on the people: "All the people went away to eat, to drink, to send portions and to celebrate a great festival, because they understood the words which had been made known to them" (Neh. 8:12). Ezra simply delivered the Word of God to the people and they rejoiced because of it.

But this practice of reading, explaining, and applying the Word didn't end there. It continued even into the synagogues of first-century

---

[17] F. Charles Fensham, *The Books of Ezra and Nehemiah* (Grand Rapids, MI: Eerdmans, 1982), 217.
[18] R. Albert Mohler, *He Is Not Silent: Preaching in a Postmodern World* (Chicago: Moody, 2008), 52.

Judaism. In fact, verse-by-verse exposition was so structured and intentional in these synagogues that the Torah was read and taught in its entirety every three years![19] And as the early church was born out of Judaism, it likewise adopted these practices, bringing expository preaching right to the doorstep of Christianity.[20]

In 1 Timothy 4:13, after the Apostle Paul wrote to Timothy to address several problems in the local church, he made the following statement: "Until I come, give attention to the public reading of Scripture, to exhortation and teaching." Without a working knowledge of the history and practices of Judaism, it's easy to breeze past this passage and not think twice about it. But this passage represents precisely the kind of expository preaching performed by Ezra, continued in Jewish synagogues, and adopted by early Christians.

Although most English versions of this passage provide a fine translation, the Greek text translated on a tighter, literal rendering actually better exposes what Paul was saying: "Until I come attend to the reading, to the exhortation, to the teaching."[21] What is important to note is that Paul wasn't referring to vague or generic practices of reading and teaching, but instead to *the* reading, *the* exhortation, and *the* teaching. He was not simply telling Timothy to read any old Scripture he'd like and then use that to launch into his own topical sermon. Rather, the presence of the definite article "the" tells us that Paul was referring to a very specific practice that he knew Timothy, a

---

[19] Philip H. Towner, "The Function of the Public Reading of Scripture in 1 Timothy 4:13 and in the Biblical Tradition," *Southern Baptist Theological Seminary Journal of Theology*, Fall 2003 (2003): 44-53.
[20] Will Durant and Ariel Durant, *The Story of Civilization: Caesar and Christ* (New York: Simon and Schuster, 1944), 596.
[21] Alfred Marshall, *The NASB Interlinear Greek-English New Testament: The Nestle Greek Text with a Literal English Translation* (Grand Rapids, MI: Regency Reference Library, 1984), 827.

fellow Jewish Christian, was well aware of—none other than the threefold public practice found in the synagogues.

Timothy was to carry out *the reading*, meaning he was to systematically and sequentially read through the Scriptures. He was to carry out *the exhortation*, meaning he was to urge the listeners to respond and conform their lives to the truths presented. And he was to carry out *the teaching*, meaning he was to inform them of theological principles and implications of the text itself (not his own ideas and opinions). Just as this served the purpose of bringing God's people to maturity in the past, so too was it to be continued in the Christian community for the purposes of spiritual growth. The threefold practice of reading, explaining, and instructing, as indicated in Scripture, demonstrates the biblical heritage of expository preaching.

Expository Preaching Is Historically Validated

The Protestant Reformation of the sixteenth century serves as an incredible example to the modern church in a number of ways, not the least of which is a return to the biblical model of expository preaching. At that time, the corporate worship service of the Roman Catholic Church included the public reading of Scripture, but rather than moving verse by verse in sequence through the Bible, the Catholic Church continued its long-held tradition of *lectio selecta*. This Latin phrase, meaning "selected readings," was instituted in the sixth century and meant that the particular passage to be read during each Catholic Mass was to coincide with the liturgical calendar.

In other words, various passages selected from across the Bible were to be read in accordance with the religious holidays on the calendar such as Good Friday, Easter, and Christmas.[22] And, as with any tradition instituted by the Catholic Church, this became normative for their church life. Thus, by the 1500s, the Roman Catholic Church was well established in the process of simply reading whichever verse was selected for that part of the year as found in their lectionary (the book containing the selected passages).

The Reformers, as they sought to correct the errors within the Roman Catholic Church, recognized the flaw inherent to the *lectio selecta* method: by only reading and teaching through passages of the Bible that were *selected*, there would always be passages *omitted*. In addition, they recognized that hand-picking texts from across the Bible would undoubtedly lead to an emphasis on the congregation's "felt needs," as opposed to their real needs.[23] As one might expect, this was unacceptable to the Reformers, who properly understood that the entire Bible was important and useful, rather than just particular verses.

As they looked back to the early church for guidance, they learned that Christian preaching was born out of the method found in the Jewish synagogues. And since the early church did not have chapter and verse numbers in their Scriptures, the Reformers saw that first-century preachers would simply mark the spot where their teaching left off each week and then resume at precisely that point during the next corporate assembly. This practice was known as *lectio continua*, a Latin phrase meaning "continuous readings." Rather than selecting only parts of Scripture to read and teach, the early church was committed to a sequential reading and teaching through all that was

---

[22] Consultation On Common Texts, ed., *Revised Common Lectionary* (Minneapolis: Augsburg Fortress, 2012), x-xi.

[23] Bryan Chapell, *Christ-centered Preaching: Redeeming the Expository Sermon*, 2nd ed. (Grand Rapids, MI: Baker, 2005), 65.

written. So, with a newfound understanding of *lectio continua*, coupled with a determination to implement it, the Reformers put it into practice without hesitation.

John Calvin, one of the most notable figures in church history, represents just how committed the sixteenth-century Reformers were. Calvin was instrumental in establishing a thriving Protestant church in the city of Geneva, in large part due to his commitment to expository preaching. Yet, after reaching literally thousands of souls with the truth of God's Word, an uprising from his opponents in the church forced him to leave the city.[24] Given literally forty-eight hours to depart, Calvin's preaching ministry ended in an unimaginably abrupt way.

However, within three years of his departure, officials in the city of Geneva begged Calvin to return in order to help re-establish Geneva as the beacon of light for which it was so well known. Calvin graciously agreed and resumed his teaching position.[25] And what did Calvin preach upon his return? What was the first text he taught? The very next verse. Despite a three-year hiatus, he was so tenaciously committed to *lectio continua* that he simply resumed his preaching at the *exact* passage that had been interrupted. Ultimately, the city welcomed Calvin back with open arms, and the legacy of Geneva's influence in church history is a testament to the power of the Word of God.

Quite simply, John Calvin was so adamant about sequential exposition that he would allow nothing to interrupt God's Word — leaving us with an example that is nothing short of inspirational. He

---

[24] Steven J. Lawson, *The Expository Genius of John Calvin* (Lake Mary, FL: Reformation Trust Pub., 2007), 12.
[25] William A. DePrater, *God Hovered Over the Waters: The Emergence of the Protestant Reformation* (Eugene, OR: Wipf & Stock, 2015), 77.

and other Reformers understood that if the Holy Spirit considered something important enough to write, they would consider it important enough to preach. Thus, history demonstrates to us the great need for expository preaching and we would be wise to follow suit. Those who engage in sequential exposition are linking arms with godly men of the past who shared the same commitment to biblical preaching.

Expository Preaching Is Logically Required

In Matthew 28:18-20, we find the epitome of the Church's purpose in the world: The Great Commission. Before ascending to Heaven, Jesus commissioned His disciples with the work of bringing others to a saving relationship with Himself and left them with this: "All authority has been given to Me in heaven and on earth. Go therefore and make disciples of all the nations, baptizing them in the name of the Father and the Son and the Holy Spirit, teaching them to observe all that I commanded you; and lo, I am with you always, even to the end of the age."

Despite what modern mantras may teach, the Church's primary purpose is not to redeem the culture, influence political policy, or resolve social injustices. Rather, the Church has been commissioned for the primary task of making disciples. And how did Christ say that His disciples were to accomplish this task? By *going*, *baptizing*, and *teaching*. Although we would find near unanimous agreement among believers that these three aspects characterize The Great Commission, it is this final aspect (teaching) that is often unwittingly neglected.

Notice that in The Great Commission, the disciples are instructed to teach others to obey *all* that Christ has commanded. Jesus didn't tell them to teach *part* of what He commanded. He didn't tell them to teach *some* of what He commanded. And He didn't provide them with a license to edit or condense the message. Rather, the entire spectrum of Christ's teachings—every doctrine, each theological point, all of divine revelation—was to be brought to bear on those who wanted to follow Him. While many would agree to this in theory, they functionally deny it in practice. How so? Because anything less than sequential exposition logically fails to pursue this task.

Non-sequential approaches to Scripture provide no legitimate criteria by which to evaluate whether or not *all* of Christ's commands are being taught. "Patchwork" preaching, selecting only certain passages to preach (rather than handling every passage in order), has no meaningful way to determine how well The Great Commission is actually being fulfilled.

Instead, it is almost as if a great many pastors view the disciple-making process as preaching a truncated Gospel message, calling people to "make a decision," and then spending the rest of their lives teaching only what they perceive to be the "necessary" elements of the faith. That is a sub-standard approach to The Great Commission.

Sure, there are doctrines of Scripture that must be emphasized—the Trinitarian nature of God, the substitutionary death of Christ, salvation by faith alone, and so on. But just because a doctrine is secondary for salvation does not mean that it is optional for discipleship. There may be secondary doctrines, but there are no secondary Scriptures. No part of the Bible can be relegated to a life on the shelf. Thus, The Great Commission is fulfilled only by teaching everything the Bible has to offer. A pastor whose preaching ministry avoids giving attention to every verse is a pastor who has effectively defaulted on The Great Commission.

And make no mistake about it—there are grave consequences for neglecting this. The Apostle Paul understood the priority of this for his ministry as well. In Acts 20, as he left the Ephesian elders to continue ministry elsewhere, he mentioned that he taught them night and day for a period of three years. He also said that he declared the "whole purpose of God" to them (the Greek word for "purpose," also translated as "counsel," refers to God's entire plan of redemption). In essence, the phrase "the whole purpose of God" represents the reality that Paul preached God's Word in its entirety. He held nothing back in his preaching. There was no doctrine that he viewed as unimportant. There was no teaching that was secondary. He taught it all. Not only did he recognize the positive benefits of the whole purpose of God (equipping believers), but he also understood the negative consequences of willfully neglecting any part of God's Word.

Paul testified that he was innocent of the blood of all men because he did not "shrink" from declaring any part of God's revelation to them. In other words, He knew that if he intentionally dodged part of God's Word, there would be significant negative consequences for him when he stood before God to give an account for his ministry. But because he had faithfully delivered it all, his conscience was clear.

Apart from teaching the Bible verse by verse, there is simply no guarantee that the entire message has been delivered. And without that guarantee, pastors ought to recognize that they may incur the guilt of neglect when giving an account to God for their ministry. The bottom line is this: there is a big difference between the full counsel of God and the hand-picked counsel of God. In order to substantiate the claim that he has preached the entirety of God's redemptive message, a pastor must give attention to every verse. Sequential exposition is the only logical means of accomplishing this.

Expository Preaching Is Authorially Intended

One final question remains: did the biblical authors themselves intend for their works to be used for expository preaching? Did they plan on their words being read, taught, and obeyed in a line by line fashion? Absolutely. A sampling of the New Testament in three key areas—the Gospels, the Epistles, and Revelation—provides a comprehensive demonstration of this.

As the only Gentile author in the New Testament, we know Luke as the traveling companion of the Apostle Paul who joined Paul during his second missionary journey (cf. Acts 16:10). Writing a two-volume history (the Gospel of Luke and the book of Acts), Luke was a historian with a keen eye and attention to detail, saying, "It seemed fitting for me as well, having investigated everything carefully from the beginning, to write it out for you in consecutive order, most excellent Theophilus" (Luke 1:3).

And his investigative commitment to detail shows. Between these two books that he authored, Luke's words account for more than one-fourth of the entire New Testament—more than any other author.[26] Not only that, but Luke's primary purpose for writing was so that his recipient (a man by the name of Theophilus) would know the *exact truth* about the Gospel message.

So how did Luke set out to accomplish that? How did he intend for Theophilus to receive his words? Luke 1:3 says that the account was written "in consecutive order," a phrase representing the Greek adverb *kathexés*. This adverb carries the idea of something occurring in a particular order.[27] Thus, what we see, by Luke's own words, is that the message was composed in a very calculated and intentional sequence for the express purpose of Theophilus understanding it properly.

---

[26] John MacArthur, *The MacArthur New Testament Commentary: Luke 1-5* (Chicago: Moody, 2009), 1.

[27] Frederick W. Danker, Walter Bauer, and William F. Arndt, *A Greek-English Lexicon of the New Testament and Other Early Christian Literature, 3rd ed.* (Chicago: University of Chicago Press, 2000), 490.

Don't misunderstand—this is not to say that everything Luke wrote was in consecutive *chronological* order. There are indeed some parts of his narrative that deviate in order to convey a particular theological truth. But what this does mean is that Luke put together his work so that it would be read in a particular *logical* order. Thus, sequential exposition follows Luke's expressly-written desire. As the primary recipient, Theophilus needed to hear and learn God's Word in the same order Luke wrote it. As secondary recipients, we too need to learn God's Word in the same order Luke wrote it.

The second major area of the New Testament is the section of epistles, written primarily by the Apostle Paul. Aside from a few personal letters, these are addressed to saints in a particular location, thus were intended to be communicated to a group of people at once. One letter in particular, Paul's letter to the church in Colossae, provides us with insight as to how he intended his epistles to be read. At the end of Colossians, we read the following: "When this letter is read among you, have it also read in the church of the Laodiceans; and you, for your part read my letter that is coming from Laodicea" (Col. 4:16).

The first thing to be noticed is that Paul commanded the church to read his letter to all the believers there. While this instruction would certainly include a straightforward reading of Paul's letter (just as any letter would), the underlying assumption is that this would also be accompanied by exhortation and teaching, just as Paul's disciple Timothy was commanded to do (cf. 1 Tim. 4:13).

But it doesn't end there. After reading and teaching through the letter, the church in Colossae had instructions to *exchange* letters with the church in Laodicea. There is some debate between scholars as to which letter came from Laodicea, but the bottom line is that these churches were commanded to preach and teach through Paul's letters one after another. This is the essence of an expositional ministry.

Preaching through the Bible book-by-book represents exactly what Paul intended for his circular letters.

Finally, the end of the New Testament contains the book of Revelation—the Apostle John's vision of the events to come. Revelation 1:3 says, "Blessed is he who reads and those who hear the words of the prophecy, and heed the things which are written in it; for the time is near." Right from the start, the Apostle John anticipated that his words would be read and taught aloud to the hearers. He even attached a word of blessing to his vision, recognizing the profound impact it would have on those who embraced it. The underlying implication, of course, is that what he wrote would be taught in its entirety.

In fact, John used a literary technique called an *inclusio* to emphasize that the entire book of Revelation was to be taught and understood as a whole unit (rather than a preacher selecting verses out of it). An *inclusio* is a word or phrase found at both the beginning and end of an author's work to serve as "bookends," signaling that the entire work is intended to be understood as a unit. Similar to an introduction and conclusion, an *inclusio* tells the reader the beginning and end of a complete text.

So, in Revelation 1:1, John said he was writing of the things which "must come to pass quickly," and then in Revelation 22:6 he stated that his vision was of things that "must come to pass quickly." By using this same phrase at both the beginning and end, John was telling his reader that the entire book was to be taught, not simply parts and pieces. This, again, is a clarion call for expository preaching.

Thus, a concise survey of the New Testament such as this plainly reveals that the authors did, in fact, intend for their works to be exposited sequentially. Knowing the exact truth that has been written requires sequential exposition, just as Luke intended. Maturing a congregation in the faith requires book-by-book preaching, just as Paul intended. Receiving God's blessing requires teaching all that is written, just as John intended. To teach the Bible verse by verse is to respect the intentions of the New Testament authors themselves.

A Commitment to Expository Preaching

The Apostle Paul had deposited the Word of God to his disciple Timothy (cf. 2 Tim. 1:13-14) and, like a mailman, Timothy was under obligation to tenaciously safeguard the divine mail so that it could arrive safely to its recipients. That need remains true today and demands a level of commitment that can only be characterized by expository preaching—saying what the Bible says, according to what the Bible says, in the manner the Bible says it, for the purpose that the Bible says it. Pastor John MacArthur's preaching ministry includes the monumental feat of preaching through every single verse of the New Testament, and his preaching philosophy affirms this perspective:

> If I received five letters in the mail one day, it would make no sense to read a sentence or two out of one, skip two, read a few sentences out of another, and go to the next one and read a few out of that, and on and on. If I really want to comprehend the letter—what is going on, the tone, the spirit, the attitude, and the purpose—I must start from the beginning and go to the end of each one. If that is true of personal correspondence, I believe it is even more important when interpreting divine revelation.[28]

---

[28] John MacArthur, "Why are you compelled to preach verse by verse through books of the Bible, unlike other notable preachers such as C. H. Spurgeon?," *GTY Resources: QA83.* Grace to You, accessed August 19, 2016, https://www.gty.org/library/questions/QA83/why-are-you-compelled-to-preach-verse-by-verse-through-books-of-the-bible-unlike-other-notable-preachers-such-as-c-h-spurgeon.

The shepherd of God must commit to leading and feeding his flock with verse-by-verse preaching through books of the Bible. It is demanded by God Himself. It is inspired by a robust theology of the Word. It is portrayed in the biblical accounts of preaching. It is confirmed by godly men of the past. It is necessary to fulfill The Great Commission. And it is the intended use of Scripture according to the writers themselves.

Those who want to know how to carry out biblical discipleship need not look any further than Paul's instructions for pastoral ministry. As parents, we must come to the unwavering conviction that sequential expository preaching is the charge given to pastors. Only then will we be convinced to follow suit with our families. If we are to lead our flocks at home the way pastors are to lead their flocks in church, we must recognize that there is only one way to teach our children the Bible—*teach them the Bible.*

Sadly, though, rather than feeding the sheep a steady diet of God's Word, many pastors provide foreign substitutes: "felt-needs" topics, narcissistic testimonies, movie-based messages, congregational "conversations," and so on. It should not surprise us, then, that of all the resources claiming to help us teach our children the Bible, many of them are also entertainment-based, sentimentally charged, and doctrinally anemic.

With that said, will you be the unfaithful herald who modifies the message before it gets to the ears of your children? Will you edit the words of the biblical authors for your own purposes? May it never be! God's Word contains everything your children need for life and godliness. This makes your charge clear: bring the Book and preach the Word! Just as the preacher must be committed to expository preaching, so too must the parent be committed to expository parenting.

3
CARRYING OUT THE TASK

"The power is in the Word of God and our task is simple. All we have to do is make the Bible's meaning plain, proclaim it with accuracy and clarity, and the Spirit of God uses His Word to transform lives. The power is in the Word, not in any technique or program."[29]

–Phil Johnson

Focus Text: *No soldier in active service entangles himself in the affairs of everyday life, so that he may please the one who enlisted him as a soldier. Also if anyone competes as an athlete, he does not win the prize unless he competes according to the rules. The hard-working farmer ought to be the first to receive his share of the crops. (2 Timothy 2:4-6)*

What exactly does expository parenting entail? Should you build a makeshift pulpit in your living room, develop a three-point sermon outline, and sit your children down for an hour-long message each day? Well, you could. But that's not the point.

Expository parenting is less about implementing the external structure of a corporate worship service and more about delivering the underlying content of an expository preaching ministry. The idea is to minister the Word at home the way an expositor ministers from the pulpit—reading the text, explaining the text, and applying the text.

---

[29] Phil Johnson, "Better Than Any Fad," *The GraceLife Pulpit*, accessed June 13, 2016, http://thegracelifepulpit.com/Articles.aspx?code=PJ-A02.

Whether you sit on the couch in the evening, gather the family at the dinner table, or set aside time right before bed, the process is straightforward: open up the Bible to where you last left off the day before, read and explain the passage to your children, and call them to obey its implications in their lives. The next day, do it all over again.

It should go without saying, but if you want to give your kids a knowledge and love of the Bible then you must teach them the Bible. There are no shortcuts, despite what many other parenting philosophies might tell you. It's not like you can select a Top 10 list of things from the Bible that are important (implying that the rest is not), or teach the Bible on a "need-to-know" basis (as if there are parts no one needs to know). The reality is that your children need to know *all of it* because all of it *is important.* Thus, you must make sequential exposition the number one priority in your home in order to deliver all of God's Word.

A commitment such as this is not complicated, but it does require forethought. Rather than bouncing from topic to topic with your kids, haphazardly opening the Bible to random passages, or dusting off the Bible only when emergencies arise, this work calls for the intentional, day-by-day, verse-by-verse delivery of the Scriptures at home. For some, the idea of Christian parenting amounts to little more than handing children a Bible and assigning it to them to be read, but shepherding a flock means that the shepherd must be actively engaged in daily care. This is foundational for expository parenting.

Furthermore, what sets the paradigm of expository parenting apart from anything else is its unchanging approach throughout your son or daughter's childhood—just like the unchanging nature of expository preaching throughout the life of a congregation. When the Apostle Paul commanded Timothy to "preach the Word," he immediately followed it up with the command to "be ready in season and out of season" (cf. 2 Tim. 4:2). Timothy needed to prepare for year-round ministry because of the fact that he was to minister year-round. He was not to deviate from the message during various periods of life, but was instead to carry out his task in every spiritual climate, whether the truth would be well-received or not.

Beyond that, Paul warned Timothy that he would have to confront those who would prefer to have their ears tickled, hearing words that would suit their wants and soothe their consciences, rather than hearing the truth of God's Word that they desperately needed. Paul had experienced this in his own ministry. He knew quite well that Jews wanted a sign from God, and that Greeks desired philosophical insight, but he gave them neither (cf. 1 Cor. 1:22). Instead, he preached Christ crucified—one message for all men. Thus, Paul wanted Timothy to know that the biblical approach to ministry has no specific audience nor expiration date. God's unchanging Word is eternally authoritative and does its effective work when it is simply unleashed on hearers from all walks of life.

Thus, the same is true of expository parenting—nothing in the approach changes based on the age of your children. In season and out of season, whether your child's little ears want to be tickled or not, your job as a parent is to preach the Word, rather than adapt the message. When your kids are young, preach the Word. When they are old, preach the Word. Simple enough, right? But one thing is certain: this is a minority perspective.

Survey the milieu of children's ministry material offered for Christian parents and you will see the same trappings that plague a majority of church ministries. Events, programs, and topical studies catered to adults are aplenty in many churches, while the sequential exposition of Scripture is nowhere to be found. In the same way, many children spend time doing biblical crafts, watching biblical movies, and even playing biblical games, rather than receiving biblical instruction.

At a young age this might take the form of a moralistic movie involving talking vegetables, a sanitized reenactment of Noah's ark, or a skin-deep lesson on manners. And as they get older, the crafts, movies, and games simply age alongside them—teens are catered to with a variety of topics such as dating, peer pressure, and self-esteem, that are thought to be particularly relevant to their demographic. But in many cases, this flurry of activity is indicative of the same root problem: a failure to recognize that the Bible itself, taught consecutively, is what truly honors God and meets the needs of His people at every stage of life.

One writer, in giving advice to fathers for leading in family devotions, correctly addresses several common excuses that fathers give for not discipling their children—feeling ill-equipped, fear of failure, and so on. But then, after offering suggestions such as purchasing a devotional workbook or exchanging personal life-stories, he concludes with, "If all else fails, just read the Bible and pray together!"[30] *If all else fails, just read the Bible and pray together?* Scripture does not portray these two elements as a last resort. On the contrary, the apostles understood that their ministry had essentially only two elements: the preaching of the Word and intercessory prayer (cf. Acts 6:4)!

To be fair, this particular writer did acknowledge that the Word of God is living and active to work even when children seem disinterested, but the solutions offered did not match that conviction. Here is the bottom line: teaching your kids the Bible and praying

[30] Bill Delvaux, "5 Reasons Fathers Don't Lead Family Devotionals," *Leading Men* (blog), Lifeway Men, February 2, 2016, http://blog.lifeway.com/leadingmen/2016/02/02/devo.

together is Plan A, and there is no Plan B.

The Method of Expository Parenting

The fundamental method of expository parenting is straightforward: teach your children the Bible verse by verse each day, just as a pastor teaches his congregation the Bible verse by verse each Sunday. Following the example of the Apostle Paul who preached the full counsel of God to the Ephesian church before departing from them (cf. Acts 20:26-29), your goal is to work your way through the entire Bible with your kids before they leave your home. Since the work of parenting occurs over a long time, in which your children are growing and maturing, it might help to think of your ministry in the home like a rock which is thrown into a pond: initially there is a small and confined ripple, but as time goes on that ripple continues to widen and expand outward, covering a greater and greater area of the pond. This describes what the overall character of your teaching should look like as you raise your children to spiritual maturity.

Initially, younger children will be learning the foundations of the Bible at a very surface level—the people, places, events, and overall narrative of God's plan of redemption. As they grow, your job is simply to leverage their accumulated Bible knowledge in order to continue teaching the Bible with even greater depth, a depth that matches the spiritual maturity and capabilities of your children. It goes without saying, but this isn't a novel idea. This isn't a newfangled technique. This is simply the faithfulness of a shepherd in tending to the sheep given to him. After all, Paul's preaching was not a flashy affair either—he simply wanted to preach Christ crucified so that his hearers would be built up by the power of God rather than the wisdom of men (cf. 1 Cor. 2:4-5).

Like the rock thrown into the pond, the ripple may be covering the same material as the years go by, but to a greater extent and degree. In many ways, this mimics the pattern set by the apostles. The New Testament writers often made mention of the fact that their letters were simply a restatement of what had already been taught in person (cf. Rom. 15:15, 2 Pet. 1:12, Jude 1:5). Much of their later work was simply to remind believers of the truths that were explained previously, knowing the tendency of fallen minds to forget the glorious truths of the Gospel.

So what is the first thing you as a parent ought to do? It's actually something you ought *not* to do—don't wait. As soon as your kids are old enough to sit up and listen to a Bible passage, they are ready for you to begin expository parenting.

When they are at a very young age, look for a basic children's Bible to teach. Select one with basic words and succinct descriptions that match a young child's attention span. Set up a daily routine based on a short amount of time and simply read to them. Most children's Bibles are divided up into narratives of a manageable length, so committing to one per day is usually sufficient. Although a preschooler may not understand many of the things you are saying, the regularity of getting out the Bible and teaching from it will convey to them that you give importance to one particular book over and above all others. This commitment to daily reading in the Bible is critical for developing the habit and expectations in your children, so don't think that this time is spent in vain. As toddlers, your kids may not be able to understand rhetoric and dialogue, but they can certainly understand behavior and affections.

Consider the words of Psalm 119:97, which states, "O how I love Your law! It is my meditation all the day." This passage perfectly summarizes the kind of mindset that you are looking to develop in your children right from the start. But the problem is obvious—try to explain this passage to a two-year-old boy and he would be off running around the house before you were even thirty seconds into it. At that age he simply cannot understand what it means to love the Law of God and meditate on it all day, and if you tried to explain it with lofty words and concepts, you would be fighting a losing battle.

However, that is not at all to say that you cannot communicate this passage to him. He may not understand the phrase "O how I love your law," but he *would* understand watching you hug his children's Bible and saying, "Thank you, Jesus." This would very clearly communicate to him the love the Psalmist expressed in the first half of the passage. Likewise, he may not understand the phrase "It is my meditation all the day," but he *would* understand that Daddy thinks the Bible is important enough to open up and read every single day. This would communicate the daily meditation the Psalmist expressed in the second half of the passage.

So at a young age, much of what you are teaching has to do with establishing a pattern of sequential exposition, which will actually communicate to your children much more than you might expect. By working your way through a Bible with them, they become prepared for the routine of consecutive exposition that will be followed for the rest of their childhood.

As they grow during the early years of childhood, you can gradually introduce them to more mature children's Bibles. Once your kids understand basic concepts, it's time to deepen your expositional ministry. Many children's Bibles, if read on a consistent basis, can be completed in a year or less. Thus, once you finish working your way through one, select another children's Bible that contains more accounts and a greater fidelity to the actual words of Scripture. And again, the pattern is no different—open up their Bible and teach them each story day after day until you've gone through the entire thing.

The distinction here is that as your children grow they become better at retaining meaningful details from the Bible, so you want to span the breadth of their Bible as effectively as possible. Because your child will be learning biblical truths for the first time, the objective is not to ask them probing, introspective questions (which will only lead to their frustration), but rather to explicitly tell them the facts and purposes of the stories that you are walking them through.

In other words, the idea is to get as much biblical "data" — solid, accurate, meaningful knowledge of God's Word — into your child as they are capable of receiving. Remember, as Christian parents you likely have years of basic Bible knowledge that perhaps you aren't even consciously aware of, yet none of this has found its way into your child's head yet. Your child doesn't know anything about Adam and Eve, Moses and Aaron, or Christ and the apostles. They have never learned about the Israelite exodus from Egypt, or the persecution of Paul during his missionary journeys. Everything in the Bible is new to them. If you can keep that in the back of your mind, it will help you remember that your goal is to lead them through all of the Bible and tell them about everything God has done in saving His people.

In the end, the younger years may look more like teaching your kids a children's Bible "story by story," but each time you teach through an entire children's Bible (which will gradually take longer as more advanced Bibles are used), you then simply select another age-appropriate Bible and repeat the process. If you implement this practice over a number of years, you will have worked your way through several children's Bibles and provided your kids with a great base of biblical knowledge.

Yet, because children's Bibles don't typically use the actual text of Scripture, any given one will have a unique set of strengths and weaknesses. This is why it's helpful to work through a large number of them rather than re-teaching the same one over and over. Some do a great job emphasizing the historical background of each story. Some include excellent discussion questions at the end. Still others are better at pointing to Christ within each account. Completing several different children's Bibles allows each one to complement the others and assist in the areas that any single one may be weak.

Once your children can read, the potential for them to learn the Bible increases dramatically. By being able to interact directly with the text themselves, they can become personally invested in the learning process. Look for a children's Bible that is geared towards young readers so that they don't feel overwhelmed—after all, if the purpose is to learn biblical content, words that they cannot pronounce or sentences that are complicated will simply become an obstacle to learning.

When it's time for your daily instruction, read through the Bible and allow them to follow along. You might even encourage them to read any given chapter either before or after you teach it to them (and certainly encourage reading any other passages as desired!). But be warned: this juncture in their childhood, the time when they begin to read on their own, also poses one of the greatest threats to your ministry—the temptation for you to disengage from discipleship.

The great allure once your children can read their own Bibles is to simply let them learn on their own, sending them off to go study it alone. And a similar mindset is found in some pastors towards their churches. Rather than continuing to expand and develop their ministry for their sheep, a mindset among many is that their job is simply to feed the congregation surface-level truth and let the congregation dig deeper on their own time. It's often believed that once sheep reach a particular level of maturity, the shepherd is no longer accountable to feed them; the sheep must simply feed themselves.

While it is certainly true that believers should study as much as possible on their own, in no way does this abdicate the pastor of his duty to teach. In fact, the etymology of the very word "pastor" won't allow for such a mentality; it is related to the Latin word *pascere,* which means "to pasture, to feed!"[31] Similarly, your child's intellectual capability does not abdicate you of your responsibility to continue leading him or her. It only makes sense, then, that when Christ commissioned Peter as a shepherd, He told him to feed both the young and the old—the "lambs" and the "sheep" (cf. John 21:15-17). So you must fight this mentality—just as the pastor's job is to escort his flock as long as they are with him, so too is it the parent's job.

The age at which you begin to teach your child from an actual, full-text Bible will certainly depend on factors particular to your family. But one thing is certain: if your children have been raised on a large number of storybook Bibles in their younger years, their capacity to learn and understand the actual Scriptures will be greatly expedited, and they will be ready sooner rather than later.

In order to make the leap from a storybook Bible, the books of Psalms and Proverbs serve as great transitions for children to prepare for a full-text Bible. Since both of these books actually consist of dozens of individual texts written at different times and by different authors, any given chapter usually serves as its own literary unit. This means that you can teach your child a chapter on its own without your child having to follow an extended discourse over an entire book. With much of the rest of the Bible, a true grasp of what is being taught requires the hearer to follow the line of thought over an extended number of chapters, tracing the logical arguments or historical

---

[31] Donald K. McKim, *Westminster Dictionary of Theological Terms*, *2nd ed.* (Louisville, KY: Westminster John Knox Press, 2014), 230.

narratives. But Psalms and Proverbs allow those with shorter attention spans to immediately enter into the text because the context for any given passage is typically self-contained in the individual chapter.

As if that weren't enough of a blessing, these two books serve very well to bolster two ends of the spiritual "spectrum" for your child— Psalms often contain very lofty truths about the nature of God and His redemptive purposes, whereas Proverbs often contain very concrete instructions that can be immediately applied in daily life. As you determine that your child needs to begin transitioning to a full-text Bible, reading and teaching through a Psalm or a Proverb (perhaps before or after a passage from their children's Bible) will prove to be an invaluable help to make this happen. Your children will begin to hear true biblical exposition from you which will prepare them for the lengthier books of the Bible in the future.

Granted, it could be argued that a full-text Bible ought to be used for instructing children from the very start. And while there is certainly some legitimacy to that argument (after all, storybook Bibles are relatively new in the history of the church), the reality is that if you were to pursue that route you would end up summarizing the Bible in much the same way that many children's Bibles already have.

Beyond that, Scripture recognizes that expository preaching requires more awareness than a small child possesses (cf. Neh. 8:2). Regardless, you ought to plan on transitioning from "milk" to "meat" as soon as is reasonably possible. The more time you have to teach the full counsel of God from the actual Scriptures, the better your ministry will be. Hence, when you determine that your child is capable of following along from chapter to chapter each day (which is almost certainly while they are in the single-digit age range), get a full-text Bible for them, open it up to Genesis 1:1, and begin.

But if it is as simple as that, why are so many parents hesitant to teach their children the Bible? Aside from time constraints and feelings of inadequacy, perhaps one of the concerns is this: *"If I teach the Bible verse by verse to my young child, we're going to come across difficult themes such as murder and sex that they've never been exposed to before!"* Exactly! Amen! Praise God! Rather than letting the world fill your child's mind with a skewed perspective of these issues, you as a parent get to preempt the world's perversion with the truth of God's Word! If your child is intellectually able to understand the concepts in a given passage, then the passage is age-appropriate. Stated differently, there is no such thing as a portion of Scripture that is "inappropriate" (and may we never characterize the Bible as such!).

On the contrary, the man who truly understands what it means to herald God's Word knows that it is not his place to determine which parts of the message suit a child's ears. A true expositor will not conceal the things of God (cf. Psa. 78:1-4). Dr. Steve Lawson puts it this way:

> We're like a skier behind a boat. We're just hanging on to the rope. We can only go where the boat takes us. We can't go in another direction. We can't go in the opposite direction. We're being pulled along by the boat. We can only ski in the wake of the boat—that's what expository preaching is. We go where the text goes, we say what the text says, we warn what the text warns, we offer what the text offers, we speak what the text speaks.[32]

Think of it like this: there is going to come a point in your child's life in which it is the first time that he or she is exposed to certain mature themes, and the older your child gets the closer it is to happening. So

---

[32] Steve Lawson, "The Meaning of Expository Preaching," *PM 501: Fundamentals of Expository Preaching*, The Master's Seminary Theological Resource Center, accessed October 6, 2015, http://www.theologicalresources.org/the-masters-seminary/24-fundamentals-of-expository-preaching.

the only question is, whom do you want to introduce your child to such difficult topics? You, the one who can properly explain what the Bible says about these issues? Or "Little Johnny," the neighbor boy who has grown up watching too much adult television and spending unsupervised time surfing the internet? By confronting these topics head-on through verse-by-verse exposition, you strip these "forbidden fruits" of their allure. You take what may otherwise only be learned about in a locker room and shine the spotlight of God's Word directly on it, just as Christians are instructed to do (cf. Eph. 5:11-14).

For example, when it comes to teaching a child about "the birds and the bees," what is a parent to do? Some fret about it to the point of avoiding the discussion altogether. Others may simply sit down to have what amounts to a really awkward, uncomfortable, and long overdue conversation. But for the expositor in the home, the solution is much simpler. When he determines that his child has questions related to marital intimacy that are more than surface-level, he simply opens his Bible to the Song of Solomon and teaches it verse by verse, using the eight chapters of divine guidance as a seamless transition into a more detailed explanation of God's plan for human sexuality. If sequential exposition is a normal part of everyday home life, there is ultimately nothing out of the ordinary when it comes to teaching Song of Solomon as opposed to any other book. A commitment to expository preaching provides the opportunity that a parent needs.

Of course, this is not at all to say that you should use graphic or lewd language in your teaching. The Bible does not go into unnecessary detail about certain topics, which leaves the discretion up to you as a parent to determine how specific your explanations are. But it does mean that you will at least touch on every theme that God deems important to address. There is no reason to leave your child in the dark, defenseless for the moment when the world does confront them with adult themes (and the age at which this occurs only seems to get younger and younger as time goes on).

So, when Genesis 19 says that God rained fire and brimstone on Sodom and Gomorrah because the men there wanted to "have relations" with Lot's angelic visitors, you need to look your child in the eyes and say exactly that, letting your parental wisdom guide the degree of your explanation. Or, when Jesus' parable in Matthew 24 says that the master of a house will find his disobedient slave and "cut him in pieces and assign him a place with the hypocrites" you need to preserve the integrity of the text by letting the vivid details speak for themselves. Your child's inevitable follow-up questions will dictate the depth of your conversation from there.

Having said all of this, if you are looking for a practical way to determine when you should begin a full-text Bible, a bit of simple math can go a long way. Consider for example, the 1,189 chapters in the entire Bible. Without a doubt, some chapters are read and understood fairly quickly in a single day, whereas other chapters may require weeks to truly grasp the heart of the content. But to provide a reasonable estimate, let's assume that you are able to teach your child an average of three chapters per week (broken down over the course of seven days makes this a very manageable number). What this would mean is that the entire Bible could be taught, to some degree of depth, in just under eight years.

Thus, to teach the entire Bible to your child while they are still at home, based on this assumption, you would need to start by the time they are roughly ten years old. And one thing is certain: a ten-year-old is more than capable of following verse-by-verse exposition! Ideally, you would begin a full-text Bible well before your child reaches the age of ten, but again, these numbers are simply meant to illustrate the kind of forethought needed.

Once your children reach the teenage years, nothing in your task changes. This age-range simply allows for the greatest depth of instruction. By this point in time, they will have had close to a decade of biblical teaching from you. Thus, they will be more than ready to fully engage in the process of sequential exposition. To that end, they ought to begin studying on their own both to prepare for and reflect on what you teach them each week. But again, just because your teens are capable of studying Scripture on their own doesn't mean that they no longer need guidance from you. Nor does it alleviate you of your obligation to continue leading them through the Scriptures. Instead, this simply means that your expository ministry will be that much more matured than it was during their younger years.

In many ways, instructing a teenager who has been raised in the Scriptures ought to resemble instructing an adult. Not only can you fully plumb the depths of God's Word and explain the detailed historical narratives, prophecies, logical arguments, and doctrines, but you can also drive home these truths by providing them with the life-changing ramifications and implications of the text. Sure, teenagers lack much of the common-grace wisdom that adults have, and certainly the challenges they face in life differ than those of adults. But as your teenagers get closer and closer to leaving your home, your instruction should reach such a level that they will be equipped to tackle all of the complex situations that adulthood will throw their way.

Help them grapple with the deep and difficult elements of the Bible. Work with them through challenging scenarios in life that may not have an explicit solution. Have them articulate apologetic arguments based on various passages that they've learned. And if, perhaps, you finish teaching them the entire Bible with a few years to spare, you can take time to revisit certain books of the Bible with a more meticulous and in-depth approach—making your expository ministry even more similar to a pastor's expository ministry in the pulpit.

In the end, the teenage years ought to be the time when they not only know the basics of redemptive history and the logical implications of Scripture for their lives, but are also able to explain, defend, and persuade others of the theological positions they've learned. By learning the full counsel of God, they will have sixty-six books' worth of divine revelation with which to be "thoroughly equipped for every good work" (cf. 2 Tim. 3:17). Ultimately, the final years under your roof ought to be the climax, the largest and widest "ripple in the pond," the culmination of all of your years of instruction that will set the course for the rest of their lives (cf. 2 Tim. 3:14-15).

The Mechanics of Expository Parenting

As you carry out this work, there is much to be said about establishing a routine for instructing your children. Aside from providing children with a sense of security and giving them a dependable expectation, sequential exposition is an exercise in consistency. It operates on the premise that the regular, verse-by-verse explanation and application of the Scriptures is the heartbeat that gives Christians vibrant spiritual life. Thus, without being obstinately inflexible, it's important to determine a daily pattern that will characterize expository parenting in your home. Although every family's time of instruction will look outwardly different, several key characteristics are helpful and important for every ministry.

When it comes time to open the Bible, how you begin sets the tone for the entire time of instruction. First, you must convey the idea to your kids that this is an important time. Nehemiah 8:5 says that when Ezra the scribe prepared to exposit the Scriptures to the Jews, he ascended the platform and opened the book, at which point "all the people stood up." Out of a sense of reverence, they stood the entire time God's Word was taught, treating the experience as if they were in the presence of God Himself.[33]

Without requiring your children to stand the entire time you teach them, the mentality behind such a posture should certainly still characterize your time of instruction as well. Teaching the Bible isn't like reading through any other book; this text stands head and shoulders above all others. Of course, the point is not to venerate the physical book itself as if it were a sacred relic, but your kids need to be reminded that God's Word is to be revered because it is just that — *God's* Word. In addition, make sure that your surroundings are free from anything that would draw your child's attention away from the Bible — turn off the television, remove the toys, and silence the phones. Your kids need to understand just how important this time is for honoring God and growing in their faith.

Nehemiah 8:6 goes on to say, "Then Ezra blessed the Lord the great God. And all the people answered, 'Amen, Amen!' while lifting up their hands; then they bowed low and worshiped the Lord with their faces to the ground." Ezra opened up his time of exposition by addressing God and offering a prayer to Him. The congregation, by bowing low, affirmed their utter dependence on God and reliance on His divine counsel.

The importance of this simply cannot be overstated. After all, our efforts to teach our children will be totally unfruitful apart from the work of the Holy Spirit. He is the one who inspired Scripture (cf. 2 Pet. 1:21), He is the one who empowers men to teach Scripture (cf. 1 Pet. 1:12), He is the one who causes hearers to respond favorably to

---

[33] John MacArthur, *The MacArthur Bible Commentary: Unleashing God's Truth, One Verse at a Time* (Nashville, TN: Thomas Nelson, 2005), 546.

Scripture (cf. 1 Cor. 2:14-15), and He is the one who continues to help believers understand Scripture (cf. 1 John 2:20). So it only makes sense to pray to Him and seek His help when dealing with Scripture.

Before opening the Bible to your passage of the day, here are some things to consider praying for with your child (giving him or her the opportunity to pray for these things as well):

Thank the Holy Spirit for providing Scripture, that you and your child may know truths about the glories of God (cf. John 16:12-15).

Thank the Holy Spirit for giving new hearts that are receptive to divine realities (cf. John 3:3, 1 Cor. 2:14-15).

Thank the Holy Spirit for interceding on your behalf when you don't know how to pray (cf. Rom. 8:26).

Ask the Holy Spirit to help you explain the Word with courage, conviction, clarity, and compassion (cf. Gal. 5:22-23, Eph. 6:18-20).

Ask the Holy Spirit to help each of you understand the passage at hand (cf. 1 John 2:27).

Ask the Holy Spirit to help you and your children apply what you learn in order to wage war against sin (cf. Rom. 8:13).

Afterward, a great idea is to show excitement for what is about to happen. The Jews gave a hearty "Amen!" after Ezra's prayer, demonstrating how excited they were to hear from the Lord. And when it comes to encouraging your children (especially younger ones), it is up to you to lead by example. You ought to show this same level of excitement, even if it might not be natural according to your personality. Simply shout, "Hooray! Bible time!" or, "Ok, here we go!"

Whatever you do to express joy in the Bible, recognize that your children will closely examine how you portray this time. So often, we speak of "making the Bible exciting," but the truth is that the Bible *is exciting* by virtue of what it is—the very words given to us from our Creator. We can't make the Bible exciting any more than we can make water wet! Thus, your job is simply to reflect the exciting nature of the Bible, which may mean, at times, that you have to express more emotion than you typically would.

Next, take a few minutes to review what was learned from the previous day's passage in order to remind your child of the context and setting that you are in. This helps establish continuity from day to day and immediately prepares your son or daughter's mind to jump right into the text. Just as an expositor in the pulpit will recreate the context for his hearers each Sunday morning, so too should you draw your child's mind back into the passage each day.

After that, it's simply time to dive in. Some passages lend themselves better to reading an entire section and then explaining and applying it all at once, while other passages are so theologically dense that they might require explanation (and perhaps application) after each verse. As you read, do your best to enunciate and emphasize the words as appropriate.

Although your children will inevitably have questions as you teach through the passage, most of the discussion will likely occur at the end when you ask them questions. With young children, stick to fact-based questions from the account ("Who," "What," "Where," "When," and "How"). This will help you gauge whether or not they have retained the basic information that you explained to them. Children at a young age simply need to learn the basic facts of the Bible so that in later years they can draw upon what they know in order to form biblical conclusions. Consider questions like, "What did this man say to that man?" or, "What city did so-and-so travel to?" By asking these questions, it will jog your child's memory and ensure that he or she has retained something from the story.

When your children are just learning the basics of the Bible, it is best to avoid asking the "Why" questions—questions regarding motive, intent, perspective, or inference (unless such a question is explicitly answered in the passage itself). In order to answer inferential questions, a person needs to have learned an established set of information from which to draw upon in making the logical conclusion. But young children haven't learned enough of the Bible to do this. To ask those kinds of questions will only lead your children to frustration and despair.

Instead, when the need arises for a deeper truth to be considered, you simply ought to provide the questions and answers during the time of instruction. You can fill in the theological blanks by explaining to them why God did what He did in a passage, or what caused a particular event to occur, or how a situation applies to our lives. Just because your kids can't answer the deeper questions doesn't mean you shouldn't teach about them—on the contrary, you should! It just means that they are wholly reliant on you for that.

As your children get older, the time of discussion ought to deepen and expand. Those in the middle years of childhood ought to be able to begin drawing logical conclusions based on what they've learned. Provided they have several years' worth of biblical instruction under their belt, they will begin to see the connections in Scripture that allow them to contemplate the implications of any given portion of Scripture.

At this stage in their childhood, they need to begin learning how to follow logical arguments, since many books of the Bible (New

Testament epistles in particular) often present a variety of logical proofs to make their point. Thus, rather than asking simple, fact-based questions, you ought to ask your older child questions that will help him or her step through logically understanding and applying the text. Perhaps you might ask, "What alternative thought or behavior should that person have pursued in the passage?" or, "What do you know about God that helps us understand this text?"

Finally, those in the teenage years ought to be able to engage in complex discussion after your time of instruction. Perhaps you might present an apologetic or historical situation related to the passage at hand. Or they might ask you about the theological implications of a passage. During these final years, in which you are preparing your sons and daughters for life on their own, your objective is to assess the wisdom they have gained throughout their childhood. You want them to take the facts learned at a young age, and the biblical inferences determined at an older age, and use them to derive the theological convictions that you've been instilling in them the entire time. Allowing them to restate the meaning of a passage in their own words and then discuss application based on it is helpful for drawing out their understanding. Ultimately, you want to be able to interact with them as you would an adult, since they are soon to be one.

Each day, as you wrap up your time together, conclude with prayer. Beyond what was prayed for at the outset, you might include specifics based on the passage that was explained. Perhaps you praise God for an attribute of His that was revealed in the passage. Maybe the text leads to conviction and confession of sin. You might ask that God would help you and your child obey the implications of the passage. Whatever the case may be, there is perhaps nothing better than a prayer based on the text that was just learned. Preaching the full counsel of God and praying the full counsel of God makes for a winning combination!

Finish by letting your children know how thankful you are for them and how grateful you are that God has given them to you as disciples. Look them in the eyes and simply tell them you love them. Make sure they know that your love for them is not only shown by cheering for them in sports, goofing around together at home, congratulating their academic achievements, or being a shoulder to lean on, but that it's also expressed by the time you spend together learning God's Word.

So is that it? Just read the Bible and pray together? Fundamentally, yes. Granted, modern church-growth advice would suggest that such a rudimentary approach to making disciples is simply not compelling enough for adults, let alone children, in our technological, entertainment-saturated culture. Whether it's a pastor riding a zip-line down into the pulpit, or a worship band playing theme music from Hollywood's latest movie release, one thing is clear: for many pastors, expository preaching is simply out of step with the modern man.[34]

Of course, the aforementioned examples are among the more egregious, but the underlying mentality characterizes many churches across the spectrum of modern Christianity. Pastor Phil Johnson wisely identifies this mindset and warns against it, saying,

> We need to stop following worldly fashions. We need to stop following evangelical fads. We need to renounce the postmodern quest for innovation. And we need to get back to the simplicity and honesty of

---

[34], Bill Blankschaen, "Zip-Line Pastor Entrances and Skyfall Worship Music," *Faith Walkers* (blog), Patheos, April 4, 2013, http://www.patheos.com/blogs/faithwalkers/2013/04/zip-line-pastor-entrances-and-skyfall-worship-music.

Paul's philosophy of ministry: preach the Word.[35]

The same applies in the sphere of parenting. Rather than embarking on a never-ending quest for novelty, captivating our children's hearts with things other than the Bible, we need to commit to the fundamentals of discipleship. And perhaps that is the reason verse-by-verse instruction, whether in the home or the pulpit, is not as widespread as it ought to be—it's not glamorous. You ought to be prepared for this reality.

On that note, what kind of mindset will you need in order to carry out this task? What will this venture demand of you as you preach the Word day after day? Consider that this paradigm differs drastically from others, many of which rely on man-centered techniques and human wisdom to address a child's perceived needs. Instead, expository parenting has a sole focus that meets the real need, a need that endures throughout childhood and into adulthood: knowledge of the full counsel of God. This is a singular devotion. And the mentality needed for such an endeavor is precisely what the Apostle Paul explained to Timothy by way of analogy.

The Mentality of Expository Parenting

When the Apostle Paul urged Timothy to find faithful men for ministry, he gave him three illustrations to demonstrate the qualities that would have to characterize such candidates. As parents, these three illustrations likewise portray what mindset is necessary for us to carry out our ministry in the home: the dedicated soldier, the disciplined athlete, and the diligent farmer.

---

[35] Phil Johnson, "Preach the Word," *The GraceLife Pulpit*, accessed June 13, 2016, http://www.thegracelifepulpit.com/Sermons.aspx?code=2013-06-23-PJ.

No soldier in active service entangles himself in the affairs of everyday life, so that he may please the one who enlisted him as a soldier. Also if anyone competes as an athlete, he does not win the prize unless he competes according to the rules. The hard-working farmer ought to be the first to receive his share of the crops. (2 Timothy 2:4-6)

The first portrait of a faithful man of God that Paul painted for Timothy is that of a soldier. The Roman Empire was one of the most successful military powers the world has ever seen, not only because of their overall strategy, but also because of the way individual soldiers were trained and organized. Any citizen who wished to become a soldier would swear an oath called a *sacramentum*, binding him to complete his service unless interrupted by either death or demobilization.[36] During his term, he had no will of his own but did the will of the general, attacking anything in sight, upon order, and to completion. Following orders without question meant that he would assume no personal responsibility for his actions in combat. His will was not his own, but was instead subject to the interests of his commanding officer. At the end of a soldier's term, his commitment was rewarded with praise from the Emperor in the form of a plot of land.[37]

And what was the minimum time of enlistment? Twenty years. Needless to say, this illustration was fitting for Timothy because of the long-term dedication that soldiers had to the cause of the empire. The ministry set before Timothy required just as much devotion to the cause of Christ. Coincidentally, twenty years is a similar modern-day minimum commitment for any father or mother who intends to raise

---

[36] Paul Erdkamp, *A Companion to the Roman Army* (Malden, MA: Blackwell, 2007), 51.

[37] J. B. Campbell, *War and Society in Imperial Rome, 31 BC-AD 284* (London: Routledge, 2002), 34.

children in godliness.

But notice that Paul also said the soldier does not get entangled in the "affairs of everyday life." Upon entering service, the Roman soldier would depart from his shop, his field, his books, and all other aspects of civilian life in order to pursue service to country. Those things were simply not compatible with his new occupation.

In the same way, every pastor must be so dedicated to his ministry that he eliminates anything that would interfere with his service to God. Therefore, as family shepherds, we too need to draw in the loose ends of our life: our close relationships, our entertainment habits, our financial priorities, our time commitments, and every other aspect that might interfere with our ministry. We too need to avoid being entangled in the affairs of everyday life. Of course, this doesn't mean we live a joyless life. After all, Paul told Timothy not to be "entangled" with these affairs; he didn't say they must be avoided altogether. But it does mean we have a mission that demands our utmost attention.

Simply put, when it comes to expository parenting, your life needs to be arranged so that nothing gets in the way of teaching your children. Sure, there are times when unexpected events may interrupt your normal schedule. Naturally, there are days that will offer less time for biblical instruction. But in general, if there is an aspect of your life that is regularly disrupting your mission of verse-by-verse teaching, you as a good soldier of Christ need to disentangle yourself from it.

Maybe that means drastically cutting back on the time you spend on entertainment. Maybe that means disengaging from some of your evening activities. Maybe that means distancing your family from someone or something that is contradicting what you teach your children. Whatever the case may be, you ought to adjust your priorities so that you will have the necessary time and ability to provide rich and meaningful biblical exposition to your children. Like a good soldier pleasing his officer, dedicate yourself to the mission so that you are sure to hear "well done, good and faithful servant" from the King (cf. Matt. 25:23).

The second portrait of a faithful man of God is that of an athlete. Like the Olympic games of today, the ancient Greek Olympic Games had strict rules for the competitors to follow. To begin with, only Greeks were allowed to participate. Non-Greeks, slaves, and those who had committed heinous crimes were barred from the games. Second, when the athletes met one month prior to the event, they would have to swear an oath that they had actually been training for the previous ten months, demonstrating that they were adequately prepared for a high level of competition in the public eye. Finally, violation of the rules could result in disqualification, fines, or even flogging.[38]

The reason for such strict regulation is that the stakes were high. Upon winning a competition, victors were welcomed back to their hometowns as local heroes, wearing a crown made of wild olive leaves. But in order to get to that point, there was an incredible amount of precision required, a commitment to following the rules. One misstep—one lapse in judgment—and months (or more likely, years) of time could be thrown away. The reward for winning was just as high as the cost of cheating.

Undoubtedly, Timothy (whose father was a Greek) would have been well aware of these implications. Timothy would have understood that every Christian pastor must be just as dedicated to the "rules" of ministry as an athlete in competition. Timothy, and those he would mentor, would not have wiggle room to invent their own

---

[38] Robert S. Dutch, *The Educated Elite in 1 Corinthians: Education and Community Conflict in Graeco-Roman Context* (New York: T & T Clark International, 2005), 273.

version of preaching. They would not have the luxury of innovating their own self-styled methodology. Instead, they would be under obligation to minister according to the pattern God had already laid out (cf. 2 Tim. 1:13-14). Paul had delivered divine revelation and Timothy's job was simply to herald that same revelation to the next generation.

In fact, there is perhaps no better illustration of expository preaching than that of the ancient Olympic competition called the *lampadedromia,* or more commonly known as the "Torch Race." In this event, athletes would receive a torch, run at their best speed for a particular interval, and then hand the torch off to the next runner in order to be the first team to cross the finish line.[39] And of course, if the torch went out at any point in time, the entire team would be disqualified from the event. Along those lines, one thing is certain: every pastor has received a 66-book "torch" for his leg of the race that must be delivered aflame.

Furthermore, Timothy would have had to demonstrate a level of discipline similar to that of the Greek athlete. Rigorous training. Focused commitment. Tenacious devotion. If that was the kind of discipline that was rewarded by the Greeks, how much more is it the kind of discipline rewarded by God? After all, the Greeks competed for a perishable crown, but Timothy was competing for an imperishable crown (cf. 1 Cor. 9:25).

Likewise, you must be just as dedicated. Expository parenting will fall apart if it is done without discipline. Like the athlete who trains day in and day out, you must teach your children the Bible day in and day out. There is no time to waste. There is no room for novelty.

---

[39] Oskar Seyffert, *A Dictionary of Classical Antiquities, Mythology, Religion, Literature & Art* (New York, NY: Macmillan And Company, 1891), 640-641.

Ignoring the guidelines could mean disqualification. When you stand before God, will you be able to say that you faithfully competed according to the rules?

The third portrait is that of a diligent farmer. The emphasis that the Apostle Paul placed in this illustration was on the attribute "hard-working," coming from the Greek verb *kopiaó*, which means "to become weary or tired by exerting oneself."[40] Thus, the purpose of this illustration was to assert that the true man of God ought to labor to the point of exhaustion. But why did Paul say that such a farmer should be the first to receive "his share" of the crops? Isn't all of the farmer's harvest "his share?" In modern times, it is often true that a farmer owns his own land and thus owns the entire harvest. But first-century farming was different than what we might expect today.

Typically, only the rich aristocrats owned land in the Roman Empire. Thus, the two kinds of farmers that you would find out working the land would either be slaves, who simply received food and shelter from their owners, or tenants, who rented the farmland from the owners (tenant farming was the basis for the parable found in Matthew 21:33-41). Although slaves were cheap labor, they were also notorious for their laziness and carelessness in the field—it's true that you get what you pay for! In fact, first-century slaves were such poor farmers that one Spanish landowner who had several estates in Italy noted, "We have abandoned the husbanding of our soil to our lowest slaves, and they treat it like barbarians."[41] With little incentive to work hard, slaves did not typically produce the greatest yield of harvest.

---

[40] Frederick W. Danker, Walter Bauer, and William F. Arndt, *A Greek-English Lexicon of the New Testament and Other Early Christian Literature, 3rd ed.* (Chicago: University of Chicago Press, 2000), 558.
[41] Will Durant and Ariel Durant, *The Story of Civilization: Caesar and Christ* (New York, NY: Simon and Schuster, 1944), 319.

Thus, instead of using slaves, some landowners opted to lease out their land to tenants. Often, the tenants would pay the landowners money in order to use the land. But another form of payment was based on an agreement in which the tenant would simply give the landowner a portion of the harvest at the end of the farming season, a practice known as *sharecropping*.[42] Since Paul spoke of the farmer receiving a "share" of the crops, this leasing system was most certainly what he had in mind.

The benefit of sharecropping was that a person with very little means could find employment with little upfront costs. Those willing to put in the effort could use land owned by someone else (as well as the owner's tools). But this form of payment also posed a moral dilemma for the tenant. The tenant could expend considerable energy working to maximize the harvest for the owner (as he likely would if the land were his own). Or, he could work half-heartedly, yielding just enough total harvest to give him an adequate share (leaving him with more time and energy for other endeavors).[43] Since he didn't own the land and merely received a portion of whatever was harvested, there would be little incentive for him to farm every inch of the land as effectively and efficiently as possible. And because it was difficult for landowners to evaluate how hard the tenants were working (especially since other factors such as weather or theft could cause low crop yield), it was equally difficult to enforce a level of work ethic for the tenants.[44]

---

[42] Michael Burgan, *Empire of Ancient Rome* (New York, NY: Facts On File, 2005), 99.

[43] Marc Bellemare, "Sharecropping," *International Encyclopedia of the Social Sciences.* Encyclopedia.com, accessed October 9, 2016, http://www.encyclopedia.com/plants-and-animals/agriculture-and-horticulture/agriculture-general/sharecropping.

[44] Dennis P. Kehoe, *The Economics of Agriculture on Roman Imperial Estates in North Africa* (Göttingen: Vandenhoeck & Ruprecht, 1988), 163-189.

So what did Paul say about this? That the hard-working farmer should receive the first share of the crops. Not only would hard work produce a greater overall quantity of crops, but Paul said that the diligent farmer should be rewarded for his faithfulness by receiving the first share. Even if he were to be paid first, a sharecropper who worked hard could be counted on by the owner to finish out the harvest with integrity.

Don't miss the critical application here: Paul's overall point was that sharecroppers who farm the owner's field with maximum effort demonstrate a level of trustworthiness that is to be commended and rewarded. He knew that believers in the church were to be treated as God's field, and that he was to farm it accordingly (cf. 1 Cor. 3:9). In the same way, the faithful man of God who ministers with maximum effort will also be rewarded for his care of the owner's property.

In 1 Peter 5:2, the Apostle Peter referred to believers in the local church as the flock *of God*. For simplicity's sake, we often think of a congregation as the *pastor's* flock. But in reality, the congregation belongs to God and the pastor is simply the temporary caretaker—just as the sharecropper farms a field that belongs to someone else.

Thus, Timothy was charged to work diligently in the ministry, knowing that he was laboring for God. Lackadaisical labor was not acceptable for the tenant farmer and neither is it for the shepherd. Pastor Steve Lawson speaks from experience when he says,

> Much diligent study is necessary in true expository preaching. I think many men are not expositors for several different reasons. One, they don't know how. Two, they've never been taught. Three, they have no

role models. But four, it's hard work.[45]

This carries great implications for us as parents too. Look around and you'll see that dysfunction characterizes many families (including those that would identify as Christian). This is the manifestation of sin, which of course affects all of us. But ask yourself this: how many of these families can legitimately say that they are committed to the Word of God? How many not only say it, but demonstrate it in the form of sequential exposition? How many Christian parents are diligently teaching their children the Word? It's possible that many parents are not even studying the Bible on their own, let alone teaching their children. Do we really need to put forth such strenuous effort? Is the amount of work worth it?

Maybe you'd rather take a path-of-least-resistance approach to parenting. Perhaps you just want to "get your kids saved," and then you can coast the rest of the way through life. It could be that you are tempted to farm like the unreliable sharecropper—just enough to meet the minimum expectations of the landowner. Teach a basic Gospel message, throw in some stories about Jonah and Samson, require manners from your children, and you will likely be perceived as a hardworking farmer by many in the Christian community.

But let Paul's words convict you to fight that mentality. Just like the sharecropper, recognize that you have been entrusted with someone else's property; your children ultimately belong to God (cf. Psa. 127:3, Ezek. 16:20-21). He is the one who will evaluate your work. But unlike the landowners, He has the ability to determine if you have given sub-maximal effort.

---

[45] Steven J. Lawson, "The Preeminence of Christ in Preaching, Part 2" (presentation, The Expositor's Conference 2011, Christ Fellowship Baptist Church, Mobile, AL, September 27, 2011).

Of course, as with any crop, you may not see the fruit of your labor immediately. It could very well be that you will never see the long-term impact your instruction has had. But don't let that deter you — your job is simply to plant the seed and water the crops verse by verse; God is the one who will bring about growth (cf. 1 Cor. 3:6). Farm with integrity and diligence so that when you give an account for how hard you worked, having cultivated the land as if it were your own, you can trust that God will reward you according to your labor (cf. 1 Cor. 3:8).

4
APPROVED FOR SHEPHERDING

"All expositors must be serious students of God's Word, willing to devote themselves to the relentless pursuit of deepening and expanding their knowledge of biblical truth. The day the preacher stops studying God's Word, whether he realizes it or not, is the day he begins losing spiritual passion and vitality in his preaching."[46]

–Steve Lawson

Focus Text: *Remind them of these things, and solemnly charge them in the presence of God not to wrangle about words, which is useless and leads to the ruin of the hearers. Be diligent to present yourself approved to God as a workman who does not need to be ashamed, accurately handling the word of truth. (2 Timothy 2:14-15)*

Consider the deadening effect on a local church if the preacher neglected his own personal study. He would lose the joy of gaining an ever-increasing knowledge of God's Word. He would sever himself from the means of sanctification provided by God's Word. He would be more susceptible to mishandling God's Word. And these negative outcomes would work their way into the congregation. The regular preaching of the Word, which ought to be the lifeline of the church, would be severely hindered by the pastor's own indifference. In the same way, your ministry to your children will

---

[46] Steven J. Lawson, *Famine in the Land: A Passionate Call for Expository Preaching* (Chicago: Moody, 2003), 88.

be insurmountably handicapped if you are not committed to regular, in-depth, personal study. Not only do you need to model verse-by-verse study for your kids, but you need to deepen your own knowledge of the Word in order to properly instruct them. You must be a man or woman of the Word if you are to train up men and women of the Word.

Although it should go without saying, it does no good to walk your children through the Bible verse by verse if you are wrongly teaching them the Bible verse by verse. The sequential nature of expository preaching is certainly a hallmark characteristic, but the ultimate purpose of expository preaching is to *expose* (accurately) what the Bible means by what it says. In other words, sequential exposition must be both *sequential* as well as actual *exposition*. Fail to account for either of these and you are not actually engaging in sequential exposition. Mishandling the Bible verse by verse is *not* expository preaching. To wrongly interpret the Bible (and teach it to your children in such a fashion) is ultimately unhelpful, or worse. As one theologian said, "A misinterpreted Bible is a misunderstood Bible, which will lead us out of God's way rather than in it."[47]

While it is essential that you have a local pastor who is teaching you the Bible, the reality is that you as a parent must still put in whatever time possible to study the Word for yourself. Your pastor will not be at your home each day when you sit down to teach your children. He will not be at the dinner table when Scripture is being applied to life's difficulties. He will not be at your daughter's bedside when she asks those deep theological questions that have been on her mind all day. Although your pastor may be available for assistance,

---

[47] J.I. Packer, *Beyond the Battle for the Bible* (Westchester, IL: Cornerstone Books, 1980), 19.

you cannot afford to handicap your ministry by outsourcing these fleeting moments of importance. Ultimately, the task of expository parenting is predicated on the assumption that you as a parent are deeply committed to ongoing study of the Word yourself.

Yet, far too often there is a self-imposed ignorance by laypeople through their own willful apathy. Rather than seeking out the deep things of God and continuing to pursue their own spiritual growth in an age of near-limitless access to information, many are content with spiritual stagnation. Confusing a child-like faith with a childish faith, some would even go so far as to claim that maturing in biblical knowledge is somehow "anti-spiritual."

In order to pursue our own spiritual well-being and the well-being of our families, we must fight this mentality. We must commit ourselves to an ever-increasing knowledge of God's Word so that we may become more effective in The Great Commission. The disciple-making process not only provides maturity to the student, but demands maturity from the teacher. You must have a firm grasp on the Bible in order to teach it, and that will only come by a life devoted to continual study.

Make no mistake about it—just as the process of sequential exposition is tiring, so too is the preparation. A story is told of someone who once approached a great Bible teacher and said to him, "Sir, I would give the world to know the Bible as you do." The teacher replied, "And that is exactly what it will cost you."[48] Yes, like everything else in the Christian life, expository parenting is costly. It demands time away from leisurely activities, and it cuts into time spent on recreational endeavors. But if a man's greatest desire is to know, obey, and teach the Bible (cf. Ezra 7:10), he will gladly rearrange his

---

[48] John MacArthur, *How to Study the Bible* (Chicago: Moody, 2009), 26.

priorities to prepare for such a noble task. Hopefully this can be said of you.

Regardless of the opportunity cost, the reality is that diligent study is not optional. Since God's Word is sharper than a double-edged sword (cf. Heb. 4:12), it must be wielded with precision. As with any blade, there is a great danger in untrained men handling such a weapon. John Calvin was right to say that a zealous man without doctrinal training is like "a sword in the hand of a lunatic."[49] Sadly, even a brief look at some of the most popular preachers today reveals a cadre of men who look more like staggering swashbucklers than skilled swordsmen. The Apostle Paul warned that any man who mishandles Scripture will stand before God ashamed. If a pastor is going to teach his flock the Bible in a God-glorifying manner, he must be an approved workman. The same goes for the parent.

Handle with Care

> *Remind them of these things, and solemnly charge them in the presence of God not to wrangle about words, which is useless and leads to the ruin of the hearers. Be diligent to present yourself approved to God as a workman who does not need to be ashamed, accurately handling the word of truth. (2 Timothy 2:14-15)*

Although persecution from outside the church makes the Christian life difficult, the most dangerous threat comes from false teachers within (cf. Jude 1:4). In fact, much of the New Testament was specifically written in order to address error in the church (cf. Col. 2:8, 2 John 1:8-

---

[49] William J. Bouwsma, *John Calvin: A Sixteenth-Century Portrait* (New York: Oxford Univ. Press, 1988), 228.

11). Physical harm may affect a Christian's body, but false teaching can do far worse to the soul.

For example, when false teachers were claiming that salvation was by faith plus works, the Apostle Paul made it clear that he would not "yield in subjection to them for even an hour" (cf. Gal. 2:5). He was on a mission from the risen Lord and would not allow anyone to twist God's Word and mislead fellow believers. In fact, he was more than willing to "endure all things for the sake of those who are chosen" (2 Tim. 2:10). His mind was made up. Endure torture *for* God's Word? Sure. Endure the torture *of* God's Word? Never.

This tough-as-nails resolve needed to find a place within the hearts and minds of other men as well, that they too would be willing to rise to the occasion. Those that were to come after Paul needed to protect the flock from Scripture-twisters, while not becoming one themselves. Thus, Paul commanded Timothy to remind other men of "these things," referring to faithfulness amidst suffering. But faithfulness to what? The Scriptures (cf. 2 Tim. 1:12-14, 2:8-9).

Paul began with the negative command, telling Timothy that the men he trains must not "wrangle about words." This phrase is actually a single Greek word which could be thought of as "word-battling," which can take many shapes and forms. In some instances, it occurs when men cast doubt upon the divine inspiration and authority of the Word; they are warring against the *nature* of God's Word. This is common among academics who mask their unbelief in grandiose arguments and terminology. At other times, this occurs when men subject God's Word to their own word (tradition, philosophy, and worldly wisdom); they are warring against the *content* of God's Word (cf. 1 Cor. 3:18-20).[50] This is a common problem among those who lack or simply disregard theological training. Either way, Timothy's job was to instruct future pastors to avoid these practices. The man who truly seeks to honor God's Word must come to it with an empty hand rather than a clenched fist.

Paul then issued his next instruction to Timothy—the positive command to handle God's Word with accuracy. Being diligent in "accurately handling" Scripture comes from *orthotomeó*, formed from the words *orthós* ("straight") and *temnō* ("to cut"), thus meaning "to make a straight cut."[51] This Greek word was used in a number of contexts such as a farmer plowing a straight trench in his field or a man slicing bread to feed his family.[52] But there was one other context in which a straight cut was required, a context well-known to the Apostle Paul: tentmaking. To provide for his own needs while doing ministry, Paul was a tentmaker by trade and knew all about precision (cf. Acts 18:3). Creating a tent required Paul to properly handle and cut individual pieces of animal skins so that they could be sewn together for the finished product; jagged cuts would render a piece unusable. Thus, an attention to detail was critical for the overall craftsmanship of a tent.

This concept applies perfectly to those who handle Scripture. Misusing the Bible, wrenching verses out of context, and all forms of "word-battling" are the functional equivalents of jagged cuts. And just as mishandling animal skins would produce an inferior tent, so too does mishandling Scripture produce a substandard Christian life—or

---

[50] John MacArthur, *The MacArthur New Testament Commentary: 2 Timothy* (Chicago: Moody, 1995), 72-73.
[51] Frederick W. Danker, Walter Bauer, and William F. Arndt, *A Greek-English Lexicon of the New Testament and Other Early Christian Literature, 3ʳᵈ ed.* (Chicago: University of Chicago Press, 2000), 722.
[52] Richard Mayhue, *How to Study the Bible* (Fearn: Christian Focus, 1997), 21.

worse.

If you are to be an expositor for your children, you need to make sure that you are accurately representing the text. You cannot afford to war against the Word, nor make jagged cuts across Scripture, but must accurately relay what God has said in the Bible. In short, you must become an approved workman.

The Approved Workman Uses Biblical Hermeneutics

The first thing that a workman must do before teaching a passage of Scripture is determine its meaning, and the reality is that the meaning of the text *is* the text. In other words, the text means what it says and says what it means—the Bible is not a lump of dough to be molded by the reader. Instead, the reality is that any given text has a fixed meaning set by the author who consciously wrote words and phrases in order to communicate particular truths to his hearers.[53] Our job, then, is to correctly interpret the words and phrases of these authors according to normal rules of language so that we can understand what they meant when they wrote. These rules of interpretation, called *hermeneutics,* allow us to correctly understand what the biblical authors intended to communicate.

The first principle, or hermeneutic, that the approved shepherd must implement is that of the *literal principle.* This principle involves interpreting language according to its normal, natural, daily use. Rather than looking for secret or hidden meanings in the Bible, the faithful interpreter seeks to understand Scripture in its straightforward, literal sense. Although the Bible is a divine book, it was not simply dropped from the sky into the laps of believers.

---

[53] Robert H Stein, *Playing by the Rules: A Basic Guide to Interpreting the Bible* (Grand Rapids, MI: Baker, 1994), 11.

Instead, the Holy Spirit used men to deliver it using human language (cf. John 15:26-27). Thus, the Bible ought to be recognized as supernatural, but not mystical. This fundamental understanding helps us avoid the temptation to "spiritualize" passages by interpreting them abstractly. A commitment to the literal principle helps us refrain imposing our own imaginations onto what we read.

Of course, this is not to say that there aren't figures of speech or metaphors in Scripture, but those are simply recognized as part of everyday human language as well. For example, when the Psalmist wrote, "From the rising of the sun to its setting, the name of the Lord is to be praised" (Psalm 113:3), we understand from a scientific standpoint that the sun does not actually "rise" and "set." Technically, the earth is rotating on its axis and we see the sun come into view on the horizon each day. But the Psalmist's purpose was not to describe the orbit of celestial bodies; it was to describe the ongoing, never-ending need to praise God. Even today, the most technical scientist would never wake up in the morning and say, "My, what a wonderful earth rotation!" Instead, natural, normal language allows for symbolic descriptions that the average person understands. At the same time, the literal principle keeps us from turning Scripture into one giant metaphor. Pastor John MacArthur speaks from experience when he warns against the danger of spiritualizing Scripture:

> I'm ashamed to admit it, but the first sermon I ever preached was a deplorable example of what not to do with Scripture. I'm glad there is no recording of it. My text was, "The angel rolled the stone away" from Matthew 28. I entitled my sermon, "Rolling Away the Stones in Your Life." I talked about the stone of doubt, the stone of fear, and the stone of anger. Doubt, fear, and anger are all legitimate topics, but they have nothing to do with that verse! I cringe when I think of it, and I still cringe

today when I hear preachers handle the text that way.[54]

Thus, one of the quickest ways to disrupt Scripture's transformative power in your child's life is to turn it into an Aesop's Fable, in which you abandon the actual meaning of the words in a passage. The authors of the Bible wrote with the intent that their readers would understand, which necessarily means that their words are to be understood according to standard, recognized definitions (unless the context clearly indicates a non-literal interpretation).[55]

Asking yourself the following questions can help evaluate whether or not a biblical author might be using a non-literal expression: Does this passage possess a degree of absurdity when taken literally? Does it possess a degree of clarity when taken symbolically? Does it fall into an established category of symbolic language? Only after asking these questions should a passage be considered for non-literal interpretation.

Since children are naturally concrete thinkers, a good way to test your commitment to the literal principle is to consider how they would naturally understand a passage of Scripture. Certainly, some passages require a level of intellectual sophistication greater than a child might possess. Yet, at the same time, the Bible assumes that a young mind is able to grapple with biblical truth (cf. Eph. 6:4). For example, when Genesis 1 says that God created the world in six days, with each act of creation followed by an evening and morning, a child would naturally understand this as occurring over the course of actual 24-hour days. No abstract insight is needed in order to understand the meaning of

[54] John MacArthur, "The Preacher and His Bible," *Expositor Magazine*, July 2015, 15.
[55] Robert H Stein, *Playing by the Rules: A Basic Guide to Interpreting the Bible* (Grand Rapids, MI: Baker, 1994), 50.

the passage. On the contrary, you would have to do quite a bit of language-bending in order to convince your child that words like "day," "evening," and "morning" don't constitute a normal, 24-hour period of time! Thus, in many cases your child's own inclination towards literalism will help you avoid telling them something other than what the text naturally expresses.

The second major principle of biblical hermeneutics is the *grammatical principle.* With this principle we examine grammar (how words are used in a passage) and syntax (how words relate to each other in a passage). This principle assists our interpretation by reminding us to pay close attention to subjects and verbs, relationships between clauses, and the flow of the text. Although this principle comes naturally to most readers (by virtue of the fact that they can read), there are times when verses in Scripture suffer the neglect of a workman who has abandoned normal rules of grammar.

Consider Jeremiah 29:11 (widely memorized in the New International Version), which states, "'For I know the plans I have for you,' declares the Lord, 'plans to prosper you and not to harm you, plans to give you hope and a future.'" Finding its place on devotional calendars and inspirational greeting cards everywhere, this passage is commonly understood to mean that despite any trials we are currently facing, God has a plan to turn our lives around for the better. Many well-intentioned believers have quoted this passage as a means of encouraging those experiencing a difficulty in life—providing hope after the loss of a job or peace amidst a strained relationship.

At face value, we must confess that this sentiment is kind, gracious, and commendable. After all, believers ought to encourage one another (cf. 1 Thess. 5:11) and surely Scripture is one of the best ways to do that. But there's just one problem—Jeremiah 29:11 has nothing to do with promising present-day believers that their lives will be prosperous. By assuming the passage is referring directly to the reader (a misuse of the Bible known as "personalizing"), many are left with an entirely faulty understanding of this passage.[56]

Instead, when the passage uses the word "you," we must examine the surrounding context to determine the reference for this pronoun. If we read Jeremiah 29:1, just ten verses prior, we see that this portion of Scripture was written to "the rest of the elders of the exile, the priests, the prophets, and all the people whom Nebuchadnezzar had taken into exile from Jerusalem to Babylon." Thus, not only does the verse refer to Jews who were held in captivity long ago, but the pronoun "you" is in the plural form (as if to say "y'all"). That is a far cry from the individual believer reading the passage today!

This is not to say that a verse like Jeremiah 29:11 is entirely irrelevant now, but by quoting it to your daughter on the day of her piano recital, or to your son after filling out a college application, you misrepresent the Bible and mislead your children. Accurate biblical instruction demands that we correctly identify word usage as found in the grammatical details.

The third primary principle of biblical hermeneutics is the *historical principle*. As we interpret the Word we must remember that we live in an "alien" culture—separated from the historical setting of the biblical authors. Our completed Bible comes to us having been written over a period of 1500 years, on three different continents, in three different languages, and by over forty authors of a variety of backgrounds.[57] We must be cognizant of the fact that the accounts

---

[56] Rick Warren, "Personalize God's Word To Change Your Life," *Pastor Rick's Daily Hope* (blog), May 21, 2014, http://pastorrick.com/devotional/english-with-tags/personalize-god-s-word-to-change-your-life3.

[57] S. Michael Houdmann, *Got Questions?* (Enumclaw, WA: Pleasant Word, 2009), 139.

depicted in an ancient text are separated from us by time, geography, worldviews, religions, politics, social structure, and culture. This means that the Bible's usage of words, phrases, and concepts may not match our modern understanding of those same words, phrases, and concepts.

For example, when Jesus told His disciples that He would make them "fishers of men," this would have conjured up a different mental image for them than it probably would for us. The disciples would have thought about their vocation as cast-and-drag fishermen, laboring as a team on a daily mission. We might be prone to picture the recreational activity of bait-fishing on a leisurely Saturday afternoon. The implications regarding evangelism differ based on which scenario is envisioned, and whether or not the historical principle is used.

We must take great care not only to interpret based on these kinds of considerations, but also do what we can to explain these nuances to our children. They have far fewer real-world experiences from which to draw upon as they envision the historical realities of a given biblical passage. Thus, pictures and other resources can be helpful aids in communicating a setting as accurately as possible to them. This could be as simple as opening an encyclopedia and showing them pictures of Roman architecture, or perhaps as involved as taking them to a farm and showing them how sheep respond to their shepherd. Certainly the idea is not to turn your time together into a major production, but well-timed object lessons can work wonders in opening up your child's mind to the biblical setting.

Finally, it is critical to examine *context* when interpreting a passage. With the advent of chapter and verse numbers we are continually faced with the temptation to select an individual verse out of context and interpret it irrespective of its surrounding verses (a practice called *isolationism*).[58] There is perhaps no surer way to come to an errant interpretation of Scripture.

Philippians 4:13 ("I can do all things through Him who strengthens me.") serves as an example of a verse commonly subject to such acontextual abuse. Despite the fact that Paul wrote this passage while imprisoned for his faith, it is often cited as a rallying point for self-willed success. For example, one church leader uses the passage to assert that we can have our "dreams fulfilled," and "climb to new heights" as we seek our own prosperity.[59] Yet, by simply considering Philippians 4:12, the student of Scripture easily learns that Paul was indicating his contentment in all circumstances, not offering a motto to empower selfish aspirations. Your children will only be edified to the extent that you safeguard your interpretations from such misuse.

Thankfully, the very nature of consecutive exposition helps keep verses in context, by virtue of the fact that it is a sequential explanation of Scripture. Therefore, the expositor has an intrinsic advantage over the topical preacher. Nevertheless, care must still be taken to properly represent each passage according to its context.

Ultimately, the process of using good hermeneutics (attention to the literal, historical, grammatical, and contextual details) to determine the author's intended meaning leads to what is called *exegesis*.[60] Derived from a Greek word which means "to lead out," exegesis is the act of leading or drawing out of a passage what it natively means. This

---

[58] Richard Mayhue, *How to Study the Bible* (Fearn: Christian Focus, 1997), 91-92.
[59] Jonathan Merritt, "Philippians 4:13: How many Christians misuse the iconic verse," *On Faith & Culture* (blog), Religion News Service, January 16 2014, http://religionnews.com/2014/01/16/philippians-413-many-christians-misuse-iconic-verse.
[60] Peter A. Lillback, Vern S. Poythress, Iain M. Duguid, G. K. Beale, and Richard B. Gaffin. *Seeing Christ in All of Scripture: Hermeneutics at Westminster Theological Seminary* (Philadelphia: Westminster Seminary, 2016), 25.

stands in contrast to imposing your own foreign assumptions onto the passage, which would be called *eisegesis*.[61] Apologist Dr. James White explains exegesis and eisegesis as follows:

> Exegesis can be defined with reference to its opposite: *eisegesis*. To exegete a passage is to *lead the native meaning out from the words*; to eisegete a passage is to *insert a foreign meaning into the words*. You are exegeting a passage when you are allowing it to say *what its original author intended*; you are eisegeting a passage when you are forcing the author to say *what you want the author to say*. True exegesis shows respect for the text and, by extension, for its author; eisegesis, even when based upon ignorance, shows disrespect for the text and its author.[62]

Exegesis, a proper interpretation of a given passage, is where every expositional ministry begins. A commitment to properly handling the Word demands that we continue to expand our understanding and skills in this area, and scores of books have been written to assist with this. As believers devoted to a life of fidelity to the Word, we must always keep these hermeneutic convictions in the forefront of our minds, lest we unintentionally abandon them.

Yet, hermeneutics and a proper exegesis are only the beginning of the expositor's work. Once we have determined a passage's *meaning*, we must then determine a passage's *purpose*. In other words, after you have correctly understood what the biblical author wrote, you then must determine why God inspired the account to be recorded. *What's the point?*

---

[61] Walter C. Kaiser, *Toward an Exegetical Theology: Biblical Exegesis for Preaching and Teaching* (Grand Rapids, MI: Baker Book House, 1981), 44-45.
[62] James R. White, *Scripture Alone* (Minneapolis, MN: Bethany House, 2004), 81.

The Approved Workman Exalts Christ

In 1 Corinthians 2:2, the Apostle Paul stated that the sole priority in his ministry was to preach Christ and Him crucified. Paul was not concerned with eloquence. He did not want to be known for sophistication. He had a disdain for worldly wisdom. Instead, if there was one thing he wanted his hearers to remember from his preaching, it was Jesus Christ. And while doing ministry, he accomplished this by preaching not only new revelation given to him by the Holy Spirit (cf. 1 Tim. 4:1), but also by preaching Christ from existing Scriptures (cf. Acts 18:28). Of course, during the early years of his ministry, the only Scriptures he had were what we now know as the Old Testament—meaning that he was able to preach Christ even from that part of our Bible. And this should come as no surprise to us. After all, it was Jesus Himself who claimed that the Old Testament Scriptures testify of Him (cf. John 5:39).

Thus, while it is absolutely true that the Bible was written by human authors, demanding that we first use biblical hermeneutics to explain a passage's meaning, our instruction to our kids can't stop there. We must also recognize that the Bible has a divine author—the Holy Spirit. His job is to point people to Jesus, which means that the words He inspired must also be used to point people to Jesus (cf. John 15:26, 1 Pet. 1:10-11). Undoubtedly then, when Paul told Timothy to be an approved workman, it would include, as its highest aim, the need to exalt Christ from the Scriptures. Paul preached Christ from the Scriptures and his disciple Timothy would have needed to follow suit. Likewise, if there's one thing that your ministry in the home should be known for, it ought to be Christ and Him crucified.

If we are to preach Christ from the Scriptures, the first thing we must be on guard against is moralism—presenting Scripture primarily as a means of behavior modification. In many ways we are all born legalists, thinking we can overcome our failures through self-effort, and this sinful inclination tends to rear its ugly head in the way we handle the Bible. The Old Testament, in particular, is subject to all kinds of abuse in this fashion, as it is often taught from a moralistic perspective (how to be better people) rather than a redemptive perspective (how God saves sinful people). Although we as adults may be able to recognize when the Bible is being misused like this, children (who live to please their parents) are much more susceptible to misunderstanding Scripture in this way. This is where we must put forth a concerted effort to redirect our children's eyes away from themselves and towards Christ. If we fail to recognize that the Scriptures testify of Jesus (cf. Luke 24:27), not only will our instruction hinder our children's spiritual growth, but in some cases, could lead to their ruin (cf. 2 Pet. 3:16).

For example, think of how many adults you know who have grown up in church, hearing all of the well-known Bible stories, yet do not understand even the basic elements of the Gospel. Ask them how to enter Heaven and they mention something about going to church regularly, giving enough money, or just being a "nice person." Or, ask them about what Jesus accomplished during His earthly ministry and they may say that He showed us how to live a good life to benefit others.

What happened here? In most cases, it was not that such people never heard the name of Jesus, but it was that the redemptive nature of the Bible was flooded out by a tidal wave of moralistic maxims. Sadly, then, when these children grow up and reject Christianity, it's based not on the actual claims of the Gospel, but on a caricatured version of the Gospel that was misrepresented in their Sunday School classes. So it is simply not enough to say we are leading our children verse by verse through the Bible if we are not identifying and explaining its redemptive nature. We see this failure time and time again, especially in well-known passages.

The account of David and Goliath provides a perfect illustration. What is the purpose of this passage? Was it recorded in the Bible in order to teach us how to "defeat our giants?" Is it really about "being a David" or "giving it your best shot" (no pun intended)? The average church-goer may nod in agreement. But such conclusions ought to sound like nails on a chalkboard to those who truly understand and believe that the Scriptures testify of Christ.

When we consider the story of David and Goliath in 1 Samuel 17, we immediately remember that the Israelite soldiers in the account were incapable of facing Goliath, a valiant Philistine warrior. The text says, "When all the men of Israel saw the man, they fled from him and were greatly afraid" (1 Sam. 17:24). Much could be said about the cowardice of these soldiers, but the bottom line is that these men were not courageous combatants ready to fight. Thus, if the purpose of this account is to teach us how to "overcome the giants in our life," then the purpose contradicts the very problem that the Israelites were facing in the first place. They *couldn't* overcome the giant in their life, which is precisely why they ran! Therefore, presenting the passage in this way is really nothing but a message of despair.

Secondly, the reality is that David himself was a sinful man just like the rest of us. By his own confession, his life was marked by sin from the beginning (cf. Psa. 51:5). Do you really want your children to be like a man who wound up lusting after a woman, committing adultery with her, and then having her husband murdered in order to cover it up (cf. 2 Sam. 11:2-15)? If the purpose of the passage is to instruct us to "be like David," then we are simply being encouraged to live like a fellow sinner, amounting to little more than exchanging our own sinful life for another. That too, is but a message of despair.

So is there actually a redemptive message to be found in the story of David and Goliath? Is there a way to exalt Christ with this story? There is, and in fact it is vitally important that we identify God's redemptive grace in the account, otherwise we will be teaching our kids to read the Bible like Pharisees. But before we identify the true purpose of the passage, at the outset we must confess the obvious reality: not every verse in the Bible explicitly mentions Jesus. Nor does every passage speak of the virgin birth, righteous life, substitutionary death, triumphant resurrection, and majestic reign of the Son of God. The Bible is simply not laid out like that.

What we do see however, are aspects of God's redemptive work all throughout Scripture, aspects which find their ultimate fulfillment in Christ. Although Jesus may not be directly mentioned or situationally present in a given account, the passage will still portray the grace of God, ultimately pointing to the Son of God.

In his time-tested book *Christ-Centered Preaching: Redeeming the Expository Sermon*, expositor Bryan Chapell explains this well:

> Jesus said that all Scripture is about him. This does not mean that every phrase, punctuation mark, or verse directly reveals Christ but rather that all passages in their context disclose his nature and/or necessity. Such an understanding compels us to recognize that failure to relate a passage's explanation to an aspect of Christ's person or work is to neglect saying the very thing that Jesus said the passage is about. Jesus said the passage is about him. If this is so, then we cannot faithfully expound any text without demonstrating its relation to him.[63]

In other words, just as it's been said that "all roads lead to Rome," so

---

[63] Bryan Chapell, *Christ-centered Preaching: Redeeming the Expository Sermon, 2nd ed.* (Grand Rapids, MI: Baker, 2005), 279.

too should every sermon lead to Christ. He represents the greatest act of redemptive grace—the Savior who provided a substitutionary atonement for sinners in need. Thus, as we teach through the Bible, we can escort our children to this grace by first identifying sinful man's desperate need in the passage at hand—an approach that Pastor Bryan Chapell calls the *fallen condition focus*.

No matter where we are in Scripture, we must affirm at the outset that the Bible is not intended to portray mankind as being spiritually capable and morally adequate. Instead it reveals just the opposite: men are utterly fallen, unable to remedy their own condition, and lost apart from God's saving hand (cf. Gen. 6:5, Jer. 13:23, Rom. 3:10). Consider this: only four chapters in the entire Bible, the first two and the last two, depict an unfallen world![64] The pages of Scripture repeatedly present mankind as hopeless creatures in need of divine rescue. Thus, the first step in determining the redemptive theme of a particular passage is to identify sinful man's need, pinpointing how the people in the particular text are portrayed as being inadequate in and of themselves. Speaking of this fallen condition focus, Chapell states:

> By identifying the fallenness, you are forced to come up with a divine solution and that divine solution is going to force you to think redemptively about the text and that ultimately is saying Christ must provide something that humanity cannot provide for itself. So, identifying the fallen condition focus, if you will, is identifying the hole that the divine grace of God must fill. Thus, the Gospel comes into play no matter where you are (in Scripture).[65]

---

[64] John MacArthur and Richard Mayhue, eds., *Biblical Doctrine: A Systematic Summary of Bible Truth* (Wheaton, IL: Crossway 2017), 47.
[65] Jeff Robinson, "Q&A with Bryan Chapell on Christ-centered preaching," *Southern News* (blog), The Southern Baptist Theological Seminary, June 3, 2010,

In other words, as you walk your children through the text, your first priority needs to be noticing the ways in which the people in the passage are shown to be utterly dependent on God to meet their need (i.e. sin, weakness, hunger, despair, displacement, confusion, or any other deficient condition).

In the story of David and Goliath, the fallen condition focus is obvious: the Israelite soldiers were cowards in danger of suffering defeat at the hands of the Philistines. They were inadequate for battle. They had no ability to conquer the larger-than-life Philistine champion. Recognizing this at the outset immediately eliminates a moralistic use of the passage. And not only does this help steer you away from such a man-centered approach, but it prepares you for the next step in preaching Christ from this story: identifying God's grace.

After correctly identifying the fallen condition, the next step is to find evidence of God's grace as the solution to man's predicament. Just as a passage has a literal, historical, and grammatical context, so too does it have a *redemptive* context.

First, any given account will contain God's grace within the specifics of the story: occasions when God sustained a life, delivered new revelation, provided rest for the weary, patiently awaited repentance, or triumphantly defeated enemies, for example. These are clear acts of unmerited favor granted to undeserving sinners within the particular setting of the passage. This is the first aspect of God's grace to locate.

Secondly, each passage also magnifies God's grace in relation to the scope of the entire Bible. For example, God sent prophets to reveal His will, priests to atone for sin, and kings to defend the nation, all of

---

http://news.sbts.edu/2010/06/03/qa-with-bryan-chapell-on-christ-centered-preaching.

whom point to Jesus Christ as the ultimate fulfillment of prophet, priest, and king for His people.

Pastor Bryan Chapell calls these two redemptive elements of any passage the *micro* and *macro* evidences of grace.[66] The micro-grace is the evidence of God's grace within the particular setting and situation of the passage, whereas the macro-grace is the passage's connection to Jesus Christ as the pinnacle of grace. Chapell explains it as follows:

> Preachers determine the meaning of a passage by seeing not only how words are used in the context of a book or its passages but also how the passage functions in the entire scope of Scripture. An accurate interpretation requires preachers to ask, How does this text disclose the meaning or the need of redemption? Failure to ask and to answer this question leads to preaching that is highly moralistic or legalistic because it focuses on the behaviors a particular passage teaches without disclosing how the biblical writer was relating those behaviors to the work of the Savior.[67]

Thus, going back to the story of David and Goliath, we ask, "Does God provide a solution to man's predicament here?" Certainly. The micro-grace (grace related to the specifics of the story) is that God used the shepherd boy David, an unlikely candidate, to face Goliath and ultimately defeat him. In doing so, God kept His covenant promise to bless the nation (given beforehand to Abraham) by once again providing peace and safety. The Israelites were frail and fallible, but God was mighty and gracious to provide a solution. God promised to

---

[66] Jeff Robinson, "Q&A with Bryan Chapell on Christ-centered preaching," *Southern News* (blog), The Southern Baptist Theological Seminary, June 3, 2010, http://news.sbts.edu/2010/06/03/qa-with-bryan-chapell-on-christ-centered-preaching.

[67] Bryan Chapell, *Christ-centered Preaching: Redeeming the Expository Sermon, 2nd ed.* (Grand Rapids, MI: Baker, 2005), 80.

preserve the nation of Israel, keeping His word even though the Israelite soldiers did not trust Him as they should have. This micro-grace solution comes directly from the initial interpretation of the text based on biblical hermeneutics.

Finally, we look to identify the "macro-grace." Here, we transition to Christ as the culmination of God's grace, by relating the redemptive element in the passage to the Bible's overall redemptive story. Undoubtedly, this is one of the most difficult steps for any faithful interpreter of Scripture. How do we properly connect a passage of Scripture to Jesus as the ultimate expression of God's grace? It's fairly easy to do in the New Testament, and for obvious reasons—the New Testament speaks freely, openly, and directly about Christ's work on the cross and His Second Coming. But what about when it comes to the Old Testament? How do we point our child's eyes to Jesus when working through some of the portions of Scripture that do not specifically mention Jesus? There are actually several ways to consider in order to preach Christ from the Old Testament:[68]

New Testament Reference. If a passage in the New Testament refers to a passage from the Old Testament (perhaps even citing it verbatim), you can quickly and easily direct your child's thoughts to Christ from the passage. For example, while teaching through the book of Jonah, you can connect his three days in the whale to Jesus' three days in the tomb, since Christ Himself made this direct reference (cf. Matt. 12:40).

Promise-Fulfillment. Some passages contain a prophecy or promise

---

[68] Sidney Greidanus, *Preaching Christ from Genesis: Foundations for Expository Sermons* (Grand Rapids, MI: William B. Eerdmans Pub., 2007), 3-6.

of God that is fulfilled by Jesus in the New Testament. For example, Isaiah 53:10-11 speaks of the one who will be punished by God as He offers Himself on behalf of sinners. Although the New Testament never quotes this passage, it is a prophecy fulfilled by Jesus on the cross, to be explained while teaching through Isaiah.

Analogy. Although there are important distinctions between the nation of Israel and the New Testament Church, there are also many similarities. For example, just as God saved the nation of Israel in order for them to be a distinct people among the nations, so too have New Covenant believers been saved by Christ in order to be a distinct people among the nations (cf. 1 Pet. 2:12). By way of this analogy, you can translate the redemptive context of the Israelites to the redemptive context that you and your child find yourselves in (the Church, bought by the blood of Christ).

Longitudinal Theme. Some passages may not explicitly refer to Christ, but the theological theme or motif is inextricably linked to Christ in such a way that the passage can be related to Him. For example, in Psalm 23, the Psalmist speaks of the Lord as his shepherd who leads him in paths of righteousness. In John 10, Jesus says that He is the Good Shepherd who knows His sheep and leads them. This theme spans from the Old Testament to the New Testament.

Redemptive-Historical Progression. In Genesis 3:15, God promised that the seed of the woman would crush the head of the serpent. Thus, from that moment on, the Old Testament shows God working in and among His people in order to bring that promise to pass. In many cases, then, you can simply ask yourself, "How does this particular passage function to set the stage for the coming of the promised Messiah?"

It is this final method that is readily employed to preach Christ from the story of David and Goliath. Here, we recognize that the God who was faithful to bless Israel as He promised Abraham is the same God who could be counted on to bless the whole world as He promised Abraham—and the promise to bless the whole world was indeed kept through the coming of Jesus Christ. The Israelites were threatened and fearful of the encroaching Philistines, but God was not. God's covenant promises to protect and preserve His people were not threatened by the immense stature of the Philistine warrior. Instead, God raised up David in order to defeat Goliath, preserve His people, become king over Israel, and prepare the way for Jesus Christ, the One whose kingdom shall have no end (cf. Luke 1:32-33).

But in addition to the redemptive-historical progression of this passage, there is also the longitudinal theme that God uses the weak things of the world to shame the strong, thus displaying God's glory through weakness (cf. 1 Cor. 1:26-31). To that end, Pastor Mike Riccardi of Grace Community Church elaborates on the motif that is also expressed by this account:

> Just as God chose the younger Abel over Cain, the younger Isaac over Ishmael, the younger Jacob over Esau, the younger Moses over Aaron, so He chooses the runt of the litter, the little shepherd boy David over the head-and-shoulders-taller-than-everybody-else Saul. God chooses the unlikely to be prominent, and in some cases, to triumph over what would have seemed to be the obvious choice in order to display His sovereign power in the fulfillment of His promises. And, ultimately, He chooses the

manger over the royal palace, humility over pomp and circumstance, the foal of a donkey over an armed chariot, and the cross over the crown — all to ensure that the people of His covenant (this time the New Covenant) would share in the fulfillment of God's promise of salvation and the forgiveness of sins.[69]

Riccardi's explanation sits well with one of the primary motifs of the book of 1 Samuel, that "God sees not as man sees, for man looks at the outward appearance, but the Lord looks at the heart" (1 Samuel 16:7).

In the end, the redemptive qualities in this account are connected to the greater redemptive story of the Gospel itself. By first applying biblical hermeneutics to the passage and then identifying the micro-grace in the passage, you can determine the macro-grace from the passage in order to exalt Christ. You can preach Christ through the story of David and Goliath.

Bear in mind that when we want to exalt Christ in a text that doesn't explicitly mention Him, we must take great care to use the text *properly* to exalt Him. In an effort to teach the Bible in a Christ-centered way (which is good and right, of course), a common temptation is to turn the Old Testament into a kind of "scavenger hunt," turning details of a passage into symbols of Christ that aren't actually intended to represent Him. One of the most common examples of this is the idea that God chose David to slay Goliath and save the helpless Israelites, which metaphorically represents God sending Jesus to slay Satan and save helpless believers.

This kind of simplistic use of the passage would certainly point our child to Christ and the Gospel, but there's a problem. This interpretation actually suffers from the same flaw as the moralistic use

---

[69] Michael Riccardi, *The Forest & the Trees* (Sun Valley, CA: Grace Books, 2016), 52-53.

of Scripture—allegorizing. The moralistic view of David and Goliath misuses the text to say that David represents believers who need to "slay" the "giants" in their life—things like debt, stress, marital problems, or health concerns. Yet, to say that Jesus is David, by coming to "slay" the "giants" of sin and Satan for us, equally casts the story into the realm of allegory. Although it is true that Jesus has conquered sin on our behalf, this aspect of the Gospel does not come from a straightforward interpretation of the text, but is instead imposed onto the text—turning the passage into an extended Gospel metaphor. Such an interpretation fails to properly connect the micro-grace to the macro-grace.

In fact, due to the very nature of allegory (extended metaphor), it's difficult for this errant approach to find a stopping point. For example, another misuse of David and Goliath takes the allegory even further. This interpretation says that since Goliath's armor was made of snake skin, his beheading after forty days of taunting the Israelites is symbolic of Jesus crushing the serpent's head after forty days of fasting in the wilderness![70] Such notions ultimately put biblical interpretation into the realm of subjectivity. There is no objective standard by which to evaluate the validity of such an assertion. Since the interpreter has dictated the symbolism, the degree to which the allegory grows is simply a function of each individual's creative fancy.

Believe it or not, yet another allegorical interpretation actually sees Jesus as *Goliath* in the story, claiming that Goliath's death as a blasphemer symbolizes Jesus's substitutionary death in the place of

---

[70] Ed Stetzer, "David and Goliath—Christ-Centered Preaching: A Recap of a Recent Panel Discussion—Part One," *The Exchange* (blog), Christianity Today, July 1, 2013, http://www.christianitytoday.com/edstetzer/2013/july/david-and-goliath-christ-centered-preaching.html.

sinners![71] There truly is no end to this kind of misinterpretation, which can only be described as symbology on steroids.

With these kinds of approaches, preaching Christ *from* a narrative really ends up inserting Christ *into* the narrative. When an interpretation artificially superimposes the Gospel onto details in a passage, it becomes nothing more than Christ-centered eisegesis. And of course, the ends don't justify the means. Honoring Christ demands that we not only exalt Him in passages throughout the Word, but do so in a way that is honoring to the Word.

A good question to ask yourself is this: am I looking for Christ in the details of the story, or am I pointing to Christ based on the overall redemptive storyline? Perhaps a good rule of thumb is this: if you have to use air quotes in order to explain how a passage speaks of Jesus, you've probably entered into the realm of allegory. The approved workman does not exalt Christ through creative license, but through faithful exegesis.

Ultimately, a proper interpretation of Scripture requires not only a correct understanding of the human author's words based on biblical hermeneutics, but also a correct understanding of the divine author's purpose—by identifying the fallen condition focus, micro-grace, and macro-grace. If we fail to identify any of these elements we have neglected to fully teach the passage to our kids. Ignoring the fallen condition focus leads to a moralistic use of the passage, skipping the details of micro-grace puts the passage in danger of becoming an allegory, and stopping short of the macro-grace fails to exalt the Lord Jesus Christ as the focal point of all Scripture. Without these aspects,

---

[71] Chris Hutchinson, "How to Preach David and Goliath with Balance: A Case Study of Finding Christ in the Old Testament (Part I)," *Featured* (blog), The Aquila Report, January 19, 2014, http://theaquilareport.com/how-to-preach-david-and-goliath-with-balance-a-case-study-of-finding-christ-in-the-old-testament-part-i.

your children may get excited about a compelling story, but they have missed the true purpose of the passage. Instead, by working to handle the text rightly you will be able to point your child's affections towards the Lord Jesus Christ in a way that not only respects the authorial intent of Scripture, but also exposes the multi-faceted aspects of God's grace as it unfolds in the Bible.

This is not to say that these steps of interpretation must be mechanically iterated through as you teach your children the Bible. Obviously we don't need to say, "Ok, son, now here's the fallen condition focus. Now here's the micro-grace. Ok, now check out this relationship to macro-grace." Instead, these key aspects simply need to be present in the back of your mind as you walk your children through each passage. A good preacher asks himself, "Would Jesus have to be crucified to make this sermon work?"[72]

Ultimately, no matter what we draw out of the text, the bottom line is that we must see Christ as the hero of the Bible, not ourselves or anyone else. He is the one for whom all things were created (cf. Col. 1:16). He is the one through whom grace is received (cf. John 1:17). He is the one by whom we are reconciled (cf. Eph. 2:16). And He said the Scriptures testify of Him (cf. John 5:39). Thus, we must take Him at His word by exalting Him with His Word. The approved workman also does this in a way that is faithful to His Word.

The Approved Workman Makes Grace-Based Application

Once you've interpreted the passage, identified the redemptive elements, and exalted Christ as the divine solution to humanity's need, you are then ready to apply the passage to your child by issuing

---

[72] William Willimon, "Interview with William Willimon: A New Evaluative Question: 'Would Jesus Have to Be Crucified to Make This Sermon Work?'" *Modern Reformation*, November/December 2000, 46.

instructions for obedience. *And only then.* In an effort to "make the Bible relevant" (again, as if it isn't already relevant), one of the greatest temptations we face is to jump straight from the reading of a passage to a direct application for our child. Because some parts of the Bible are relatively obscure, being distant in both time and culture, it's common to rush past otherwise profound details in a passage in order to tell our children something immediately usable in their lives.

And let's face it—the desire to equip our children with biblical commands for godly living is good and right. After all, it is our duty to teach our children both to hear *and* obey the Bible (cf. Jas. 1:22). It's not as if we can passively read Scripture and then move on with our day like it has no implications for our lives (a common pitfall when it comes to reading the Bible as "daily devotions"). Following Jesus doesn't simply mean contemplating what He's done for us and then living a life of complacency—that's nothing more than using grace as an excuse for sinful indifference.

Yet, once we understand that disobedience on account of grace is nothing more than licentiousness, we must also see that attempted obedience apart from grace is legalism. Children must first come to recognize their inability to remedy their lost condition, followed by an understanding of the redemption and transformation found in the Gospel, before they can understand that good works occur as a result of grace. After all, without faith it is impossible to please God (cf. Heb. 11:6) and those in the flesh cannot please Him (cf. Rom. 8:8). Thus, apart from God's saving grace, even our most sincere obedience is worthless in God's sight (cf. Isa. 64:6, Phil. 3:8).

So when it comes to exhorting our children to godly behavior, we must make *grace-based* application. After, and only after, you have taught your children about God's grace in a passage should you then explain to them how they are to obey the principles and precepts they have learned. This ensures that your children do not misunderstand their response to the passage as a means of earning, or even maintaining, approval from God (cf. Gal. 3:3). Instead, they will see that submission to Christ's commands is the evidence of living by faith, finding delight in serving the One who saved them from their sins (cf. Gal. 2:20, 1 John 5:3).

A proper understanding of this is rare, however. With widespread usage, the trite phrase "love God, love others" is often trumpeted as a summary of the Christian ethic. Yet, as Jesus explained in Matthew 22:40, that phrase on its own is simply a summary of the Law and the Prophets—a standard that we have all failed to achieve. There is no grace in that isolated command; it is a standard that only serves to condemn us for our failure to perform it (cf. Gal. 3:10). After all, anyone with an ounce of honesty has to admit that he *hasn't* loved God and loved others the way he ought.

Thus, whenever the apostles issued commands, they always couched their instruction in divine aid provided through the Gospel. This means that the Christian ethic is not simply to "love God and love others because we're supposed to," (even though that is a true, albeit imprecise, statement). Rather, the Christian ethic is this: "We love, *because He first loved us*" (1 John 4:19). The imperative for believers (that we are to love others) is based on the indicative of the Gospel (that Jesus Christ first loved us). This is the essence of grace-based obedience.

Such a paradigm of grace-based obedience is not only found in single verses, but also serves as the template for entire New Testament letters. For example, in the book of Colossians, Paul spends the first two chapters exalting Christ and demonstrating His supremacy over all things. Then, after Paul indicates the glorious work of Christ found in the Gospel, he transitions in the final two chapters to instruct believers how to live an exalted life in light of that reality.

So, as we teach our children, it is not only helpful, but it is mandatory, that we provide them with instruction that is based on God's grace found in the Gospel. Our kids ought to know that the reason we love our enemies is not simply because "it's the right thing to do," but because "God demonstrates His own love towards us, in that while we were yet sinners, Christ died for us" (Rom. 5:8). Do you see the difference? One is an instruction based on Law, the other is an instruction based on the Gospel. Pastor Bryan Chapell states it succinctly as follows:

> Christ-centered preaching does not abolish the normative standards of Christian conduct but rather locates their source in the compelling power of grace. In Christ-centered preaching, the rules of Christian obedience do not change; the reasons do. Believers are exhorted to serve God in response to his sure mercy rather than in payment for his conditional favor.[73]

Dr. Stephen Olford, notable expositor of the past, provides similar insight:

> It is possible to preach commitment, responsibility, lifestyle, or challenge without any significant reference to Christ Himself, His redemptive activity, and the resources available in Him. To put it another way, just as you can miss the glorious foundational truths of God's mercy, grace, and promise in the exposition of an Old Testament text, the same can be true in one's approach to the New Testament. We are not so concerned about one such message to committed Christians who understand God's mercy, grace, and promise in Christ; but, to consistently preach "Be,"

---

[73] Bryan Chapell, *Christ-centered Preaching: Redeeming the Expository Sermon, 2nd ed.* (Grand Rapids, MI: Baker, 2005), 312.

"Do," "Change" messages without the essential truths that make such directives *meaningful* and obedience *possible* is to miss the forest for the trees.[74]

Olford's words could not be more insightful. These "Be" sermons— "Be Good," "Be Better," "Be Like"—are dominant approaches that characterize many churches. And because these kinds of messages are almost always devoid of prerequisite grace, they are spiritually deadly to the hearers. Sunday after Sunday, many believers gather in church only to be saddled up and beaten down with instruction after instruction—pray more, study harder, serve longer. They are never taught about the grace of God that provides the forgiveness for their failures and the impetus for their success.

Pastor John MacArthur likewise emphasizes the need for redemptive, grace-based application:

It seems to me that many are content to talk about things that are important things that we need to know. But they are secondary matters. They call people to better spiritual devotion. They call people to more faithfulness to the Lord, to greater obedience, to greater holiness, but without the vision that is essential to that sanctification which is the vision of Christ in all His fullness and all His glory. Messages on better Christian living are important. Messages on having more faith are strategic. Messages on being less anxious and more joyful, more thankful, we must hear those messages. We do need more discipline. But all those injunctions and all those good intentions and instructions are weak when they are disconnected from the critical motive behind their pursuit which is the knowledge of the glories of Christ that generates

---

[74] Stephen F. Olford and David L. Olford, *Anointed Expository Preaching* (Nashville, TN: Broadman & Holman, 1998), 133-134.

love for Him which then becomes the driving force in obedience.[75]

Returning to the story of David and Goliath, the reality is that there certainly are instructions for your child to obey; there are aspects of the passage that can and should direct your child's thoughts and behavior. And as you teach, you cannot simply do a verse-by-verse commentary of the text, you also need to draw out and drive home its implications. But they must be given *after* the divine solution has been explained. Your children must come to understand that Christian obedience is a *response to,* not a *reason for,* God's love in their lives.

Thus, rather than teaching your child a moralistic principle from the story of David and Goliath, the first point of application ought to be in explaining that God providentially protected His people in order to keep His covenant promises, teaching us that we can and should trust Him to keep His promises to us today.

The second point of application is related to the theme of God using the weak to shame the strong. Just as God raised up an unskilled shepherd boy to deliver His people (a foolish choice by the world's standards), so too does He provide salvation through the Gospel (a foolish message by the world's standards). We must abandon the way that seems right in our own eyes, and instead entrust our lives to the word of the cross (cf. 1 Cor. 1:18).

Furthermore, it is even legitimate to use David himself for application. After all, the New Testament relies upon both positive and negative examples from the Old Testament in order to explain godly

---

[75] John MacArthur, "An Introduction to Christ in the Old Testament," *GTY Resources: Sermon*, Grace to You, September 27, 2016, https://www.gty.org/library/sermons-library/90-430.

living (cf. 1 Cor. 10:6, 1 John 3:12, Luke 17:32).[76] In 1 Corinthians 11:1 the Apostle Paul explicitly stated, "Be imitators of me." But notice how the verse ends: "…just as I also am of Christ." Even when using himself as an example, Paul made sure his instruction was framed within the context of salvation.

Thus, rather than simply telling our children to "be like David," a more helpful phrase would be "learn from David." In other words, since David was a sinful man, yet still used by God to accomplish important things, there are both positive and negative behaviors that he exhibited in his life. David is not like Jesus in that we can simply say, "Be like him." When David honored God, led with integrity, or repented of his sin, our children ought to learn that they can and should do these things with the Holy Spirit's help (cf. Heb. 11:32). But when David engaged in polygamy, plotted to murder a woman's husband, and lived in hypocrisy, our children obviously ought to avoid his example.

A foundational understanding of godliness will allow you to derive principles from a passage in order to teach your children God-honoring thoughts, words, and actions. No matter what, though, your application must always begin at the foot of the cross and work its way out from there.

Present Yourself Approved to God

It's no wonder that Paul instructed his disciple Timothy to "be diligent" in handling Scripture properly. Proper interpretation is hard work and it's been well said that the Bible does not yield its fruit to the

---

[76] Mark Dever, J. Ligon Duncan, III, R. Albert Mohler, Jr., C.J. Mahaney, John MacArthur, John Piper, and R.C. Sproul. *Preaching the Cross*. Wheaton, IL: Crossway, 2007. 64.

lazy.[77] Just as pastors must continue to study and expand their knowledge in order to rightly handle God's Word, so too must we as parents.

In a moment of honesty, we would have to admit that it would be much easier to march through the Bible and simply say to our kids, "Do this. Don't do that. Do this. Don't do that." Explaining the context, properly exalting Christ, and determining age-appropriate, grace-based application is time-consuming. But bludgeoning our children with verse-by-verse moralism would be, quite simply, a sinful use of the Bible.

There is no doubt that the opportunity costs are high in order to be a skilled exegete and expositor for your family. But what other options do you have if you want to raise your children to know and love the Lord? Teach the Bible incorrectly? Teach it superficially? Not teach it at all? No, you must be diligent to present yourself approved to God as a workman who does not need to be ashamed, accurately handling the word of truth.

To become approved for shepherding will likely mean that you need to put in a great deal of time in your own study before and after teaching your children. Whether it's consulting commentaries, listening to additional sermons throughout the week, or taking notes in your Bible, being diligent involves continuing to develop your own knowledge so that you are prepared. Sequential Scripture-twisting is simply not an option for the shepherd in the home. The warning that Pastor Steve Lawson issues to pastors applies to parents as well:

> There is coming a final day of accountability for every expositor in which he will be made subject to the searching scrutiny of the Lord Jesus Christ.

---

[77] Howard G. Hendricks and William Hendricks, *Living by the Book* (Chicago: Moody, 1991), 80.

Though all his sins have been forgiven and there is no condemnation for those who are in Christ, the preacher nevertheless will stand one day before the One who enlisted him, as a servant to his master, and give an account for his ministry. On that last day, every preacher will be judged, though not for the size of his congregation, nor the number of his staff. He will not be examined for the volume of his budget, nor for the upward mobility of his flock. In large measure, he will be reviewed for his handling of the written Word of God.[78]

Sadly, many modern sermons do not reflect such sobriety. Is the exodus from Egypt really about being like Moses and confronting the "Pharaohs" in your life? Did Jesus calm the storm on the Sea of Galilee so that we would trust Him to calm the "storms" in our life? Are you supposed to "find your Boaz" based on the book of Ruth? Such blatant silliness is not as uncommon as it should be.

But even with good intentions, many preachers fail to abide by biblical hermeneutics, interpreting verses out of context. Some regularly neglect the redemptive nature of the text, focusing on the imperatives in Scripture apart from the gracious indicatives that precede them. Others abandon application entirely, opting for a "let go and let God" approach to Christian living. By becoming an approved shepherd you will not only be able to correctly handle the Word, but you will be equipped to evaluate how others have interpreted the Bible to know if they are handling it correctly.

In the end, the purpose in teaching your children the Bible is not merely to apply principles for particular issues they are facing, but also to help them think rightly about the God who made them. For that reason, it's important to recognize that deep and meaningful theology

---

[78] Steve Lawson, "The Preacher and His Accountability," *Expositor Magazine*, July 2015, 7.

is a necessary component of godly instruction. Thus, while expository preaching begins with properly interpreting a text, exalting Christ from the passage, and issuing grace-based instruction to the hearer, it doesn't stop there—it must be accompanied by sound doctrine.

5
MINIATURE THEOLOGIANS

"Many people believe that theological study holds little value. They say, 'I don't need theology; I just need to know Jesus.' Yet theology is unavoidable for every Christian. It is our attempt to understand the truth that God has revealed to us—something every Christian does. So it is not a question of whether we are going to engage in theology; it is a question of whether our theology is sound or unsound."[79]

–R.C. Sproul

Focus Text: *…preach the word; be ready in season and out of season; reprove, rebuke, exhort, with great patience and instruction. (2 Timothy 4:2)*

By teaching through the Bible verse by verse, your kids will be learning how redemptive history unfolds—that is, the way in which God has brought about the salvation of His people throughout the ages. They'll see Adam and Eve's sin in the Garden, followed by God's promise to send a Savior to crush the serpent's head. They'll learn about the promises of land, descendants, and worldwide blessing given by God to Abraham. They'll discover the salvation of the Israelites out of the land of Egypt, the sending of prophets to the kingdoms of Judah and Israel, and the return of the Israelites from captivity. On into the New Testament they will be taught about the earthly ministry of Christ, the work of the apostles, the future

---

[79] R.C. Sproul, *Everyone's a Theologian: An Introduction to Systematic Theology* (Orlando, FL: Reformation Trust, 2014), 12.

Millennial Kingdom, and the eternal state. Ultimately, they will witness the promises made in the Old Testament and the promises kept in the New Testament.

And each redemptive period of the Bible, if it is taught properly, will be used to point your child's heart towards Jesus Christ—not only His perfect life, atoning death and triumphant resurrection, but also the way in which everything in the Bible finds its fulfillment in Him. They will have a firm grasp on the Bible's salvific storyline.

Yet, at the same time, there is more to the Bible than just a "story," more than just a narrative.[80] Yes, the storyline is *foundational* to our understanding of what God has done in and through His Son. Certainly, all of the Old Testament types and shadows of Christ are essential to properly understanding what the Bible teaches. And we must always consider the ways in which all things will culminate in the return of Christ. But the Bible tells us more than that. The Bible teaches us *doctrine*. The Bible teaches us categories of theological truth. And because all Scripture is in harmony with itself, that means that the entire Bible works together, systematically, to provide a cohesive and logical explanation of all areas of theology.

This "system" that the Bible teaches is what we would call *systematic theology*—the organization and summary of various doctrines taught in the Bible.[81] Systematic theology is concerned with theological categories such as the doctrine of God ("Theology Proper"), the doctrine of man ("anthropology"), and the doctrine of salvation ("soteriology"). Systematic theology uses the entire Bible to provide a comprehensive answer to particular doctrinal questions.

---

[80] John MacArthur, *Parables: The Mysteries of God's Kingdom Revealed Through the Stories Jesus Told* (Nashville, TN: Thomas Nelson, 2015), 195.
[81] Wayne A. Grudem, *Systematic Theology: An Introduction to Biblical Doctrine* (Leicester, England: Inter-Varsity, 1994), 24.

To illustrate this, imagine that the Bible were an automobile. If you worked at a car manufacturing facility, you would have the opportunity to see the car created and assembled from start to finish. You'd see it begin as the raw material. You'd see the frame fashioned into its proper form. You'd watch robotic arms perform welds and attach the various components to the car. You'd see the paint booth apply a dazzling coat of color. And finally, you'd see the finished car roll off the assembly line. By working at the automotive plant, you'd gain an in-depth understanding of all the various parts and pieces of the car and how they fit together. You'd know how the car began, where it ended, and what each step looked like along the way. This process represents the unfolding storyline of redemption that your children will learn as you teach them the Bible verse by verse.

On the other hand, consider the different perspective you'd have if you worked at a car dealership. You would still have an intimate knowledge of the vehicle, but it would be in a different way. As a salesman, you may not have watched as all the different sections were fitted together, but you would know all about the specifications and technical details of the car—the size of the engine, fuel economy characteristics, and various luxury accessories. Not only that, but you would also be able to explain how the car functions as a finished product, which features stand out, and how it compares to other vehicles. This knowledge represents the function and purpose of systematic theology.

So, which perspective of the car is better? The answer is neither. It's not that one of these is necessary and the other is unnecessary; on the contrary, they are both critically important but in different ways and for different reasons. The same is true of the instruction you give your children. They need verse-by-verse instruction in order to understand the narrative of redemption as it unfolds throughout the

Bible, but they also need doctrinal instruction in order to understand the theological categories taught by the Bible. Pastor and theologian R.C. Sproul comments on these two aspects as follows:

> At many seminaries, the systematic theology department is separate from the New Testament department and the Old Testament department. This is because the systematic theologian has a different focus than the Old Testament professor and the New Testament professor. Biblical scholars focus on how God has revealed Himself at various points over time, while the systematician takes that information, puts it all together, and shows how it fits into a meaningful whole.[82]

Expository Preaching Is Doctrinal Preaching

...preach the word; be ready in season and out of season; reprove, rebuke, exhort, with great patience and instruction. (2 Timothy 4:2)

So how do these two aspects work together? In the landmark passage on expository preaching (2 Tim. 4:2), the Apostle Paul charged Timothy to "preach the Word," which has been shown to mean that pastors are to teach sequentially through the Bible. The outcome of this is that the hearers will come to a knowledge of God's redemptive plan both in the past and the future. Being led through the Bible unfolds the history of what God has done to save His people from their sins. Consecutive expository preaching provides the important knowledge of Scripture's redemptive storyline.

But notice that after Paul told Timothy to "preach the Word" he didn't leave it at that. Paul also gave Timothy instructions regarding

---

[82] R.C. Sproul, *Everyone's a Theologian: An Introduction to Systematic Theology* (Orlando, FL: Reformation Trust, 2014), 7.

additional aspects that were to characterize his preaching. Timothy was to preach when it was popular as well as when it was not ("in season and out of season"). He was to refute error ("reprove"), convict of sin ("rebuke"), and urge his hearers to pursue godliness ("exhort"). He was to be compassionate and enduring with his hearers ("with great patience"). And finally, he was to accompany his preaching with *instruction*.

This final characteristic ("instruction") comes from the Greek word *didache*, which is related to the act of teaching and refers to a set pattern of Christian beliefs or practices.[83] The idea behind this word is that the entire Bible, functioning as a single unit, teaches a "set" or "system" of collective truths. Although the Bible was written by dozens of authors over hundreds of years, the reality is that it teaches unified truths — truths about who God is, who man is, how one can be saved, what the future holds, and so on. The authors explain a consistent set of truths about reality. Thus, to "preach the Word with instruction" means to herald God's Word *while also* including and explaining systematic truths that help the hearers understand lofty theology. In other words, expository preaching, if performed according to Paul's instruction, will also be doctrinal preaching.

What Paul was saying is that it would not be enough for Timothy simply to stand and explain the Scriptures line-by-line, urging his people to obey what they heard. Yes, that was and is the foundational element of sequential exposition — reading and teaching the Scriptures verse by verse is the critical first step. But along with these things, Timothy was to accompany his preaching with *instruction*. He was to help his hearers have a thorough understanding of not only the

---

[83] Frederick W. Danker, Walter Bauer, and William F. Arndt, *A Greek-English Lexicon of the New Testament and Other Early Christian Literature, 3rd ed.* (Chicago: University of Chicago Press, 2000), 241.

particular passage at hand, but an understanding of the passage as it sits in harmony with the rest of Scripture. All of the biblical testimony as a "set" was to be included as he preached the biblical testimony in "pieces." This would not only ensure that his teaching remained within the bounds of orthodoxy; it would also provide tremendous maturation for his hearers.

Returning to the analogy of the automobile, imagine how enriched a worker at a manufacturing facility would be by having the knowledge of a salesman. Not only would he know how the car is assembled at each stage of production, but with a salesman's knowledge, he would have a better grasp of the final product's performance characteristics. He would be able to envision the completed car, giving him a better appreciation of the process used to create it. And he would recognize the value of his work by contemplating the price tag associated with the finished automobile.

This same paradigm ought to be leveraged by the preacher while teaching through the Bible. He ought to use the Bible as a *whole* while teaching the Bible *in parts,* so that his hearers might gain a systematic understanding of doctrine as they learn the redemptive storyline of Scripture.

While preaching through the book of Leviticus, the preacher may draw from the book of Hebrews as he explains the doctrine of the atonement (and theological words like "propitiation" and "intercession"). While preaching through the Gospel of John, the preacher may incorporate material from Romans and Ephesians in order to explain the doctrines of election and predestination. Whatever the case may be, the fact is that no passage sits in isolation; no theological truth exists in a vacuum. Instead, all of the Bible can (and must) be used to explain individual verses.[84]

In fact, this concept is so important that in order to be qualified to be an elder, Titus 1:9 says that a man's theology must be in accordance with "the teaching" (the Greek word *didache* again used here). In other words, the evidence that a man can be a pastor is that his beliefs line up with the systematic theology of the apostles.

Titus 1:9 goes on to say that the reason the pastor must possess this qualification is so that he can then go on to "exhort in sound doctrine." A commitment to the systematic truths of the Christian faith is necessary so that those same systematic truths can be taught to other believers. The application for today is that legitimate expository preaching must also be doctrinal. If doctrine is not being taught, expository preaching is not occurring as it should. Every pastor who is faithfully preaching the Word should be raising up doctrinally mature congregants.

Bringing Theology Home

At this point you may be thinking, "But I'm no theologian!" Or you might be tempted to say, "Well, I'm not really all that into theology." But those assertions simply aren't true. The moment you or I say something about the nature of God, man, church, salvation, or really any meaningful aspect of reality, we have made a theological assertion and have entered the realm of theology. So it's not so much about whether you and I as parents hold theological convictions, but rather, whether or not such convictions are biblically accurate. Thus, you *are* engaging in theology as you teach your child the Bible. You simply need to be aware of this reality in advance because it will shape

---

[84] Martyn Lloyd-Jones, *Preaching and Preachers* (London: Hodder and Stoughton, 1971), 66.

and strengthen your commitment to doctrinal precision.

With this in mind, as you teach your children through the Bible, you are going to come across some passages that require a more in-depth explanation in order to communicate their significance. In some cases, there may be overarching themes or doctrines that need to be fleshed out in greater detail so that your kids don't miss out on the depth of the particular passage. At other times, you may need to reconcile one truth in Scripture with another found elsewhere. But to deviate from the passage at hand in order to address these concerns in detail would undoubtedly impede your progress through the Bible. You would find yourself quickly heading down rabbit trails to explain each point. On top of that, you would likely overwhelm your kids by trying to work your way through multiple passages of Scripture at the same time in order to develop a theological point completely.

For example, Psalm 51:5 states, "Behold, I was brought forth in iniquity, and in sin my mother conceived me." In this pivotal passage, King David was expressing an aspect of the doctrine known as Total Depravity—that is, the theological truth that all men are born guilty, sinful, spiritually dead in their sins, unable to please God, and unwilling to be reconciled to Him. This naturally raises questions. *How is it that King David was born in sin? And how could a child be this guilty and sinful from his earliest moments in life?*

Well, in order to provide a comprehensive answer you would need to draw on a variety of passages such as Genesis 3:1-19, Ephesians 2:1-3, and Romans 5:12-14. These passages, among others, collectively explain that because the first man, Adam, represented the entire human race in the Garden of Eden, his rebellion against God by eating the forbidden fruit consequently cast all of humanity into rebellion as well. His first act of sin was on behalf of all mankind, which brought about the Fall that renders every human guilty and sinful from the time of conception. This also means everyone is born spiritually dead and alienated from God, captive to sin in every aspect of our being.

Much more could be said about the doctrine of Total Depravity, but the point is this: in order to fully explain all of this theology to a child, you would have to deviate considerably from the original passage you were teaching (Psalm 51:5). Not only that, but you would be heaping an overwhelming amount of information onto him or her all at once.

But what if there were a way to give your kids theology in advance? What if you could prepare your children with these kinds of doctrines so that as you teach through the Bible, they are already familiar with the theological terms you will use? What if you could gradually introduce these terms and ideas so that they slowly build up like a set of blocks being stacked upon each other? If we consider how a pastor accomplishes this, we'll have a good idea as to how we are to accomplish this.

When pastors preach from the pulpit, they will point out key doctrines and theological themes as they work their way through the Bible. This is essentially what it means to use the Bible to teach the Bible. Because the pastor has a comprehensive, systematic understanding of the entire Bible, he is able to recognize the way in which various passages of Scripture relate to one another, and can use that knowledge to properly and effectively explain each text.

Returning to the example, the doctrine of Total Depravity teaches that men are born spiritually dead in their sins as a result of the Fall, unable and unwilling to repent and seek after God. On that basis, we can understand why men must be born again if they are to enter into the Kingdom of God; every man is in need of a new heart and spiritual life. The Holy Spirit, therefore, is the one who does this—He causes men to be born again, brought out of depravity and into spiritual life (cf. John 3:5). This is the doctrine of Regeneration. Once you come to understand both doctrines, you can "systematize" them by noticing their cause-and-effect relationship—the doctrine of Total Depravity is what necessitates the doctrine of Regeneration. Because men are born spiritually dead, the Holy Spirit must cause men to be born again.

Of course, these doctrines may not be known by the average hearer, nor are they defined in Scripture like a textbook. Therefore, a pastor must explain these doctrines during the course of his consecutive exposition. While teaching through a single passage, the pastor's job is to enlist the aid of other passages in order to explain the theological implications at hand. While expositing the third chapter of Romans (which teaches the doctrine of Total Depravity), the pastor may point out to his hearers that the doctrine of Regeneration is necessary because of what the text says about mankind's fallen condition. Likewise, while expositing the third chapter of John (which teaches the doctrine of Regeneration), the pastor may point out to his hearers that the doctrine of Total Depravity is what necessitates the new birth spoken of in the text. To explain doctrine during the course of an expository sermon is to point the hearer's mind to the lofty theological implications of the text that may not be readily apparent.

Just as a pastor utilizes this type of systematic theology in his preaching, so should you utilize systematic theology while teaching your children. Imagine if you were working through the book of John and came to chapter three in which Jesus tells Nicodemus that a man must be born again if he is to see the kingdom of God. Perhaps your child may ask, "Why do people need to be born again to enter Heaven?" The answer to that question involves all that has been said about the doctrine of Total Depravity. But again, that would require considerable effort to communicate to your child in the moment.

Instead, the solution is to provide your child with that theological answer *beforehand*. Before you ever reach the third chapter of John, teach them that the reason why we must be born again is because we are all born guilty and sinful, needing new hearts before we can be fit for Heaven. By doing this, you won't have to work through this theological answer while in the middle of your passage; you simply refer them back to the answer they've already memorized.

This means you have to teach your children basic systematic theology *in addition* to daily Bible instruction. Perhaps your initial thought is, "How in the world can you teach a young child systematic theology?" That might sound like a tall order, but don't let the phrase "systematic theology" mislead you. For kids, this kind of instruction simply goes by a different name—the often neglected and almost entirely forgotten practice known as *catechism*.

What Is Catechism?

It may be that you have very little knowledge of catechism; perhaps you have heard the term in passing or faintly know that it is some type of religious instruction. Or, it may be that you have more memories of catechism than you'd ever care for—you're thinking back on a time of cold-hearted discipline in an overbearing religious upbringing, rather than joyful education in a Christian home. Whatever the case may be, you would do well to visit this concept with fresh ears.

Christian catechism can be defined as a set of doctrinal questions and answers that provides a basic theological framework of Christianity. Beyond addressing fundamental questions of the faith such as "Who is God?", "What is sin?", and "What must you do to be saved?", a catechism also asks important questions such as "How can God justify you?", "How were sinners saved before Christ came?", and "What happens to our bodies when we die?"

In Galatians 6:6, Paul told Christians that "the one who is taught the word is to share all good things with the one who teaches him." The teaching spoken of in this passage comes from the verb *katécheó* which means "to communicate information."[85] More specifically, it is often used in reference to those giving and receiving basic Christian instruction for new converts. The concept here is a reference to oral instruction by nuanced repetition: teaching, by word of mouth, foundational truths of the Christian faith. In other words, this verb quite simply means "to catechize." Thus, catechism is not only a biblical concept; it is also a biblical word. Ultimately, catechism (more formally known as "catechesis") is the process of a teacher communicating Christian doctrine to a student in a systematic, repetitive, and oral fashion.

Rather than haphazardly teaching random and disconnected things from the Bible, the goal of catechism is to teach biblical doctrine in a straightforward and logical fashion through a series of questions and answers that build upon one another. And since catechism questions are intended for oral instruction, the common practice is for the teacher to ask a theological question and for the student to recite back the memorized answer. The teacher and student go back and forth through a series of questions and answers, reciting them on a regular basis so that the content becomes ingrained.

Take, for example, the doctrine of the Trinity: the Being of the one true God exists eternally as three distinct, coequal, coeternal, consubstantial Persons—Father, Son, and Holy Spirit.[86] The Father is

---

[85] Frederick W. Danker, Walter Bauer, and William F. Arndt, *A Greek-English Lexicon of the New Testament and Other Early Christian Literature*, 3rd ed. (Chicago: University of Chicago Press, 2000), 534.
[86] James R. White, *The Forgotten Trinity* (Minneapolis, MN: Bethany House, 1998), 26.

truly God, the Son is truly God, and the Spirit is truly God. Yet, the Father is *not* the Son, the Son is *not* the Spirit, and the Spirit is *not* the Father. They are each distinct Persons and yet they are one with each other as the divine Being of God. This foundational doctrine of Christianity is clearly one of the most difficult to wrap our minds around. At the same time, because God is distinct and unique from His creation, it shouldn't surprise us that our minds have difficulty grasping this truth. In fact, if we *were* to fully grasp it, in many ways it would undermine the very reality that God is, by nature, distinct and different from His creation!

With that in mind, consider trying to explain this doctrine to a five-year-old who is still learning basic math—you have a recipe for a mental meltdown! *How is it that there is only one God and yet the Father, Son, and Spirit are all God?* Perhaps you might be tempted to use down-to-earth analogies to explain the Trinity to your children (comparing God to water, an egg, or a shamrock). Yet, as already stated, the truth is that God's existence is anything *but* "down-to-earth." He is the transcendent Creator in Heaven and thus defies being compared to any creaturely example.

For example, think through what it would look like to compare the Trinity to an egg. An egg consists of a shell, the yolk, and the white, and together they constitute an egg. But there's a problem with the analogy: the shell, yolk, and white are not *each* fully "egg." In addition, each component does not consist of the same substance (the shell is made up of a different substance than the yolk, which is of a different substance than the white). Thus, this analogy truly fails to illustrate the nature of God's existence (worse yet, it actually depicts a heretical view of God known as Tritheism).[87]

This puts us in a predicament: we want to avoid using analogies for the doctrine of the Trinity, yet this doctrine is so foundational to the faith that we can't put it off until later in our child's life. Instead, we can only explain this reality using words and concepts based on the Scriptures. How can this be accomplished? Consider the doctrine of the Trinity taught by way of a catechism, based on the following questions and answers:

Question: "Are there more gods than one?"
Answer: "No. There is only one true God."

Question: "In how many Persons does this one true God exist?"
Answer: "Three."

Question: "Name these three Persons."
Answer: "God the Father, God the Son, and God the Holy Spirit."

By basic memorization you can teach your children an accurate description of God. Does this mean your kids actually understand this truth simply because they've recited the answers? Not likely—they are simply repeating what has been drilled into their heads. But, because you are also teaching them through the Scriptures, their understanding will begin to solidify when you come to accounts that illustrate and portray the Trinitarian nature of God.

Here's an example of how this plays out: by teaching through Matthew 3:13-17 (the account of Jesus' baptism), your kids will hear

---

[87] R.C. Sproul, *Everyone's a Theologian: An Introduction to Systematic Theology* (Orlando, FL: Reformation Trust, 2014), 54.

about the Father speaking to the Son and sending the Spirit to descend upon Him. By memorizing the aforementioned catechism questions ahead of time, your kids will already know that there is only one true God, and that each of the three Persons described in the passage is truly divine. But now with the passage at hand, your kids will witness these three Persons existing and interacting simultaneously during the baptism event. Doctrinal facts about the Godhead were committed to memory in advance, and now those doctrines are being depicted in a narrative—the Father says of the Son, "This is My beloved Son, in whom I am well-pleased," and the Spirit descends upon the Son as a dove. The Bible confirms what your children had memorized in their catechism, and the truth begins to take shape in their young minds.

Thus, what you have done is *explained* the doctrine of the Trinity by rote memorization beforehand, using a catechism, and then *illustrated* the doctrine of the Trinity using verse-by-verse teaching through the Scriptures. In the end, this is exactly how the doctrine of the Trinity must be understood—since nothing in creation serves as an adequate analogy to describe God. Instead, the doctrine of the Trinity is a *revealed truth*—something that is learned only through divine revelation, by reading and understanding what God has said about Himself as recorded in Scripture.[88]

How does this work out in a practical sense? Once your kids have memorized catechism answers, you can then briefly interrupt your verse-by-verse teaching with the particular catechism questions that are related to the passage you are currently teaching. This has the benefit of not only ensuring that they are listening intently to your instruction, but also helps them understand the theology that is being

---

[88] James R. White, *The Forgotten Trinity* (Minneapolis, MN: Bethany House, 1998), 28-29.

explained.

Consider again the doctrine of the Trinity. While teaching your child about Jesus' baptism, you might explain Matthew 3:16 and then say, "Look son, Jesus was baptized, and when He came up out of the water the Spirit of God descended on Him. You know Jesus is God, but it also says that the Spirit of God was there. Are there more gods than one?" Your child responds with the memorized answer, "No. There is only one true God." You then continue on to Matthew 3:17, and explain that the "voice out of the heavens" spoke to the Son. You pause and turn to your son, saying, "In how many Persons is this one true God?" He responds with "Three," at which point you follow up with, "Name these three Persons." He says, "God the Father, God the Son, and God the Holy Spirit." After that, you turn back to the text, reiterating that it mentioned the Son being baptized and the Spirit descending upon Him. But you finish by saying, "Then who is the 'voice out of the heavens' in this passage?" If your son has been listening closely, thinking about his catechism answer, and using a bit of logic, he will respond with, "God the Father!"

Even though the passage doesn't explicitly say "God the Father," your child's systematic understanding of the nature of God (learned via catechism) allowed him to recognize this account as a clear expression of the Trinity. Rather than trying to come up with your own sophisticated-sounding analogy for the Trinity (which would have only been inadequate and sub-biblical at best), you simply let the words of Scripture provide the illustration. You equipped your child with a bit of systematic theology in advance, and then allowed the Bible to fill in the details for you.

Certainly this is a simplistic example (despite the profundity of the doctrine of the Trinity!), but it is given simply to show how to include doctrinal instruction with biblical exposition. Perhaps at times you may have to be a bit creative in order to link a particular catechism question to the text. At other times it may be that the theology of the text is straightforward enough that it doesn't require a particular doctrinal question. But more often than not, there will be plenty of ways to introduce catechism questions into your daily exposition of the Scriptures.

As you leverage the tremendous power of catechism alongside sequential exposition, it will train your children to think systematically and doctrinally. They will not only ponder the immediate teaching of each passage, but also its theological implications. The benefits simply cannot be overstated. Preaching the Word sequentially produces a chronological knowledge of God's redemptive plan, and teaching a catechism produces a categorical knowledge of God's redemptive plan—both working together to enlighten the mind of your miniature theologian.

Implementing a Catechism

Although there are a variety of ways to catechize your child, the driving emphasis must be on "repetition, repetition, and repetition." The ultimate purpose of catechism is to ingrain systematic truths into the minds of your children so that these truths are immediately accessible to them as you teach through the Bible.

The first step to take is, of course, to select a catechism. The most obvious way to do this would be to get a copy of your church's catechism, if they formally hold to one in particular. Many churches align themselves with historic creeds and confessions of the past, which often include an associated catechism (i.e. the Westminster Confession of Faith). If your church does not have an official catechism, then the next best thing to do would be to discuss various options with your church's leaders. Ask your elders for suggestions as to which catechisms would most closely match the theological perspectives of your church. Perhaps there is a particular catechism that is used in a Sunday School or children's ministry setting that you could adopt in your home. If all else fails, you may just have to do some research on your own to determine which catechisms correspond to your own personal convictions and the things you aim to teach your children.

There are a number of good historic catechisms to choose from such as the Westminster Shorter Catechism, Westminster Longer Catechism, Heidelberg Catechism, and the 1689 London Baptist Catechism. One in particular, the Joseph Engle's 1840 Catechism for Young Children (with updated language), stands out as one of the best and most popular catechisms.

Bear in mind that catechisms aren't divinely inspired—even the best of the best may require minor adjustments in order to ensure theological accuracy. Some might contain certain questions and answers that do not line up with what you intend to teach, and can simply be modified as necessary. After all, biblical fidelity is of greater importance than historical allegiance whenever the two cannot be reconciled.

Once you have a catechism selected, it would be helpful to divide it up into sets of approximately five questions. So, for example, if your catechism were to consist of one hundred total questions, you might consider grouping the questions into twenty sets (ideally, the questions in each set would be doctrinally related). Remember, rather than existing as a collection of questions in a random order, most catechisms will work through questions and answers in a theologically specific sequence, touching on various elements of the faith in order. That should help determine how to divide up the questions into sets.

To begin, simply teach your children the first set of five or so questions. Sit down with your children and read both the questions and answers out loud. Have them read along with you if they can. Repeat the set several times, and then ask the questions and see if your children can recite the answers from memory. That completes the first day of catechism (yes, it's that simple!). The next day, do it all over again—ask the questions, wait for the answers, and provide help as needed. That completes day two. Continue this daily process of reading the questions, hearing your child recite the answers, and helping as needed, until the day comes when your child can recite the answers to the entire first set of questions all on his or her own.

One critical aspect of recitation that ought to be understood is that the answers to the questions need to be precise. Since the goal is to commit these to memory, answers cannot be considered correct unless they match the wording of the answer *exactly* (with the exception being words like "the" or "a," which are often inconsequential). Once your children are able to accurately repeat back the answers to each of those questions, add the next set of questions of the catechism into your daily training. And notice that this is *adding*, not *replacing with*, the next set of questions.

In other words, once the first set of five questions is successfully recited, routine catechism should then contain ten questions (five from the first set, and five new questions). Each day when you begin catechism training, you start back at the very first question. You ask each question in sequence until you get to the latest questions. Once you get to the latest questions (those that your children are still learning), you provide assistance as needed.

Obviously, what this means is that each additional set of questions makes the task of catechism not only longer each day, but more difficult. In reality, there may come a point at which it becomes cumbersome to work through every question each time you do catechism. In that case, you may decide that some days will only be spent working on the latest set of questions. Regardless, the goal is mastery of the entire catechism, which means that continuing to recite past sets of questions is a critical and necessary part of the process.

Regardless of how you structure it, the process of catechism ought to be a blessing, not a burden, for your children. Becoming a catechism taskmaster is a good way to turn a joyous occasion into a dreaded event. The words of Colossians 3:21 serve as a healthy and necessary command to us as we implement this kind of structured and systematic way of teaching our children: "Fathers, do not exasperate your children, so that they will not lose heart." Catechism should never be used as a punishment or form of discipline, nor should it become a bludgeon that stifles your child's personality or natural affection for the things of God. Instead, if done in a spirit of love and kindness, it will become a time of incredible delight.

Consider a few other ideas that can contribute to the joy of this form of theological instruction:

Provide children with God-centered encouragement along the way. As they progress in their catechism, saying, "Wow, you're awesome!" is a nice compliment, but ultimately directs their celebration inward rather than upward. Instead, use the process to celebrate God and what He's doing in their lives. After a day of successful catechism, have them join you in prayer to thank God for His enabling work in their lives. This will help continue to point their hearts and minds back to Christ, which is the ultimate goal anyway.

Use candy or other small gifts as incremental motivation. Whether it's a piece of candy for a job well done on a particular day, or a larger gift such as a new Bible for greater mastery of the catechism, a simple gift is a great way to celebrate what God is doing in your child's heart and mind.

Add variety to the catechism every now and then. Although the bulk of instruction ought to be straightforward and routine, mixing things up can go a long way. Have your child ask the questions and you provide the answers. Allow a younger child to quiz an older child (or vice versa). Make it a king-of-the-hill competition (one child keeps answering questions until they get stumped, at which point it becomes the next child's turn). There are all kinds of creative ways to use a list of catechism questions.

Ask your child to recall a Bible story that touches on the particular catechism question. Although the purpose of catechism is to help explain the Bible, we ought to also recognize that the Bible can and should help explain the catechism questions. A great way to continue demonstrating the link between sequential exposition and systematic theology is to ask your child if he or she can remember a Bible story that is related to the doctrine of the particular catechism question.

Support the catechism's theology through the use of hymns. Buy an old hymnal and tailor your bedtime song selections to the particular doctrine you wish to emphasize. For example, if you taught your child the account of Jesus' baptism, explaining the doctrine of the Trinity with the related catechism questions, you could finish your time together by singing the well-known hymn "Holy, Holy, Holy" together. Your child will be greatly edified not only by learning sound doctrine, but also by singing it.

Give your child the opportunity to ask you the hardest theology question he or she can think of. Undoubtedly, your training and doctrinal instruction will conjure up all sorts of questions in the minds of your kids. What better way to draw these out than by issuing a "stump dad" challenge? This allows them to talk through whatever they've been contemplating, and gives you the opportunity to assess the depth of their understanding.

At certain times during your church's worship service, quietly ask your child catechism questions. For example, the ordinance of communion often leads to a number of questions from children, especially the younger ones. Thus, as the elements are being handed out you might ask your child questions from the catechism such as, "What does the bread represent?", "What does the juice represent?", or, "Who may rightly take the Lord's Supper?" These are likely the same kinds of questions many children will ask on their own anyway, but by asking these according to the catechism, you can help your children realize that they already know the answers. This empowers them to observe this important ritual with the theological background needed to recognize what is happening and why.

All of these suggestions are simply offered to demonstrate why catechism ought not be a killjoy that robs children of youthful zeal. Yes, it will begin as little more than rote memorization for younger kids. But as you live life together and exposit the Scriptures for them day by day, they will begin to understand something about sound doctrine that many people unfortunately do not—it is very accessible, highly practical, and truly enjoyable.

Instruction Throughout the Ages

The Apostle Paul required his disciple Timothy not only to preach the Word to his congregation, but to accompany his preaching with sound doctrine (the Greek word *didache*). As parents, we must follow suit by catechizing our kids. In fact, the connection between *didache* and catechism has already been identified by faithful saints throughout the ages.

For example, one of the earliest documents used for Christian education, created at the turn of the first century, is known as "The Didache" and is actually regarded as the first catechism![89] In more recent periods of church history, great confessions of faith (such as the Westminster Confession of Faith) have been accompanied by time-tested catechisms. During both the Reformation and Puritan eras, pastors were even known to write their own catechisms in order to equip their congregations. Parents would then use these catechisms at home, recognizing that it was their *duty* to catechize their children. Fathers were advised to catechize their children—whether together or individually—for forty-five to sixty minutes, at least once a week.[90] Consider, for example, the introduction to the 1840 Engle's First Catechism:

> To parents and teachers: You have an awfully responsible office in being entrusted with the training of immortal spirits for the service of God on earth and for glory in heaven. The temporal welfare and the eternal salvation not only of your own children, but of future generations, may depend upon your faithfulness in the discharge of this duty. The

---

[89] Philip Schaff and Henry Wallace, eds., *Nicene and Post-Nicene Fathers, 2nd ed., Vol. VII: Cyril of Jerusalem, Gregory Nazianzen* (New York City: Cosimo, 2007), xii.

[90] Joel R. Beeke, *Parenting By God's Promises: How to Raise Children in the Covenant of Grace* (Orlando, FL: Reformation Trust Pub., 2011), 83.

prosperity, and even the continuance, of the church of God on earth are connected with the religious education of the rising generation.[91]

Clearly, the use of catechisms has a long and rich history. As saints of the past have pointed out, catechism can be a source of delight when implemented in the right way. And this delight also goes for parents, not just children. There are perhaps few things more heart-warming than hearing your child say words like "bathtism," "justication," or "10 Amandments." Mispronunciation of theological terms is a reassuring sign that your children are learning the things of God at the perfect time—when they are young.

Just like we prefer to buy our children shoes that are a little bit oversized in order to get extra use as they grow into them, so too should we teach them doctrine that is advanced so that they have time to "grow into it." And they certainly will grow into it. But the difference between shoes and doctrine is that once your children grow into the shoes that you've provided, the shoes have met their maximum use; they're at the end of their life cycle. On the other hand, when it comes to theology, your kids will be growing into knowledge upon which they will rely for the rest of their lives.

Provided you've put in the effort to catechize your children during their younger years, their theological understanding will serve them even before they leave home. The teenage years will lend themselves to being a time of incredible growth because your kids will be more than ready to read a formal systematic theology book. You can rest assured that if a student is capable of learning trigonometry or biology then he or she is capable of learning ecclesiology (the doctrine of the

---

[91] A.W. Mitchell and Joseph P. Engles, *Catechism for Young Children: Being an Introduction to the Shorter Catechism* (Philadelphia, PA: Presbyterian Board of Publication, 1840).

Church), pneumatology (the doctrine of the Holy Spirit), or eschatology (the doctrine of the end times). And rather than viewing systematic theology as an esoteric subject meant only for pastors and seminarians, your kids will recognize that they are simply learning the deep truths of the Bible meant for believers of all ages to learn, ponder, and ultimately enjoy to the glory of God.

But all of this must begin at a young age. Even in their younger years, if your children have thoughts about God, then they are engaged in theology. Your job, then, is to systematically teach them so that their theology is accurate and meaningful. Surely this is accomplished when you preach the Word…"with instruction."

6

FULFILL YOUR MINISTRY

"Whether you're a pastor, an evangelist, Sunday school teacher, a mom, a dad—as religious authorities, we cannot continue confirming the salvation of people simply based upon their own interpretation of how sincere they were when they made a decision. We can't keep doing this. 'Well then preacher, what must we do?' Using the Word of God, teaching God's Word, we help men, women, and children discern if there is true repentance. Through the Word of God, we help them discern if there is soul-saving faith."[92]

–Paul Washer

Focus Text: *But you, be sober in all things, endure hardship, do the work of an evangelist, fulfill your ministry. (2 Timothy 4:5)*

Having given Timothy a string of pastoral duties to carry out, Paul rounded out the list with the charge to "fulfill your ministry" in 2 Timothy 4:5. The Greek verb for "fulfill," as found in this passage, carries the idea of adding to something in order to complete what is lacking.[93] Paul had given Timothy a large number of orders, and with this final command, Paul let it be known that

---

[92] Paul Washer, "The Great Commission—The Impossible / Possible Task" (G3 Conference 2015, Georgia International Convention Center, Atlanta, GA., January 22, 2015).

[93] Frederick W. Danker, Walter Bauer, and William F. Arndt, *A Greek-English Lexicon of the New Testament and Other Early Christian Literature, 3rd ed.* (Chicago: University of Chicago Press, 2000), 827.

Timothy's ministry was not like a multiple-choice question—no aspect was optional. Thus, Timothy's ministry required obedience in every area of pastoral duty: preaching the Word, refuting error, administering the ordinances, maintaining order and discipline in the church, and various other duties. But in addition to those facets, Paul pointed Timothy's attention to one thing he could not afford to forget: doing the work of an evangelist.

So, what does an evangelist do? The other two New Testament uses of this word provide us with clarity. Acts 21:8 tells us that Philip was an evangelist, and we see him leading the church in the work of evangelism (cf. Acts 8:35). And the second instance, Ephesians 4:11-12, tells us that an evangelist's job is to equip the rest of the church for the work of evangelism. Why would other Christians need to be equipped for this? Because evangelism is the duty of every Christian (cf. Matt. 28:18-20, 1 Pet. 2:9). Nowhere in the Bible is there such a thing as the "spiritual gift of evangelism" (often attributed simply to those with outgoing personalities). Evangelism is nothing more than the act of proclaiming the Gospel to unbelievers who desperately need to hear it. The office of evangelist (which *is* found in the Bible) is different from the act of evangelism. The former is a person who leads and prepares the church for the latter.

Therefore, all believers have both the privilege and responsibility to evangelize—which included Timothy. By commanding Timothy to do the work of an evangelist, Paul wanted to remind him that there would always need to be an evangelistic focus of his ministry that continued looking to reach unbelievers with the good news of the Gospel. Yes, as a pastor, Timothy's primary focus needed to be on edifying believers within his local congregation. But it would have been shortsighted for him to neglect those outside the church who had yet to hear about Jesus. Even more, it would have been naïve for him to assume that everyone within his congregation was actually saved. In order to fulfill his ministry, Timothy needed to make sure that there was a component of his preaching addressed to the lost. And that need continues today.

Simply put, a pastor's job is not complete until he has done the work of an evangelist. Dr. Steve Lawson affirms this when he says, "We're preaching to people that they might be won to Christ. We urge, we compel, we summon. Every expositor must be an evangelist. We don't get a free pass on this. We don't just delegate this to others."[94]

This means, by extension, that a parent's job is not complete until he or she has also done the work of an evangelist. In fact, perhaps the worst thing any parent could do in the task of discipling children would be to assume that they have adopted the Christian faith simply by growing up in a Christian home. A great number of faulty testimonies begin with, "Well, I've been a Christian all my life..." when the reality is that there is no such thing. God's Word says that we are all born in sin (cf. Psa. 51:5), spiritually dead (cf. Eph. 2:1-3), and in need of a new birth (cf. John 3:3). So there must come a point in time when your children hear the Gospel and respond to its claims with genuine repentance and faith. Just as the pastor cannot assume that everyone in his church is saved, neither can we assume that everyone in our homes is saved.

The Seeker-Sensitive Movement

In order to understand what true evangelism is, it's first helpful to

---

[94] Steven J. Lawson, "The Marks of Expository Preaching, Part III," *PM 501 - Fundamentals of Expository Preaching*, The Master's Seminary Theological Resource Center, accessed August 19, 2016, http://www.theologicalresources.org/the-masters-seminary/24-fundamentals-of-expository-preaching.

consider what evangelism is *not*. Because of the "seeker-sensitive" attractional model of church growth that has taken root in modern Christianity, much of the legitimate work of biblical evangelism has gone by the wayside. Instead of leaving the four walls of the church building in order to find unbelievers to evangelize, seeker-sensitive philosophy holds that churches ought to attract unbelievers to come in and join believers in the Sunday worship service. Rather than *going and preaching* (as the biblical accounts of evangelism depict), the modern method of reaching the lost is by *staying and inviting*.

Today, many churches have crafted a Sunday service in such a way that it is intended to provide unbelievers with a non-confrontational, comforting, and enjoyable experience that caters to their felt needs rather than their real needs. Congregants are often encouraged to invite as many unbelievers as they can to come along and join them on Sunday mornings in what is intended to be a time of worship to God. But because the goal is to get unbelievers to attend for as long as possible (in the hopes that they may somehow progressively become Christians), the offense of the cross and the calling of sinners to repentance inevitably takes a backseat; entertainment often takes its place.

To be fair, the desire to be around unbelievers for the purpose of evangelism is good and right. In John 17, Jesus prayed that Christians would be kept safe from the world, yet *not* taken out of the world. Thus, it's obvious that as believers we cannot, and should not, isolate ourselves from the world as monks and monastics from past centuries have done. We must engage with the unbelievers whom God puts in our path. But in order to do that, we are commanded to make disciples by "going" (cf. Matt. 28:18-20). Yet, the seeker-sensitive model of church growth has totally inverted this idea.

To that end, seeker-sensitive philosophy correctly recognizes that the church and the world ought not be completely isolated from one another. But instead of adopting the biblical solution of sending the church out into the world, the seeker-sensitive paradigm invites the world into the church. The inherent flaw with this thinking is analogous to the difference between putting a boat into water versus putting water into a boat. One allows the vessel to stay afloat, while the other sinks the ship. The truth is that biblical evangelism is a task that is accomplished by being *sent* (cf. Rom. 10:14-15).

These issues of evangelism and church function have great implications for you as a parent because the errors of the seeker-sensitive movement are also the same kinds of errors that we can run into in our homes. At its heart, the seeker-sensitive model functions on primarily three faulty premises. The first faulty premise is the assumption that people are born seeking for God; this is the essence of why it is called "seeker-sensitive." This perspective asserts that unbelievers are actually seeking righteousness, forgiveness, and the things of God. The second faulty premise in this methodology is the concept of assimilating unbelievers into a church congregation based on relationships rather than the Gospel. The idea behind this is that when it comes to these so-called seekers, a cordial relationship with them will convince them to embrace Christianity. The third faulty premise that it operates under is the idea that becoming a Christian occurs incrementally over an extended period of time. Salvation is viewed as a process in which unbelievers gradually develop a saving relationship with Jesus Christ along a "spectrum" of faith. It is assumed that, over time, Christianity will become more appealing to the unbeliever who participates in church life. Know this: these three unbiblical concepts are precisely what you must avoid as you labor to evangelize your children.

Regarding the first faulty premise, Romans 3:11 flatly tells us that no one seeks for God. Thus, as a parent, you must recognize that your children are not born loving God. They are born spiritually dead and children of wrath just as we all are (cf. Eph. 2:1-3). And the Apostle John tells us that everyone who does evil hates the light and runs from God because they do not want their sins exposed (cf. John 3:20). In other words, unbelievers aren't looking for God any more than criminals are looking for the police. Unbelievers are not "seekers," and as your child grows and matures, you will see the evidence of this until he or she is genuinely saved.

Secondly, Romans 1:16 tells us that the Gospel, not relationships with Christians, is the power of God unto salvation. Thus, as a parent, you must recognize that your children do not become believers simply by virtue of being in a Christian family. Nor is the power of the Gospel somehow augmented or enhanced because your child has godly parents. Being in a family of Christians is not the same as being in the family of God. In fact, many children who have grown up to reject Christ often cite the failures of their Christian parents as a form of hypocrisy that justifies their own unbelief. The bottom line is that God's Word, not family life, is what converts the unregenerate heart (cf. Rom. 10:17).

Finally, John 3:3 tells us that unless a person is born again, he cannot see the Kingdom of God. The reality is that a man is saved when the Holy Spirit grants him a new heart, at which point his entire spiritual perspective changes and he embraces the Gospel. He passes from spiritual death to spiritual life, from hatred of God to love of God, and from loving sin to leaving sin (cf. John 5:24). At the moment of re-birth, he is enabled by God to respond to Christ's demand: denying himself, taking up his cross daily, and following the Savior (cf. Luke 9:23). What this clearly represents is a point *in time*, not a process *through time*, in which a man forsakes everything in order to follow

Christ. Yes, it's true that we don't become perfect this side of Heaven. Christians still have sin in their lives and must battle against the flesh daily (cf. Rom. 7:22-23). But the moment when God regenerates and saves a man is just that—a moment. No one gradually repents and believes in Christ, as if in percentages: 10% loving sin and 90% loving Christ, or 50% forsaking one's life and 50% clinging to one's life, or 80% following the Lord and 20% following Satan. No, that is not at all how conversion works—99% saved is 100% lost, and this stark reality applies to your children as well. No one can serve two masters (cf. Matt. 6:24), thus you must recognize that until your children submit to the Lordship of Jesus Christ, they are still under the dominion of Satan. Do not confuse maturity or morality with salvation.

Ultimately, because the priority of seeker-sensitive methodology is to fill a church building by assuming people are searching for holiness, by believing that relationships are the means to convert people, and by thinking that salvation occurs gradually in someone's life given enough time, the result is that legitimate evangelistic work is altogether abandoned. This movement rarely gets around to confronting men and women with the true Gospel, because it assumes that the unbelievers who were invited in are already seeking for God. This methodology rarely gets around to presenting the exclusive demands of following Christ, because such a confrontation would disrupt the relationships that are being developed with the unbelievers present in the church. And this methodology rarely gets around to calling for self-examination and exposing false conversion, because it is assumed that belief in Christ is simply an ongoing process rather than a clear-cut conversion.

All in all, the urgency and sobriety of self-denying, cross-bearing, penitent faith does not fit the seeker-sensitive worldview. If the goal is to get as many unbelievers into the church as possible, the demands of

Christianity only get in the way. Likewise, if your goal is never to offend your child with the truths of Christianity (in order to avoid potentially jeopardizing the relationship), the demands of Christianity will only get in the way. But if you care more about souls than relationships, you must evangelize your children biblically. You must fulfill your ministry by doing the work of an evangelist. Four crucial areas can be identified for accomplishing this: preaching the biblical Gospel, calling for a biblical response, counting the biblical costs, and examining biblical fruit.

Preaching the Biblical Gospel

"What is wrong with the world?!" That is perhaps the most common response whenever a national or international tragedy occurs. Often it is said as an expression of surprise, as if the latest news—whether it be war, terrorism, systemic injustice, or any other number of social issues—has suddenly indicated that things in this world may be "less than ideal." It's the cry of despair when a person realizes that the world is not as pleasant as assumed to be, that people are not actually as good as once thought.

The Bible sets forth a similar question (cf. Psa. 2:1-3). But it also goes on to provide the answer, an answer that has characterized every age of mankind since the beginning of time. Romans 3:10-18 summarizes it succinctly: "…as it is written, 'There is none righteous, not even one; there is none who understands, there is none who seeks for God; all have turned aside, together they have become useless; there is none who does good, there is not even one. Their throat is an open grave, with their tongues they keep deceiving, the poison of asps is under their lips; whose mouth is full of cursing and bitterness; their feet are swift to shed blood, destruction and misery are in their paths, and the path of peace they have not known. There is no fear of God before their eyes.'"

Is this the diagnosis that the world wants to hear? Of course not. Such a characterization is not well-received by the typical unbeliever ("seeker" or otherwise). The lost simply don't want to be told that they are sinners, so it only makes sense that a seeker-sensitive church would need to abandon such an offensive message if it is to create a culture in which unbelievers feel welcome.

Moreover, is this the diagnosis that parents of young children typically want to hear? Hardly. It's certainly understandable why parents would have a hard time coming to terms with the fact that their bright-eyed toddler has a heart that is spiritually dead. Few want to be told that their infant is, as one pastor said, a "viper in a diaper."[95] Yet, a commitment to the biblical Gospel demands that we properly recognize our child's spiritual condition as such. We must acknowledge what the Bible plainly states: once the first man Adam sinned, he set every single one of us at enmity with God (cf. Rom. 5:12).

Thus, rather than being born morally innocent (or even neutral), children actually enter the world as co-combatants and co-conspirators in rebellion against God. They, like everyone else, are born in a state of guilt worthy of eternal punishment. Granted, they don't manifest their sinfulness to the degree that adults do, but their hearts are surely corrupted by sin. It's a difficult pill to swallow, but it is a necessary conclusion if we are to pursue the proper remedy.

In fact, only with that foundational understanding is the Gospel truly understood to be the good news that it is. Romans 5:17-19 states: "For if by the transgression of the one, death reigned through the one, much more those who receive the abundance of grace and of the gift of

---

[95] Voddie Baucham, "The World, the Flesh, and the Devil" (presentation, Overcoming the World: 2014 National Conference, Saint Andrew's Chapel, Sanford, FL, March 13-15, 2014).

righteousness will reign in life through the One, Jesus Christ. So then as through one transgression there resulted condemnation to all men, even so through one act of righteousness there resulted justification of life to all men. For as through the one man's disobedience the many were made sinners, even so through the obedience of the One the many will be made righteous."

Despite mankind's sinful condition, the Son of God entered the world at just the right time as the one and only perfect man Jesus. Living a life of perfection, Jesus succeeded where Adam, as well as each of us, failed. He then willingly died on a cross, taking upon Himself the wrath of God deserved by sinners. On the third day after His death and burial, Jesus rose from the grave, proving that He was who He said He was (God in the flesh) and did what He said He did (gave His life as a ransom for many). The blood He shed on the cross was a payment for sin, and the resurrection confirmed that the payment was accepted by God the Father on behalf of sinners. Because Jesus satisfied God's justice by taking upon Himself the punishment that was due guilty men, He can provide us with what Adam could not—eternal life.

It really should go without saying, but the success or failure of any Gospel ministry depends first and foremost on an accurate understanding of the Gospel. Get the fundamentals wrong and all is lost. To this end, we must dogmatically shun any so-called gospel that deviates from the message of Christ crucified to save sinners. Whether it's the "Therapeutic Gospel" (Jesus wants to help you find your self-worth amidst feelings of brokenness and inadequacy), the "Activist Gospel" (Jesus wants us to develop social and political solutions to redeem and transform the culture), or the "Moralist Gospel" (Jesus gives us a second chance to become better people), scores of counterfeit gospels masquerade in modern Christendom.[96] Instead, the true Gospel is a message of salvation, forgiveness of sin, reconciliation with God, and restoration of all things. Therefore, a biblical Gospel message must speak of sin, wrath, the cross, Christ, resurrection, righteousness, eternal punishment, grace, and atonement.

Despite what we may assume, children *can* grasp these concepts — and don't let anyone tell you otherwise. As theologian A.W. Pink rightly said,

> The glorious character of God, the requirements of His holy Law, the exceeding sinfulness of sin, the wondrous gift of His Son, and the fearful doom that is the certain portion of all who despise and reject Him are to be brought repeatedly before the minds of our little ones. 'They are too young to understand such things' is the devil's argument to deter you from discharging your duty.[97]

As you teach your child the Bible, there is no warrant for watering-down these key aspects of the Gospel. Sin is not an "oopsy-daisy;" sin is rebellion against a holy God. Salvation is not a "do-over;" salvation is the atoning work of Christ on behalf of sinners. It may seem expedient to reduce the message down to a slogan such as "God loves you and has a wonderful plan for your life." It's likely that you could cultivate a positive response much quicker using a shallow, inoffensive message. But as with most shortcuts, it will cost you more in the end, and it can take years of correction to undo the damage caused by an

---

[96] Trevin Wax, "Which Counterfeit Gospels Are Most Prevalent Today?," *Kingdom People: Living On Earth as Citizens of Heaven* (blog), The Gospel Coalition, January 20, 2011, https://blogs.thegospelcoalition.org/trevinwax/2011/01/20/which-counterfeit-gospels-are-most-prevalent-today.

[97] Jeff Pollard and Scott T. Brown, *A Theology of the Family* (Wake Forest, NC: National Center for Family-Integrated Churches, 2014), 346-347.

errant gospel presentation.

Ultimately, the biblical Gospel is the most important thing your children need. A good home life is surely a blessing, a quality education can provide them with wonderful opportunities, and an abundance of friendships may be encouraging, but your kids need more than the earthly comforts offered by shallow seeker-sensitivity. Your kids need salvation from the wrath of God. And that comes only by way of the true Gospel: that God saves sinners from their deserved condemnation by providing for them what they could not provide on their own—pardon and purity, righteousness and reconciliation— through the sacrifice of His own Son, Jesus Christ. This is the message that must be communicated to men, women, and children of all ages.

Calling for a Biblical Response

If the number one error in evangelism is the woeful neglect of an accurate Gospel presentation, perhaps the second greatest error is in the response that is called upon from the hearers. Imagine that you find yourself with a life-threatening illness. You go to the doctor, he gives you a thorough examination, and then provides the diagnosis. Finally, he says, "Well, I have some bad news and some good news. You are very, very sick, but there is a cure for what you have." He then writes a prescription for medicine that is backed by extensive research and is known to heal every single person who has used it.

But imagine that once you finally obtain the medicine from the pharmacist, you end up applying it incorrectly. Perhaps it's an oral medication and you try to take it intravenously. Or maybe it's a transdermal cream and you use it like an eye-dropper. Whatever the error is, the bottom line is that you had the correct diagnosis and knew of the correct cure, but you responded wrongly to the information. Not only did your condition remain unimproved, but you may have even created further health problems by your misuse of the medicine!

In many ways it would be your own fault for assuming you knew how to use the prescription. Your responsibility as a patient means you should have asked for as much clarity as needed. And if the doctor's guidance was not thorough enough, he or she might also share in the blame. But do you know what would be worse? If you actually had asked for help and were given blatantly *wrong* instructions. That could be clear grounds for a medical malpractice lawsuit.

Similarly, an untold number of people have heard the Gospel message, but have been called to respond to it in sub-biblical or unbiblical ways. This has the potential to undermine evangelism just as quickly as a false gospel. Consider a man who hears about the holiness of God, the sinfulness of man, and the substitutionary death of Christ. At that moment, he is in the same position as the Philippian jailor who was desperate to respond to the Good News: "What must I do to be saved?" (cf. Acts 16:30). The heart that has been truly convicted will want to know what to do with this message of forgiveness. Yet what are the responses we often hear in modern evangelistic methods? Consider the following list, which represents some of the most popular phrases and terms used:

"Repeat this prayer."
"Fill out a decision card."
"Walk down the aisle."
"Come up to the altar."
"Ask Jesus into your heart."
"Give your heart to Jesus."
"Make Jesus your Lord and Savior."
"Accept Jesus into your life."

"Bow your head, close your eyes, and raise your hand."
"Say 'Yes' to Jesus."

One would think that John 3:16, the most famous verse in the Bible, would at least be enough to clarify the issue to some extent: "...that whosoever *believes* in Him shall not perish..." Yet, in many pulpits, even a simple instruction such as "believe in the Lord Jesus Christ" is abandoned in exchange for the aforementioned trite and trivial catchphrases.

But if, perhaps, belief in Christ is called for by the preacher, it is all-too-often portrayed as little more than mental assent. Yet, even demons give mental assent to the claims of Christ; they are fully aware of who Jesus is and what He accomplished on the cross (cf. Jas. 2:19, Acts 16:16-17). Thus, for us to agree that Jesus is the only Savior and that He died on the cross to save sinners is but a necessary prerequisite to saving faith. We must then fully entrust our lives to Him, calling upon Him with the intention of entering Heaven solely by His merit. Saving faith has no backup plan. Saving faith has no alternative. Saving faith is not like a game of chess, in which a player prepares for his second, third, and fourth moves well in advance. Saving faith has one and only one move—to cast oneself entirely upon the mercy of Jesus Christ through faith in His shed blood on the cross.

Furthermore, the need for repentance is also glaringly absent from many evangelistic presentations, despite the fact that it was preached by the Old Testament prophets (cf. Isa. 30:15, Ezek. 18:30) and the New Testament apostles (cf. Acts 3:19, 17:30). Often times, the concept of turning from sin is either totally absent in evangelism, or downplayed to the point of irrelevance—and it's no surprise why. The great twentieth-century expositor Dr. Martyn Lloyd-Jones spoke of true repentance this way:

Repentance means that you realize that you are a guilty, vile sinner in the presence of God, that you deserve the wrath and punishment of God, that you are hell-bound. It means that you begin to realize that this thing called sin is in you, that you long to get rid of it, and that you turn your back on it in every shape and form. You renounce the world whatever the cost, the world in its mind and outlook as well as its practice, and you deny yourself, and take up the cross and go after Christ. Your nearest and dearest, and the whole world, may call you a fool, or say you have religious mania. You may have to suffer financially, but it makes no difference. That is repentance.[98]

If Lloyd-Jones' definition of true repentance sounds harsh, it is only further evidence that biblical evangelism has been all but abandoned by the modern church at large. In reality, Lloyd-Jones was a masterful and meticulous expositor whose language was thoroughly biblical. Looking at Scripture, he saw repentance not as a work to earn salvation (as it is often mischaracterized), but as the surrendering and forsaking of sin. He recognized that repentance is about *abandonment*, not *accomplishment*. Men in Ephesus burned their magic books in response to the Gospel (cf. Acts 19:19). Zacchaeus reimbursed those he had defrauded (cf. Luke 19:8). The Thessalonians abandoned their idols while turning to God (cf. 1 Thess. 1:90).

Rather than portraying the demands of the Gospel with over-nuanced and watered-down words of his own imagination, Lloyd-Jones called men to respond to the Gospel using the same terminology and examples that he saw in Scripture. He stuck to the text, expositing the words of Scripture, in order to call for a response from his hearers. The seriousness of sin-hating repentance and the necessity of soul-

---

[98] Dr. David Martyn Lloyd-Jones, *Studies in the Sermon on the Mount* (Grand Rapids: Eerdmans, 1959), 248.

saving faith simply flowed from the pages of the text rather than from Lloyd-Jones' own fancy.

Likewise, the man who is committed to expository preaching will be protected from the number of false and shallow Gospel responses that abound in modern Gospel presentations. After all, John the Baptist didn't say, "The time is fulfilled, and the kingdom of God is at hand; now walk down the aisle and kneel at this altar!" Jesus didn't say, "All authority in Heaven and earth is given to Me; now go and make disciples, teaching them to ask Me into their hearts." The Apostle Paul didn't say, "God now commands all men everywhere to repeat this prayer and fill out a decision card!"

Instead, when the Philippian jailor asked, "What must I do to be saved?" the response from Paul was, "Believe in the Lord Jesus, and you will be saved" (cf. Acts 16:31). Other ways that the Bible portrays men responding to the Gospel include: repentance toward God and faith in our Lord Jesus Christ (Acts 20:21), repenting and believing the Gospel (Mark 1:15), confessing Jesus as Lord and believing that God raised Him from the dead (Romans 10:9), and receiving Jesus Christ by believing in His name (John 1:12). The faithful preacher must call men to respond using biblical language.

As parents shepherding our flocks, we too must stress the appropriate biblical response to the Gospel—repentance and faith, turning from self and turning towards Christ, confessing sin and calling upon the Savior. Since we want to see our children soundly saved as soon as possible, we simply cannot afford to neglect a biblical Gospel call. Our children must not only trust in Jesus alone for their salvation, they must simultaneously hate and forsake their sins. It is a package deal, like a two-sided coin. And it was Jesus Himself who reminded the Jewish crowds, "Unless you repent, you will all likewise perish" (cf. Luke 3:5). How then could we willfully neglect this and still sleep at night? We simply cannot afford to trivialize the requirements Scripture sets forth to all who would desire forgiveness of sin. The terms of surrender have been set by King Jesus and we are not authorized to diminish them in any way for anyone, our own children included.

When it comes to a legitimate Gospel response, tradition, sentimentalism, and sheer ignorance have proven to be opponents unwilling to go down without a fight. So fight them we must. A verse-by-verse ministry in the home will assist you in this fight by helping you avoid the errant phraseology and methodology that is rampant in modern evangelism. Rather than making up your own phrases to express how your kids must respond to the Gospel, simply rely on the same terminology used in the Bible as you teach through it. The Scriptures will be your safeguard as you correctly explain to your children what it is that they must do in order to be saved.

In doing the work of an evangelist, you must transition to the Gospel call. It is not enough simply to tell your children the Gospel; you must urge, compel, and summon them to repent of their sins and believe in Christ. If you pattern your language after superficial, seeker-sensitive services, you are liable to engage in spiritual malpractice. Your kids will understand the diagnosis but misapply the prescription. On the other hand, if you pattern your language after what you see in Scripture, you will end up calling your children to respond to the Gospel in a way that is accurate and faithful to what God requires.

Counting the Biblical Costs

The Gospel message makes it clear that there is a great cost in not following Christ: everything. It will cost you *everything* not to follow the Lord Jesus Christ. Sure, you could scheme your way into gaining the whole world, but if you die in your sins you will lose it all, including your own soul (cf. Mark 8:36). The lake of fire awaits those who die unrepentant, and the absolute horror of God's wrath simply cannot be described.

And yet, in total irony, there is also a great cost to those who *do* wish to follow Christ: everything. It will cost you *everything* to follow the Lord Jesus Christ (cf. Matt. 10:16-39, Luke 14:26-27). Not only does a man have to abandon his old life in order to be saved, but once he is saved and becomes a disciple of Jesus Christ, he must recognize that the Kingdom of God is entered through much tribulation (cf. Acts 14:22). In fact, the Apostle Paul reminded Timothy that *everyone* who desires to live a godly life will be persecuted (cf. 2 Tim. 3:12). It is a divine guarantee that if you are pursuing the Christian life to its fullest, you will suffer for it.

If the first aspect of evangelism (the biblical Gospel) describes what God has done, and the second aspect (the biblical call) describes what we must do, the third aspect (the biblical costs) can be thought of as *what others will do*. As Christ and His apostles preached and called men to repent, they made it clear that forgiveness, reconciliation, and a clean conscience were offered to those who responded in faith. But they did not portray the life of a believer as a casual stroll in the park. On the contrary, they made it crystal clear to their hearers that the life of a Christian would be filled with trial and persecution.

They wanted their hearers to be able to evaluate what exactly the Christian life would entail so that the hearers could determine whether or not eternal life was worth the cost of temporary discomfort. And to those who understand the Gospel, this tradeoff should come as no surprise. After all, Jesus' life was one of shame before glory (cf. Heb. 12:2), humiliation before exaltation (cf. Phil. 2:8-9), and suffering before splendor (cf. Isa. 53:3). In commissioning His disciples, Jesus made it clear that their lives would follow suit (cf. Matt. 10:22-25).

Sadly, today there are an untold number of preachers who are not following this evangelistic caution, but are instead offering their hearers just the opposite: health, wealth, and prosperity. This so-called "Prosperity Gospel" (which is no gospel at all) is one of the great stains and blemishes on modern Christianity.

Although this false gospel would have probably gained less traction in the first century, it finds its acceptance in modern industrialized nations of today. The United States, for example, has provided the "luxury" (no pun intended) of earthly prosperity and Christianity to coexist in the lives of many people for many years. "Come to Jesus and He'll fix your marriage." "Try Jesus for thirty days and see how your life improves." "Commit your finances to the Lord and He will multiply it and bless you in return." What kind of costs are these? Would Jesus have really needed to warn His hearers if this is what the Christian life involved? It cost Jesus Christ His very life in order to obey the will of the Father; do we really think God demands less of us?

The reality is that Jesus promised His disciples two things: tribulation and salvation. Nothing more and nothing less. Just as the world hated Jesus, so too will it hate the one following Him (cf. John 15:20-21). Relational difficulty is simply par for the course. The Christian is one who may lose his job on account of his Savior. He may be ostracized by society because of his faith. His spouse may even abandon him (cf. 1 Cor. 7:15). Regardless of what form persecution takes place, the pattern left by Christ is that of a crown of thorns, not a bed of roses. Thus, once the Gospel message has been rightly declared and the Gospel call has been properly set forth, the preacher must help his hearers count the biblical cost of following Jesus Christ.

In the same way, as you walk your children through the Bible, you too must explain to them what it will cost to follow Jesus. Spanning across the pages of Scripture, we see both Old Testament and New Testament saints suffer for their faith. Jesus lamented the way in which the Jews had stoned the prophets God sent them in the past (cf. Luke 13:34). Paul cited a litany of difficulties he faced in his missionary journeys (cf. 2 Cor. 11:23-27). And the writer of the book of Hebrews gives one of the most impressive accounts of enduring faith in the eleventh chapter (a chapter often called "The Hall of Faith") as he recounts the unfathomable suffering of those who were tortured, mocked, and even sawed in two for their faith. The Bible presents examples of men who understood that they were merely sojourners in this world, men who took their eyes off of momentary suffering and focused instead on a heavenly city that is to come (cf. Heb. 11:16).

Therefore, no matter what passage you are teaching, you can almost always find an example of someone who exchanged comfort in the present for glory with God in the future—Jesus Himself being the prime example, of course (cf. Heb. 12:1-3, 1 Pet. 4:13). You would do well to point out these examples to your children and explain that these men and women counted the cost and were willing to make the payment.

Since children are already more emotionally susceptible to peer pressure and ridicule than adults, it is absolutely critical to explain to them that the life of the Christian will not alleviate such concerns, but in many ways may only intensify them. Believing in Christ does not provide us with relational tranquility, nor will it do that for children. They need to hear and understand what it will cost them to follow Jesus.

Yes, this may seem counter-intuitive at first. Perhaps your initial thought is that such radical demands would scare away your children. But as you point out all of the suffering that believers face, what it actually does is exalt Christ and demonstrate just how precious He is to those who truly love Him. That these godly men and women in Scripture would be willing to throw away everything in order to be with their Savior paints a portrait of just how amazing the Gospel offer truly is. Persecution doesn't devalue the Gospel—on the contrary, it elevates it. As one man said, "A religion that gives nothing, costs nothing, and suffers nothing, is worth nothing."[99] By explaining the cost of following Christ, you not only magnify the greatness of the Gospel, but also force your children to make a sober evaluation of whether or not momentary affliction is worth eternal salvation.

Soft-selling the demands of discipleship and what it means to live a Christian life may initially produce a positive response from your child, but like the seed cast among thorns in Jesus's parable of the sower, such a response will eventually get choked out by the trials of life or the pleasures that the world has to offer (cf. Luke 8:14). Instead, if you present the costs to your children up front (rather than burying them like fine print at the bottom of a contract), your child will have already abandoned an attachment to this world long before being tested by tribulation and temptation. His or her heart will be the fertile soil in the parable, the kind in which the seed of the Gospel takes long-term root. When it came to difficulties in the Christian life, the Apostle Paul was able to say, "For I consider that the sufferings of this present time are not worthy to be compared with the glory that is to be revealed to us" (Rom. 8:18). May it be so for your children as well.

Examining Biblical Fruit

Finally, if there is one deadly threat to evangelism in the home, it is the threat of false conversion. Growing up in a Christian household,

---

[99] David Platt, Daniel L. Akin, and Tony Merida, *Exalting Jesus in James* (Nashville, TN: B&H Publishing Group, 2014), 27.

rather than never hearing the Gospel until adulthood, is surely one of the greatest blessings any person could have (cf. 1 Cor. 7:14). And yet, it is not without its dangers. Unlike adult converts who often come to Christ through a "crisis moment," children who come to faith in Christ typically do not have such a radical conversion story. And since such childhood testimonies often lack a vivid lifestyle contrast, it can be very difficult to pinpoint when true saving faith has occurred. There is rarely a crisis moment associated with the conversion event.

Sadly, then, in an effort to artificially manufacture a conversion event (sometimes called a "spiritual birthday") for a child, the great temptation faced by many parents is to pronounce the salvation of their children simply based on a vocalized commitment or tearful prayer. In this case, a child has an emotional moment when he "asks Jesus into his heart" and from that point on he is metaphorically stamped "saved"—no questions asked. This one-time event then becomes the account upon which the child relies as evidence of his salvation. And ultimately, his conversion is never questioned so long as he continues behaving fairly well.

But the Bible does not portray this method of "sealing the deal" as proof of genuine conversion. Instead, the testimony of the apostles is that a man must examine himself to see whether he is truly in the faith (cf. 2 Cor. 13:5). Professing Christians are not called to evaluate their lives in the past to find an exact moment of conviction and remorse; they are called to evaluate their lives in the present to find evidence of genuine repentance and faith. By that standard, we cannot afford to declare our children saved based on a one-time affirmation of the Gospel message; we must help them examine themselves in search of biblical fruit.

With this in mind, it could be said that the knowledge of our salvation is like traveling from one country to another. For some people, it is like driving by car—you see the clear signposts that differentiate each country and you know the exact moment when the international border was crossed. But for others, it is like flying by airplane—you know with absolute certainty that you took off in one country and landed in the other, but you have no idea where the transition occurred. Yet, in either case, one thing is unmistakable: where you are is not where you've been. That is how we must view the Christian testimony, particularly when it comes to our children.

Because they are growing up under your faithful ministry, it may be impossible to determine the *exact* day genuine repentance and faith occurs. Yet, that ought not to be a point of concern. We shouldn't find that troubling. Although we see dramatic conversions in Scripture, points in time when men drop to their knees in submission to Christ, there is nothing that requires us to determine, with chronological precision, when our child's heart was made new in Christ. Twentieth-century theologian J. Gresham Machen likewise asserted this position:

> Some Christians, indeed, are really able to give day and hour of their conversion. It is a grievous sin to ridicule the experience of such men. Sometimes, indeed, they are inclined to ignore the steps in the providence of God which prepared for the great change. But they are right on the main point. They know that when on such and such a day they kneeled in prayer they were still in their sins, and when they rose from their knees they were children of God never to be separated from Him. Such experience is a very holy thing. But on the other hand it is a mistake to demand that it should be universal. There are Christians who can give day and hour of their conversion, but the great majority do not know exactly at what moment they were saved. The effects of the act are plain, but the act itself was done in the quietness of God. Such, very often, is the experience of children brought up by Christian parents. It is not necessary that all should pass through agonies of soul before being

saved; there are those to whom faith comes peacefully and easily through the nurture of Christian homes.[100]

Make no mistake about it—conversion does indeed occur in a moment in time, a point when our children are born again, transferred out of the kingdom of darkness, and granted repentance and faith. But that does not mean we, in our finite human understanding, will always be able to pinpoint that moment. The evidence that true conversion has occurred often requires time to uncover. The truth is that no pope or priest can absolve a man of his sins, no traveling evangelist can declare a person saved by repeating a prayer, and no parent can confer salvation to a child. Instead, we each must evaluate our lives with the Bible, as if standing in front of a mirror, to determine whether or not we have genuine, soul-saving faith in the Lord Jesus Christ.

To help our children with this, we must preach the Word of God to them and observe how the Holy Spirit convicts them as He sees fit. That is not to say that you should cast doubt upon, or be antagonistic towards, your child's profession of faith. On the contrary, you ought to show incredible excitement about their outward love for Jesus! But the Bible simply does not provide us with the license to guarantee their salvation—they must make their own calling and election sure (cf. 2 Pet. 1:10).

One of the analogies that the Bible uses to explain saving faith is that of a race, and it is a fitting analogy because endurance and perseverance are key characteristics of true faith (cf. 2 Pet. 1:6, 1 John 2:28). Just as it is necessary for a runner to strain towards the finish line and complete the race, so too must the believer continue pursuing Christ with diligence his entire life. Those who fall away from

---

[100] J. Gresham Machen, *Christianity and Liberalism* (Grand Rapids, MI: Wm. B. Eerdmans Publishing, 2009), 118-119.

Christianity do not demonstrate that they've lost their faith, but rather that they never had it to begin with (cf. 1 John 2:19).

So when we consider the lives of our children, we need to recognize that they are running in a race. And it's their own race; we cannot run the race for them. Nor can we declare mid-race that they've crossed the finish line. But what we can do is stand on the sidelines and cheer with all our might. We can whoop and holler when they pass by in order to encourage them during the difficult legs of the race. We can applaud, show excitement, and perhaps even hand them a water bottle as they round a corner. Although we can't tag ourselves in and run in their place, our emphatic joy as a spectator is undoubtedly an integral aspect that God uses to keep them going (cf. Heb. 12:1).

With that in mind, when your children say they love Jesus, the response ought to be "Yes! Amen! Now keep loving Him every day of your life!" We ought to give them the midrace encouragement to press on—"Praise God! This is wonderful! Keep going!" Certainly we shouldn't say, "Well son, I highly doubt you're saved; you barely understand the Gospel." Yet, we must likewise avoid saying, "Ok, well you're saved and on your way to Heaven!" A child who professes his love for Christ should most certainly be encouraged, but a one-time statement from a child who is known to repeat virtually anything cannot be used to substantiate true conversion. The obvious reality is that children can be led to say almost anything—whether simply by following an example, giving in to peer pressure, wanting to appease their parents, or being coerced. Yes, we are saved by faith *alone*. So it is not as if your child has to work or mature enough to be saved or savable. But we must ensure that what our child possesses is a true faith, not a false faith (cf. Jas. 2:17).

To boil it down, as parents we ought to *affirm*, but not *confirm*, a child's salvation. Only the Holy Spirit working through the Scriptures can provide your children with confirmation of their salvation. Until a child can articulate the Gospel and demonstrate fruit worthy of repentance, we must tread lightly on the issue. Both parental and pastoral wisdom should be administered on a case-by-case basis for each child to determine the best course of action when a child professes faith. There is simply no such thing as an exact "age of accountability." Some children are aware of their sinful condition at a much younger age than others.

Pastoral wisdom from John MacArthur sheds further light in this regard:

> People ask me all the time, "At what age can someone be saved?" I'm not prepared to say that; I don't think there is any age. But I think at certainly the age of seven or eight or nine or ten it is possible for a child to come to Christ. You're not going to fully know that until they reach an age of independence, say around twelve or thirteen, where they can make their own choices and behave with a little more freedom and respond to their peer pressure around them. Then you're going to know the real working of God has been done by the responses that they make when you're not literally the only controlling element in their life. But early on they can be saved and you need to be looking for evidences of that working in their heart which will come to full flower, perhaps around twelve or thirteen. That's why we wait 'til then to baptize people, because at that point you can begin to see these evidences independent of total parental control.[101]

As you work your way through the Bible, explain the various examples

---

[101] John MacArthur, "Evaluating Your Child's Spiritual Condition," *GTY Resources: Sermons*, Grace to You, accessed September 27, 2016, https://www.gty.org/library/sermons-library/80-216/evaluating-your-childs-spiritual-condition.

of biblical fruit—things such as commitment to Christ in the face of persecution, ongoing growth in the knowledge of Scripture, continual love towards fellow saints, and growing hatred of sin. Explain that these are evidences of true faith and ask them if they see these same characteristics in their own lives. The following are a few examples of helpful diagnostic questions for a child who professes faith in Christ:[102]

"What do you enjoy most in your Bible reading?"

"What are your strongest temptations to sin?"

"What do you like most about church?"

"If you weren't being raised in a Christian home, what would you miss about it most of all?"

"If a friend of yours asked you how to become a Christian, what would you say?"

Ultimately, our dependence on God's Word for the task of examination must be upheld as the final authority. We simply cannot develop our own spiritual litmus test by which we confirm the salvation of our children. Inevitably, it would be insufficient. After all, do your children believe in God? Good! But so do the demons (cf. Jas. 2:19). Do they fear God's wrath? Great! But so do the demons (cf. Luke 8:31). Do they know sound doctrine? Wonderful! But so do the demons (cf. Acts 16:16-19). In fact, Satan himself talks to God (cf. Job 1:7), quotes Scripture (cf. Matt 4:6), and goes to church (cf. Acts 5:3), but ultimately his affection for Christ is feigned (cf. John 13:27, Matt. 26:48). Thus, what defines a true Christian is not only a fear of God and His wrath, but also a desire for God and His righteousness (cf. Matt. 6:33, 2 Pet.

---

[102] Dennis Gundersen, *Your Child's Profession of Faith, 4th ed.* (Sand Springs: Grace & Truth, 2010), 95-96.

3:13). Your children must demonstrate true biblical fruit in keeping with repentance.

After you've preached the biblical Gospel to your children, called them to repentance and faith, and helped them evaluate the costs, one of the most important things you can do in shepherding your flock is to help them determine whether or not God has graciously granted them a new heart. But don't force them to come to a conclusion on the matter while they are young. As the years progress, if your teenage child exhibits fruit of genuine salvation, professes faith in Christ, and submits to the ordinance of baptism, they ought to be comforted in times of doubt—not by ignoring or overlooking whatever may trouble them about their walk with Christ, but by helping them continue looking to Jesus as the one in whom they have confidence of their salvation (cf. Heb. 12:2, Jude 24-25). At that point you can praise the Good Shepherd for tracking down and redeeming yet another lost sheep (cf. Matt. 18:12-14).

Expository Preaching Is Evangelistic Preaching

Perhaps you never realized it, but accomplishing these four aspects of biblical evangelism happens naturally through expository preaching. Look again at these elements: preaching the Gospel of Jesus Christ, calling for repentance and faith in Jesus Christ, counting the costs of following Jesus Christ, and examining lives for evidence of Christlikeness. What do these all have in common? *Jesus Christ.* Evangelistic work is all about Jesus. Therefore, expository preaching is, by definition, evangelistic preaching because the Scriptures testify of the Savior (cf. John 5:39, Luke 24:27, 1 Cor. 15:3-4). This means that as you preach the Word to your children, with a focus on the Lord Jesus Christ and His redemptive work, you will naturally be engaging in one or more of these elements of evangelism.

So how does this work? As we rightly handle the Word, we ought to remember to identify man's fallen condition and God's redemptive grace in each passage. But this is not only important for proper interpretation, it's also important for evangelism. Once you've preached Christ as the fulfillment of the passage's grace, you can then easily use the passage to segue to the Gospel message.

For example, in Numbers 21, a bronze serpent was lifted up in the air by Moses to save every Israelite who turned and looked upon it—foreshadowing the need for all men to look to the Son of God who was lifted up (cf. John 3:14-15). The Gospel message immediately comes to the forefront in this passage. You can seamlessly transition to evangelism by calling upon your son or daughter to look to the Savior as well.

But what about books like Leviticus and Deuteronomy? Surely these books of Old Testament Law are not evangelistic, are they? Think again. After all, it was the Apostle Paul who said that "the Law has become our tutor to lead us to Christ, so that we may be justified by faith" (Gal. 3:24). In that case, as you walk your child through dozens of commands given to the nation of Israel, first point out the Israelites' inability to keep them all, and their need of priestly sacrifices. Then, you can point out your child's inability to keep God's Law, and his or her need for a greater High Priest who provided a once-for-all sacrifice.

In the end, there is no discrepancy between expository preaching and evangelistic preaching. Teaching through the Bible affords you the perfect opportunities to evangelize your children; there is no need for a separate Gospel ministry in your home. If you are properly explaining the Scriptures, then you will always be identifying God's redemptive purposes in the world. And once you've identified the redemptive element of a particular passage, you are set to launch into evangelism. Biblical exposition is inherently evangelistic.

How Will They Hear Without a Preacher?

As far as the Apostle Paul was concerned, Timothy's job as a pastor was incomplete until he did the work of an evangelist. Timothy could have been a masterful motivator, an elegant orator, or a passionate preacher, but fulfilling his ministry demanded that he also remember to diagnose the condition of his hearers and prescribe the Gospel remedy. Men and women needed to be brought to saving faith before discipleship was even possible. Along those lines, we as Christian parents are commanded to raise up our children in the fear and admonition of the Lord, and their conversion must be our number one priority in order to fulfill that command.

Yet, far too often, evangelism in the Christian home ends up looking more like a seeker-sensitive church service: trite Gospel presentations, superficial responses to Christ, concealed costs of discipleship, and non-existent self-examination. Parents then operate on the underlying assumption that a long-term relationship with their child will make up for a lack of accurate and intentional evangelism. Make sure your home is different. Committing to the exposition of the Scriptures will relieve you of the burden of trying to concoct your own evangelistic techniques. The Bible will pierce the hearts of your children and do the work of conviction and conversion for you. As you preach the Word, the rebellious heart will be bored to tears, but the receptive heart will be brought to tears.

No, you cannot manufacture repentance and faith in your child; salvation is of the Lord and He saves those whom He chooses, when He chooses. There is simply no guarantee that God will save your child, nor is He obligated to do so, since it is all according to His grace (cf. Rom. 9:14-16). Nevertheless, let the following caution echo in your mind: "How then will they call on Him in whom they have not believed? How will they believe in Him whom they have not heard?

And how will they hear without a preacher? How will they preach unless they are sent? Just as it is written, 'How beautiful are the feet of those who bring good news of good things!'" (Rom. 10:14-15). As your children grow up in your home, remember that they cannot be saved unless they hear the Gospel message and respond to it by calling on the name of the Lord. Your children need to hear from a preacher. You be that preacher.

7

HOMEMADE SEMINARY

"We can no longer coast along and ignore biblical truth when deciding where and how to educate our children. The Bible is not silent on this issue. Do everything in your power to place your child in an educational environment that supplements and facilitates their discipleship."[103]

–Voddie Baucham

Focus Text: *Now you followed my teaching, conduct, purpose, faith, patience, love, perseverance, persecutions, and sufferings, such as happened to me at Antioch, at Iconium and at Lystra; what persecutions I endured, and out of them all the Lord rescued me! Indeed, all who desire to live godly in Christ Jesus will be persecuted. But evil men and imposters will proceed from bad to worse, deceiving and being deceived. You, however, continue in the things you have learned and become convinced of, knowing from whom you have learned them, and that from childhood you have known the sacred writings which are able to give you the wisdom that leads to salvation through faith which is in Christ Jesus. (2 Timothy 3:10-15)*

It doesn't need to be said, but the task of sequential exposition is no small undertaking. If a pastor is to teach through the entire Bible, it is obvious that it will take time, discipline, and determination. Unlike other methods of teaching that might take shortcuts through

---

[103] Voddie Baucham, *Family Driven Faith: Doing What It Takes to Raise Sons and Daughters Who Walk with God* (Wheaton, IL: Crossway, 2007), 128.

the Bible, expository preaching requires an attention to detail that, without a doubt, requires a long-term commitment.

To that end, one argument that is often made against expository preaching is that it is simply unimaginable to think that a pastor could ever make it through the entire Bible with his congregation. On top of that, some might say it's impractical even to attempt it. After all, to teach through even *one* book of the Bible would require months (or perhaps years) to accomplish, right?

At face-value, this would seem like a reasonable objection. And in many cases, it is certainly true that even a single book of the Bible demands much of a pastor's life in order to preach it. Therefore, if this objection has merit, it would serve as an obstacle for expository parenting as well. But when we consider the underlying assumption behind this objection, we find where the true error lies.

As we consider modern church trends, statistics suggest that pastors and congregations both prefer shorter sermon lengths. One survey shows the following three typical ranges for sermon length: twenty to twenty-eight minutes, forty-five to fifty-five minutes, and a fifty-five minute range and up (no constraint). But out of those three categories, the greatest favorable response appeared to be in the twenty to twenty-eight minute range.[104] Both pastors and congregations seem to prefer, if given the choice, to have a sermon that clocks in at less than half an hour. In fact, one church, taking advantage of this trend, advertises itself as "30 Minute Worship" and offers the restless attendee just ten minutes of singing, fifteen minutes of

---

[104] Thom Rainer, "3 Major Trends in Sermon Length," *CP Opinion* (blog), The Christian Post, February 2, 2015, http://thomrainer.com/2015/01/three-major-trends-sermon-length.

preaching, and five final minutes of reflection![105]

When you combine this preference with the noticeable decline in Sunday night services, and the almost unheard of weeknight services, you are looking at about thirty minutes' worth of biblical exposition out of the 10,080 possible minutes available each week. And that is, of course, assuming that the thirty-minute message is expositional in nature—many of those in the survey who preferred the longer time range also asserted that meaningful exposition is generally impossible in under thirty minutes.

With that in mind, we revisit the initial objection to consecutive expository preaching: "It is impossible and impractical for a pastor to teach through the entire Bible." Well, if the underlying assumption in that objection is that there are only twenty-eight minutes available each week to pursue such a monumental task, then it's a valid concern. But such a constraint is unwarranted and unnecessary. Similar things can be said of the parent's ministry in the home.

Making Time for Exposition

John Calvin is most widely known for his theological writings (particularly for his work entitled *Institutes of the Christian Religion*) and for the doctrinal system that bears his name ("Calvinism"). But because of these, his pastoral work—and more specifically, his commitment to sequential exposition—is unfortunately often overlooked. While he certainly ought to be recognized for his tremendous theological contributions, it must be understood that those contributions were made possible because Calvin was first and foremost a man who submerged himself in the Scriptures, subsequently coming up to the

---

[105] Thomas White and John M. Yeats, *Franchising McChurch: Feeding Our Obsession with Easy Christianity* (Colorado Springs, Co.: David C. Cook, 2009), 34.

surface only to submerge his hearers in the Scriptures. In other words, his lofty theology was simply a product of relentless studying, teaching, and preaching the Bible verse by verse. But his commitment to declaring the full counsel of God's Word was not of his own accord. It wasn't a novel idea that originated with him. He learned it from the Apostle Paul, a man who taught "night and day" while in Ephesus (cf. Acts 20:20, 27).

Rather than preaching a thirty-minute message once per week, Paul put in the daily work needed to deliver the full counsel of God. Undoubtedly, the amount of time he spent preaching was astronomical compared to what the typical pastor of today spends. That is not to say that pastors today are not putting in many hours on the job—they are, but many are simply spending time on the wrong things. The apostles devoted themselves to prayer and the ministry of the Word (cf. Acts 6:40), whereas many pastors today are devoting themselves to programs and events. But men like John Calvin recognized that the Apostle Paul was his example to follow. And follow him Calvin did.

After his three-year banishment and subsequent reinstatement to the pastorate in Geneva, Switzerland in 1561, John Calvin returned to the pulpit as a man on fire. Not only did he pick up his expository preaching ministry in the very next verse he left off at three years prior, but he began to blaze trails across books of the Bible through his *daily* sermons.[106]

Calvin knew that sequential exposition was his duty: "What order must pastors then keep in teaching? First, let them not esteem at their pleasure what is profitable to be uttered and what to be omitted; but

---

[106] Charles Haney, "The Preaching of John Calvin," *Past Masters* (blog), Preaching: The Professional Journal for Ministry Leaders, September 1, 1997, http://www.preaching.com/resources/past-masters/the-preaching-of-john-calvin.

let them leave that to God alone to be ordered at his pleasure."[107] On that basis, he recognized that the only way to bring his congregation to a mature faith and deep biblical knowledge was to expedite his communication of the truth to their hearts and minds.

Thus, Calvin not only began to preach twice on Sundays, but every other week he would preach daily, which averaged out to more than 250 sermons per year (consider that this figure represents five times the amount of many pastors today!).[108] On his "off weeks" he would lecture to his students, meet with other church leaders, and perform other pastoral care work. Examples of his 25-year-long expositional legacy include: 123 sermons in Genesis, 86 sermons in the pastoral epistles, 200 sermons in the book of Deuteronomy, 48 sermons in Ephesians, and 43 sermons in Galatians (among other notable accomplishments).[109]

Both pastors and parents would do well to follow Calvin's mindset. For pastors, the solution to the problem is simple: preach longer, and more often. Certainly, the point is not to increase time for the sake of increasing time, but the reality is that gradually shorter sermons will not serve the ultimate goal of preaching through the entire Bible. Detailed exposition through the pages of Scripture simply requires time, and the amount allotted for this in many churches is, quite honestly, inadequate.

For parents, the answer is that we, too, need to maximize the amount of time we have for discipling our flocks. We are simply

---

[107] John Calvin, *Commentary Upon the Acts of the Apostles Vol. II.*, vol. 19 of *Calvin's Commentaries,* ed. Henry Beveridge (Grand Rapids, MI: Baker, 2005), 251.

[108] Herman J. Selderhuis, *John Calvin: A Pilgrim's Life* (Downers Grove, IL: IVP Academic, 2009), 112.

[109] John Piper, *John Calvin and His Passion for the Majesty of God* (Wheaton, Ill.: Crossway, 2009), 47-48.

deceiving ourselves if we think that a five-minute pep talk on the way to soccer practice constitutes sufficient Christian discipleship.

Yet we must ask ourselves, is it even possible for our children to learn the entire Bible in eighteen years? Who has time for this? Well, to begin with, briefly consider how much time it would take to teach your kids each day if you had a wide span of age ranges (from the younger years, to the middle years, to the older years):

The younger years: for children in the age range of roughly two to six years old, working story-by-story through a children's Bible and briefly pointing out basic themes might take approximately five to ten minutes.

The middle years: for children in the age range of roughly seven to twelve years old, working verse by verse through a full-text Bible, with catechism questions, and moderate depth of discussion might take approximately thirty minutes.

The older years: for children in the age range of roughly thirteen to eighteen, working verse by verse through a full-text Bible at a slower pace, accompanied by meaningful theological discussion might take approximately an hour.

So, at the *most*, if you have kids in each of those ranges that require varying degrees of instruction, you could be looking at about an hour and forty minutes of total time. That may be a lot to ask on a daily basis, but it's not unreasonable as a worst-case scenario.

Yet, even better, what if your child could be learning the Bible and studying theology during the school day? *"But, the school teachers would never allow that!"* It's true, they likely would not. But again, there may be an underlying assumption here that must be addressed. Are you assuming that your child is being educated by someone else, outside your home? Is that a valid assumption? Better yet, is that a *biblical* assumption? What if you were the teacher?

Unlike a pastor or Sunday-school leader who may only have a few hours each week to teach your children, you have opportunities around-the-clock, should you choose to act upon them. Thus, the potential for you to minister the Word to your children is unmatched by anyone else. And that is by design. God has placed you in your family for the purpose of leading your kids through the Word day in and day out, illustrating the redemptive work of Christ in and through each passage, and walking right alongside them as they grow and mature in their faith.

The amount of time available for daily discipleship with your children will never be paralleled at any other time in their lives. So, what if you taught your children the Bible every day as part of their overall school curriculum? What if you provided your children with a Christian worldview even for subjects such as math, science, and history? What if education were simply a subset of the larger work of discipleship? Teaching your children the full counsel of God is a tall order if it has to be squeezed in between public school, sports, hobbies, and friends. But if it's part of daily home education, you have all the time in the world.

The Rod and the Staff

One of the fundamental assumptions that must precede any discussion of education is that the Bible truly is sufficient to instruct us in this area. Take a moment to ask yourself this question: "Do I believe that the Bible sufficiently provides the answer for how I am to educate my children?" Regardless of our position, by necessity we must be able to substantiate our convictions with a systematic argument made from Scripture alone. With that said, it must be acknowledged that nowhere in the Bible does a single verse state, "Thou shalt homeschool." Nevertheless, it must also be acknowledged that the Christian life is not lived by a need for such proof-texting (after all, there is no single passage that succinctly defines the doctrine of the Trinity, either). There is much in the Bible that is determined by the logical application of biblical statements.

Certainly, there may be particular circumstances (such as in the case of a single-parent home) that necessitate a particular educational route. Yet, we ought not use difficult circumstances as normative or ideal for determining how we educate our children. Nor should the issue of education simply be relegated to the category of "adiaphora" (a spiritually or morally neutral issue). If we will give an account to God for how we use our own time (cf. Eph. 5:16) and from whom we receive counsel (cf. Psa. 1:1), then there is no doubt that we will give an account to God for how we have managed those same things in the lives of our children. Education is simply not a "shoulder-shrug" issue.

More importantly, when education itself is understood to be a form of discipleship, and we recognize that a student becomes like his teacher when he is fully trained (cf. Luke 6:40), a great deal of clarity is given to this issue. Education is not simply about imparting facts; it's also about imparting a worldview. And imparting a worldview is not an insignificant endeavor; it is the very act of discipleship. This is ultimately the greatest impetus for reconsidering, rather than assuming, how our children ought to be educated. Pastor Voddie Baucham explains:

> Contrary to popular opinion, there is no such thing as amoral education. All education teaches and shapes morality. It is impossible to separate

one's view of God, man, truth, knowledge, and ethics from the educational process. Every day that our children sit behind a desk, they are either being taught to know, love and obey God or they are being taught to love and obey someone or something that has usurped God's proper role.[110]

All other concerns aside, the full testimony of Scripture makes it clear that a secular public school education will not contribute to raising your children in the fear and admonition of the Lord, but instead will prove only to be an additional obstacle to overcome (cf. Prov. 13:20, 1 Cor. 15:33). Therefore, in addition to the issue of time needed for discipleship, there is another aspect: spiritual safety. After all, David spoke of the Lord as a shepherd and stated that the "rod" (a club used to ward off attackers) and the "staff" (a long stick curved on one end used to lead the flock) are *both* comforts (cf. Psa. 23:4). In other words, a true shepherd must provide both nourishment and safety; he carries both a rod and a staff.

For similar reasons, we see many of the New Testament epistles end with stern warnings for believers to stay away from those who would seek to undermine everything that had just been written. The apostles knew that an unnoticed wolf posing as the shepherd would quickly lead to spiritual disaster (cf. Matt. 7:15, 2 Tim. 2:16-18), and as true and faithful shepherds they were bound to prevent that from happening. For example, at the end of Romans, the Apostle Paul tells the church to *avoid* anyone who contradicts his instruction in the letter (cf. Rom. 16:17). At the end of 2 Peter, the Apostle Peter warns believers to *be on guard* so as not to be carried away by error (cf. 2 Pet. 3:17). At the end of 2 John, the Apostle John commands believers to *reject*

---

[110] Voddie Baucham, *Family Driven Faith: Doing What It Takes to Raise Sons and Daughters Who Walk with God* (Wheaton, IL: Crossway, 2007), 127.

anyone who does not abide in the teaching of Christ (cf. 2 John 9).

With that in mind, just as the pastor must both feed and protect his disciples, so too must the parent. We must consider both aspects of shepherding, particularly as we consider where children receive their education. And training up your kids at home lends itself to both of those aspects. Homeschooling will give you the time needed to teach your children the Bible, while at the same time protecting them from the kind of influences that will undermine everything you teach them.

Like digging a hole only to fill it back in, we put our ministry at a great disadvantage if we teach our kids the Bible verse by verse only to have others "unteach" them the Bible verse by verse (and the parable of the sower in Matthew 13:1-23 confirms this). Rather than The Great Commission being a legitimate reason for placing our children in such a situation, The Great Commission is actually the reason for *not* placing our children in such a situation. Pastor Voddie Baucham clarifies why:

> Many object to homeschooling or private Christian schools based on the fact that God has called us to be "salt" and "light" and to evangelize the world. Ironically, this is precisely why we chose homeschooling. The Great Commission states: "Go therefore and make disciples of all nations, baptizing them in the name of the Father and the Son and the Holy Spirit, *teaching them to obey all that I command you*" (Matthew 28:19-20, emphasis added). How is this likely apart from Christian education? How can I effectively "make disciples" of my children if I send them off to the government school forty-five to fifty hours per week? The Nehemiah Institute, The National Study of Youth and Religion, and the Barna Report have shown us clearly that our children do not even understand—let alone obey—all that the Lord has commanded. Moreover, how can our children evangelize our government schools if they don't know what they believe and why they believe it? Not to mention that all of the evidence currently points to the fact that our

children are the evangelized, not the evangelists, in our nation's schools. They are the ones being carried away by every wind of doctrine.[111]

Concerned by the fact that he sees few children who actually possess a biblical worldview while in public schools, Pastor Baucham continues:

> Let me be clear—I applaud men and women whom God has called to teach in government schools. These people are front-line warriors, and they need to be right where they are. However, there is a big difference between sending fully trained disciples into enemy territory and sending recruits to our enemy's training camp. If we do the latter, we shouldn't be surprised when they come home wearing the enemy's uniform and charging the hill of our home waving an enemy flag.[112]

Interestingly enough, even many unbelievers recognize that when a child first goes off to kindergarten at a public school, there is a "passing of the baton," a form of graduation, in which the parent is no longer the primary instructor for the child. Surely, as Christians we must also confess this reality!

Truth be told, many moms and dads do in fact feel the heartbreak over this proverbial changing-of-the-guard. They can see that all the time spent at home, all the one-on-one instruction, all of the round-the-clock discipleship, is over. They recognize that things will never be the same. They shed tears at the thought of such an abrupt change in the relationship they have with their child. Once school is in full swing, the problems sometimes multiply—bullying, immoral influences, physical dangers, peer pressure, uncaring teachers, and so on.

---

[111] Voddie Baucham, *Family Driven Faith: Doing What It Takes to Raise Sons and Daughters Who Walk with God* (Wheaton, IL: Crossway, 2007), 125-126.
[112] Voddie Baucham, *Family Driven Faith: Doing What It Takes to Raise Sons and Daughters Who Walk with God* (Wheaton, IL: Crossway, 2007), 128.

But with compassionate honesty, I would submit to you this—such grief is often self-imposed. Where did we get the idea that after five years of training within our home, the sixth year would bring an end to it? Where did we come up with the practice that our kids "graduate" from our homes by the time they finish preschool? How did we determine that our children need to go to others for their education (aka discipleship)? These are ideas that come from culture, not Scripture. After all, if we understand homeschooling simply to be the education and care of children at whatever stage of development they're in, we would have to confess that, in reality, every family begins as a homeschooling family. Many simply choose to abandon it after a few days, a few weeks, a few months, or a few years.

So, rather than engaging in a form of "dueling discipleship," in which our children are first mistaught during the day and then retaught by us in the evening, we ought to consider what alternatives we have. When we do, we see that the virtues and benefits of homeschooling within the broader purpose of expository parenting are simply too rich to ignore.

Daily Discipleship

As we return to Paul's second letter to Timothy, we see the virtue of daily discipleship. We see the outcome of parental instruction. We see the benefits of a childhood that is saturated in the Word. And these are the same qualities that could accompany your ministry to your children in a homeschooling environment. After all, think about it this way: if Paul viewed his disciple as a spiritual son, how much more should you view your actual son as a disciple? By way of reminder to his disciple Timothy, the Apostle Paul stated:

Now you followed my teaching, conduct, purpose, faith, patience, love, perseverance, persecutions, and sufferings, such as happened to me at Antioch, at Iconium and at Lystra; what persecutions I endured, and out of them all the Lord rescued me! Indeed, all who desire to live godly in Christ Jesus will be persecuted. But evil men and imposters will proceed from bad to worse, deceiving and being deceived. You, however, continue in the things you have learned and become convinced of, knowing from whom you have learned them, and that from childhood you have known the sacred writings which are able to give you the wisdom that leads to salvation through faith which is in Christ Jesus. (2 Timothy 3:10-15)

Just prior to making these statements, Paul explained that Timothy's future would be difficult as widespread apostasy would continue. There would be a number of people who made an initial profession of faith but then turned away (demonstrating that they were imposters who were never truly saved to begin with). Not only would these men abandon the faith, but they would wreak havoc on Timothy's ministry if gone unnoticed. In 2 Timothy 3:2-5, Paul went through a laundry list of sins that characterize such men (lovers of self, disobedient to parents, reckless, and so on), and the reality is that you have probably seen these characteristics demonstrated by people in your life, including those who grew up in your church. Typically, those who leave the faith reveal their true hearts within a few semesters away at college. During those first years of adulthood, we often see the fruit of how parents have either fulfilled or neglected their duty to disciple their children.

In fact, it should be recognized that once young college students leave their parents' home they will have increased freedom and decreased accountability, which will be the ultimate test of whether or not their faith is genuine. While an unconverted heart may be able to go undetected during childhood, that same heart will eventually reveal itself in the unchecked opportunities that adulthood has to offer. Sadly, many who go off to college reveal that their faith was nothing more than a well-developed façade. And many times we are shocked, wondering how it is that a child who grew up in a Christian home quickly turned his back on the faith in adulthood.

But wait just a minute—did this child *actually* grow up in a Christian home? What do we mean by that? Is a Christian home one in which biblical instruction occurs for a couple hours on Sunday morning, followed up with doses of Christian radio and devotional books in between school and sports throughout the week?

If we were honest about it, we would have to admit that a majority of homes that claim to be "Christian homes" are hardly that at all. In many of these homes, there is little, if any, intentional discipleship occurring. Perhaps parents assume that their Christian convictions will be transmitted to their children simply by osmosis—treating a child's unconverted heart like a steak that simply needs to marinate in the "sauce" of a Christian environment long enough. Of course, nothing could be further from the truth. Instead, there must be an intentional commitment on the part of parents to develop the spiritual character of their children. And that intentional commitment must go deeper than whimsically bouncing around the Bible in random spurts at random times throughout the year.

Paul recognized something similar to this when he instructed Timothy. He knew that evil men and imposters were going to become increasingly worse and that Timothy would need to be ready for the coming spiritual onslaught. Furthermore, Timothy's commitment to Christianity would be exponentially tested once Paul was no longer available for counsel and guidance. Thus, in order to prepare Timothy for the spiritual apostasy that was to come, the Apostle Paul referred him back to two times of intense daily discipleship in his life: the time

Timothy spent with Paul, and the time Timothy spent with his godly mother. In effect, Paul was saying to him, "You have known the truth your entire life; consider not only the time spent with me, but also your entire childhood under the instruction of your godly mother. Others will fall away from the faith, but you've come too far to turn back now. Press on."

Continuing in What You Have Learned

The Apostle Paul was well aware that only a firm spiritual foundation in Timothy's life would allow him to withstand the apostasy that would characterize so many around him. Thus, he poured his life into this young man—beginning with sound doctrine. The first thing Paul referred to in 2 Timothy 3:10 was his "teaching," coming from the Greek word *didaskalia*. This Greek word refers to any kind of systematic instruction in general, but Paul's use of it had a clear context. The teaching that Timothy is said to have followed was none other than the apostolic testimony from Paul: the "things which you have heard from me" that Paul spoke of in 2 Timothy 2:2. Paul reminded Timothy of the Christian doctrine he learned because it would provide him with the spiritual protection for future years in ministry. Standing firm against Satan's schemes requires the believer to be fully armed, and God's Word is a critical element (cf. Eph. 6:10-17). Thus it only makes sense that Paul would begin the list with *didaskalia*—thorough biblical instruction.

But Paul didn't stop there. After all, instruction without example is hypocrisy. This would be like Paul telling Timothy what to do without living it out in his own life. So if the first term, "teaching," referred to the *content* of Paul's ministry to Timothy, the remaining items in the list could be thought of as the *character* of Paul's ministry to Timothy. Paul went on to write about all that Timothy observed while they ministered together, listing things such as "conduct" (godly behavior), "purpose" (godly focus), "faith" (godly commitment), "patience" (godly restraint), "love" (godly compassion), "perseverance" (godly endurance), "persecutions" (godly hardship), and "sufferings" (godly anguish). Timothy was an eyewitness to these aspects of Paul's faith in action.

These aspects were just as important as the first, because example without instruction is superficial. This would be like Paul living out his life without any theological content to undergird it. But Paul didn't fail in either way. He taught Timothy how to live, and showed Timothy how to live. He was able to deliver both the content of the Christian faith as well as the character of the Christian faith to his disciple. And how was he able to do this? How was Paul able to demonstrate all of these aspects to his disciple? How is it that Timothy was able both to learn and see such a multi-faceted ministry in the life of Paul? *Because he was with him.*

Notice in 2 Timothy 3:10, Timothy is said to have "followed" Paul's teaching and conduct. And lest we immediately jump to a metaphorical understanding of the word "follow" (that Timothy simply "learned" from Paul), we must first recognize that Timothy *literally* followed Paul. They spent time together. They traveled together. They obeyed Christ together. He *followed* Paul both in teaching and in conduct. This was full-time, daily discipleship that began years prior during Paul's second missionary journey (cf. Acts 16:1-3). Do your children literally follow you in this manner?

A common argument against homeschooling is that it "shelters" children from the world. Here is how the reasoning commonly plays out: your children go off to public school where they will be confronted and perhaps ostracized for their faith. They are introduced to all forms of immorality. They are taught anti-biblical perspectives. They are inculcated with an unbiblical worldview. At the end of each school day or week you attempt to address and counter-teach the things they have been learning. And the argument is that this is both good and necessary because otherwise your children will be totally unprepared for when they are out in the "real world" and have to interact with unbelievers on their own.

But the logic of this argument breaks down quickly. Being on your own among unbelievers early in life does not prepare you to be on your own among unbelievers later in life. A child learns how to do laundry by working with his parents as they do laundry. A child learns how to cook food by cooking alongside his parents. A child learns how to be self-sufficient not by being left to himself, but just the opposite — observing the self-sufficiency of his parents. The same is true in the spiritual realm. Thus, aside from the fact that this common objection is a pragmatic argument (rather than a biblical argument), consider again Paul's example with his disciple — Timothy *followed Paul* in persecutions and sufferings. Timothy *wasn't* alone in his younger years.

By way of analogy, imagine the task of swimming representing your son's life in the world, and swimming lessons represent your child's education. In this analogy, sending your child to public school represents the equivalent of putting your child into a pool alongside other non-swimming children in order to learn how to swim. Many would opt for this route because it helps your child learn to "fit in" with the others; he's not the oddball being taught to swim some other way. He's getting plenty of social interaction and he looks just like all the other kids.

Now it's true that if you go this route your son will fit right in with other children — but it's because he will be floundering in the water right alongside all the other non-swimmers. Here he is with no idea what he's doing (like all the other children), flailing his arms, splashing away, trying to stay afloat. He's on the verge of drowning, and at the very best, he treads water just long enough to avoid going completely under during his lesson. After the lesson, you spend time patting your son's back trying to help him cough out all of the water he inadvertently took in during the unhelpful lesson. Perhaps, even worse, you spend time performing first aid since your son was close to becoming a drowning victim. Clearly this kind of training is not an acceptable option.

But when it comes to the other end of the spectrum, there are parents who are absolutely terrified at the thought of their child getting into the water; they are paralyzed with fear that their children actually might drown. And what do they do? They never put their child in the pool. They stand at the edge of the pool, high and dry, with their child. They watch the other kids try to learn to swim while they themselves never touch a drop of water. This kind of parent has reacted so negatively to the idea of swimming that the child never gets into the pool, and ultimately never learns anything about swimming. Once the child in this scenario is forced to swim on his own, he will have no idea what to do either.

So, what's the solution? That you as a parent get into the water with your child. In some sense, it's true that your child might stick out from the others because you're the only parent in the pool. But what will happen? Your child will not only experience the water, but will learn to swim within the safety of your counsel. He'll still be experiencing the water, he'll still be facing the danger of drowning, and he'll still learn the necessary techniques for swimming. But it will be accompanied by your secure instruction and proper example.

This is what homeschooling provides. The family that is homeschooling for the right reasons does not shut off the lights and hide in the basement from the world. Rather, the homeschooling family recognizes and directly addresses the sinfulness in the world (and in the child's heart!). The homeschooling family talks about the ugly realities that occur in everyday life. The homeschooling family is in and among a fallen world. And that is the functional equivalent of what Paul and Timothy had.

Paul didn't shelter Timothy from the ugly realities of Gospel ministry. Paul clearly said in 2 Timothy 3:11 that Timothy followed his persecutions and sufferings. He didn't shy away from showing Timothy the cost of following Christ. He brought Timothy along with him during his missionary journeys so that Timothy could see and participate first-hand in ministry life. Timothy knew all about Paul's beatings and ostracism, among other things (cf. 2 Cor. 11:25), and he undoubtedly experienced some of it as he traveled with Paul for many years. Timothy was in the thick of conflict with unbelievers, learning from his mentor how to live as a light in a dark world.

And the time they spent together was absolutely critical because as Paul was preparing to depart the world, he knew that Timothy was going to have to suffer persecution on his own. But he was confident that Timothy would be able to stand up to the task because Timothy had already experienced such persecution during their travels together; he knew how to handle it because he had already been involved in it. Rather than facing trial and tribulation on his own in his earlier years, he endured it side-by-side with Paul.

So when it comes to educating our children, one of the purposes of homeschooling is that you are providing around-the-clock mentoring. Like Paul's discipleship of Timothy, you have the wonderful opportunity to explain the content of Christianity as well as demonstrate the character of Christianity. And rather than viewing this as an obligation (even though it is), we ought to view it as an incredible privilege. It should be our greatest desire to spend as much time with our kids as God has given us, stewarding the time we have with our children to the best of our ability.

On the other hand, children in other educational routes have that amount of time with their parents drastically reduced. In fact, throughout the average week, kids in public schools are typically spending more waking hours *away* from their parents than *with* them. And since no education is without a worldview, you can bet that they are being discipled there. The problem is that it is likely not the kind of discipleship you'd desire. In effect, rather than following *your* teaching, conduct, purpose, faith, patience, love, perseverance, persecutions, and sufferings (as you follow Christ on a daily basis), your kids are receiving the teaching, conduct, and purpose from an educational system that is not Christ-centered or Christ-exalting. They're also experiencing persecution and suffering in and from that same system without a mentor. This has nothing in common with Paul and Timothy's relationship.

Instead, Paul was so confident in his way of discipleship that he allowed Timothy to serve as his pastoral proxy when correction was needed in a church (cf. 1 Cor. 4:17). He taught Timothy and he spent time with Timothy, thus he knew he could count on his disciple to faithfully represent him. This is how Paul did discipleship. It was both educational and experiential.

But before we give Paul all of the credit for Timothy's strong spiritual foundation, we must recognize that he wasn't the only one who made this investment in Timothy's life. Timothy was undoubtedly matured under Paul's ministry, yet at the same time he was already a well-respected Christian even before ever encountering Paul (cf. Acts 16:1-2). How did that happen? Timothy had already been brought under the ministry of the Word by his mother.

Knowing the Scriptures from Childhood

In 2 Timothy 3:15, Timothy was reminded that his faith in the Messiah did not begin when he first heard the name "Jesus." Timothy's faith in the Messiah began well before the fuller details of the Gospel arrived at his door. Paul says that from *childhood* Timothy had known the sacred writings. The term "childhood" comes from the Greek word *brephos,* which means "infant" (even used in passages such as Luke 1:41 to refer to a child still in the womb).[113] This indicates that Timothy was instructed in the things of God at a very young age. He was raised by his mother to know the "sacred writings," which is the term used by Greek-speaking Jews to refer to the Old Testament Scriptures.[114]

All this to say that Timothy had been taught God's Word for many years. In fact, devout Jews immersed their children in Scripture so much that nursing infants were said to "drink in the Law" with their mother's milk.[115] Even though Timothy's father was not a believer, Timothy's mother made sure that from the very start he would be taught the truth—truth that would serve him for a lifetime.

This again indicates a picture of discipleship that was much more than a bumper-sticker ministry, much more than a once-a-week faith, much more than a Sunday-school coloring book. While many of the Jews in Timothy's day were pursuing righteousness by works of the Law, Timothy had learned of his need for the Savior. He had been taught that the Law was not a means of salvation, but that it was instead a guide to lead him to Christ (cf. Gal. 3:24). He realized that

---

[113] George W. Knight, III, *The Pastoral Epistles: A Commentary on the Greek Text* (Grand Rapids, MI: W.B. Eerdmans, 1992), 443.

[114] John MacArthur, *The MacArthur New Testament Commentary: 2 Timothy* (Chicago: Moody, 1995), 138.

[115] John MacArthur, "Compelling Reasons for Biblical Preaching, Part 1," *GTY Resources: Sermons*, Grace to You, accessed August 19, 2016, https://www.gty.org/library/sermons-library/90-351.

animal sacrifices could not truly take away his sins, and that he needed a better sacrifice to deal with them once and for all (cf. Heb. 10:3-4, 10). He learned that Abraham was not declared righteous by his works, but by faith alone (cf. Rom. 4:2-5). Timothy learned all of this and more from his mother, who was a believer under both Old and New Covenants.

Ask committed believers of today who had a Christian upbringing and they will likely tell you that they were deeply impacted simply by observing the life of their parents. For some, it was seeing their dad deep in study before breakfast. For others, it was the bedtime hymns sung with mom. Whatever the case may be, the example of godly parents adds tremendous sobriety to the claims of Scripture. Yes, the Scriptures themselves are what convert children (cf. Rom. 1:16, 1 Pet. 1:23), but the examples found in godly parents are often the means God uses for children to give serious consideration to the message of Scripture. It is one thing for a child to *hear* how the Bible has impacted his dad's life; it's quite another for a child to *see* how the Bible has impacted his dad's life.

Is this what you want for your children? Do you want them to have learned the Scriptures since infancy? Do you want to develop in them a firm grasp of the Gospel that will provide wisdom leading to salvation? Is your great desire to see them overcome the wave of apostasy that will characterize so many others in their generation? Then you must teach them the "sacred writings" (which, by logical extension, also now includes the New Testament). You must exposit the Scriptures day in and day out. But you must do so within the context of a life lived *with* them as well. This means that you ought to remove any obstacle that would prevent you from performing the kind of daily discipleship that characterized Timothy's relationship with his mother.

It seems that we often distinguish between quality time and quantity time spent with our kids. Which is better? The obvious answer is that both are necessary. You cannot simply pursue one to the detriment of the other. Timothy undoubtedly received both, which gave him the wisdom that led to his salvation (cf. 2 Tim. 3:15). Timothy's mother labored in the Word and undoubtedly led him day by day, teaching him diligently in accordance with the Scriptures— Scriptures which included the book of Deuteronomy, a book that hosts one of the landmark passages for biblical discipleship and child-rearing.

Teaching Them Diligently

In Deuteronomy 6:6-7, Moses was preparing the Israelites to enter the Promised Land after their forty-year wandering in the wilderness. In order to ensure that they would not abandon all that he had taught them, they were reminded of the need to diligently train up each subsequent generation in the knowledge of God. Deuteronomy 6:6-7 reads, "These words, which I am commanding you today, shall be on your heart. You shall teach them diligently to your sons and shall talk of them when you sit in your house and when you walk by the way and when you lie down and when you rise up." Far from being an afterthought, the religious instruction of children was to be a way of life.

Viewing the education of their children very seriously, Israelite families understood what it meant to "teach them diligently"—a Hebrew phrase that refers to sharpening a tool or knife.[116] Just as a blade needs to be sharpened in order to serve its purpose, the spiritual

---

[116] J. I. Packer and Merrill C. Tenney, *Illustrated Manners and Customs of the Bible* (Nashville: T. Nelson, 1997), 453-454.

direction given by parents was for the purpose of "sharpening" their kids to function properly as a member of the covenant community of God. And just as a sharp knife will naturally become dull with daily use, so too does a child (and an adult for that matter!) need constant sharpening. Thus, the reference to teaching "when you sit at your house, walk by the way, lie down, and rise up" conveyed the idea that these commandments were to be taught and explained from the start of the day to the end, during work and during recreation, and at home and abroad.[117] It was a side-by-side discipleship in which parents would lead their children throughout the day, every day.

Based on this paradigm, we are simply deceiving ourselves if we think the modern-day application of this text is fulfilled by talking to our children about God "while we drive them to school, when we drop them off at soccer practice, when we pick them up from a friend's house, and after they've done their homework." Intermittent instruction is a far cry from Moses' intent. For the Israelites, communicating the tenets of the Old Covenant was not simply to be a *part* of daily life, it *was* daily life.

And what about parents who were "too busy" for this? Or what about the parents who were not "professional" teachers (also known as the "Myth of the Expert")? No exceptions were made. Boys were primarily cared for by their mothers until age five, at which point the father then assumed full-time responsibility. Since there were no official schools at that time, instruction simply took place amid daily life.

Now ask yourself this: would it have been sufficient for the parents to instruct their children for a brief five minutes during

---

[117] John MacArthur, *The MacArthur Bible Commentary: Unleashing God's Truth, One Verse at a Time* (Nashville: Thomas Nelson, 2005), 207.

breakfast? Of course not. Or what about sending their children off to be educated by the local Canaanite community? Unfathomable. Those Canaanite communities were supposed to have been conquered and destroyed by the Israelites, after all!

In fact, Moses went on to say in Deuteronomy 6:8-9, "You shall bind them as a sign on your hand and they shall be as frontals on your forehead. You shall write them on the doorposts of your house and on your gates." In effect, his words were to be metaphorically bound as a sign on their hand (symbolizing the Law's jurisdiction over their actions), set as frontals on their foreheads (symbolizing the Law's jurisdiction over their thoughts), and written on their doors and gates (symbolizing the Law's jurisdiction at all times and all places in life). God's Law was to be taken seriously, which is why it demanded diligent, day-by-day instruction from the parents.

Undoubtedly, Timothy's mother, Eunice, knew this portion of the Law well. She understood the requirement to teach her son diligently. And although we can't say for sure how much Timothy's relationship with his mother paralleled the model found in Deuteronomy 6, one thing we do see is that the multigenerational command to "teach your sons and grandsons" was certainly followed. Timothy's family included the multigenerational examples of faith found in Eunice (Timothy's mother) as well as Lois (Timothy's grandmother). He was influenced by two older generations of faithful Jews, just as the Law intended. For this reason, Paul commended Timothy for continuing in the faith of these women. He looked favorably on the amount of discipleship Timothy received at home from them.

It's true that we as Christians are not legalistically bound by this Old Covenant command in Deuteronomy. Having been buried with Christ in His death and risen with Him in new life, we are now free from the Mosaic Law and the condemning work of the Law written on our hearts. Instead, we find ourselves under the New Covenant (cf. Rom. 6:13-14). But consider this: if the Old Covenant expected full-time discipleship, how much more should the New Covenant, which is a better covenant (cf. Heb. 8:6), solicit this same investment? Yes, there is great freedom in Christianity. Yes, we live according to the Spirit and not by the letter of the Law. But Christ has given us the Scriptures so that we would glorify God in all aspects of our life. Thus, we must take the lead in communicating them to our children.

A common cliché says, "It takes a village to raise a child," and while that may sound good on a bumper sticker, it actually has little in common with the biblical paradigm for raising children. Certainly, you need to be a part of a believing community. And yes, it's important that your kids are under the authority of local pastors. But the instruction of children falls first and foremost on the shoulders of the father, second on the shoulders of the mother, and third on the shoulders of the grandparents. It is not first the responsibility of the church. And it is much less the responsibility (or the right) of the government. The responsibility falls on us. That is the Deuteronomy 6 model that guided Old Covenant believers like Lois and Eunice, and that is the model that surely compels us as believers under the New Covenant today.

A Godly Foundation

Ultimately, we see that it would not have been enough for young Timothy simply to look back with fondness on the daily discipleship and training that he had with Paul and his mother. Yes, those memories of instruction during his formative years were critical for him. But spiritual nostalgia would have been insufficient to bolster Timothy's faith. He was told to *continue* in the things he had learned (cf. 2 Tim. 3:14). He had heard God's Word, he had believed God's Word, and he simply needed to continue obeying God's Word in order to persevere in the future.

Your children face the same issue. If they are to persevere in their faith, they not only need to hear the Word, but they need to believe and obey it. Obviously, you as a parent cannot believe or obey God's Word for them; they must respond in that fashion on their own. Yet, at the same time, they cannot believe or obey what they don't know. That's where your commitment to expository parenting comes into play. In order for your child to have a firm foundation that stands strong when trials and temptation come—and they will come—it starts with hearing the Word from you. If you are planning to exposit the Scriptures verse by verse to your children, teaching them doctrine, demonstrating Christian conduct, and giving them a firm spiritual foundation, you need to maximize the amount of time you have with them. Your children need to be not only under your roof, but under your ministry. And an educational environment based in the home meets the need.

With that said, one thing must be understood: if left to themselves, your children *will* continue in what they've learned—and it won't be pretty. Proverbs 22:6 stands as perhaps one of the most beloved of all parenting verses in Scripture, stating, "Train up a child in the way he should go, even when he is old he will not depart from it." This verse has undoubtedly been used to provide hope for an untold number of parents who find themselves grieving over a wayward son or daughter, as it is understood to be a promise that their child will ultimately return to the Lord.

But the stark reality is that this verse is actually a warning, not a comfort.[118] A tighter translation of the passage would read as follows: "Start out a youth according to his own way; even should he grow old,

---

[118] Eric Davis, "Reconsidering Proverbs 22:6 & the 'Way He Should Go,'" *Shepherding* (blog), The Cripplegate, June 8, 2016, http://thecripplegate.com/reconsidering-proverbs-226.

he will not turn from it."[119] Notice that the phrase "the way he should go" is better translated as "his own way." In other words, if a child is trained up according to *his* way (raised how he wants, a way that coincides with his natural fallenness), this passage warns us that he will not simply grow out of it, but will instead maintain his futile thinking on into adulthood. Like concrete left out to dry, childhood folly only solidifies with time. And at the risk of pushing the analogy too far, it should be noted that concrete left to dry on its own (rather than being properly cured under a watchful eye) ends up being structurally weaker in the end.

We must be honest in recognizing that as a child attends public school on his own, accompanied by peers whose hearts are also bound up in foolishness (cf. Prov. 22:15), he is most certainly being trained up according to his own way. He is learning the ways of the world, incorporating the world's ideals into his own psyche, and being affirmed in it by those around him.

The bottom line is that our priority must be to give our children as much of a godly foundation as we possibly can. Our goal should be to develop a young man or woman who has been trained up in such a way that by the time adulthood comes, he or she is ready to hit the ground running not only as an educated, well-rounded, mature member of society, but more importantly, as an equipped, dedicated, contributing member of a local church. There is simply no reason, nor legitimate excuse, that we as Christian parents would continue to produce eighteen-year-old young adults who require another twenty to thirty years of discipling in a local church before they have any kind of ability to rightly interpret Scripture, evangelize the lost, serve in

---

[119] Dan Phillips, *God's Wisdom in Proverbs: Hearing God's Voice in Scripture* (The Woodlands: Kress Biblical Resources, 2011), 367.

ministry, and disciple other believers. That kind of timetable not only stunts the individual's growth, but also cripples the effectiveness of the local church. You can do better. This is your opportunity. You can turn your home into a seminary.

Creating a Seminary at Home

One of the remarkable things about expository preaching is that the very act itself instills a love of learning in both the teacher and the hearer. God's grace acting through His Word in the lives of His people gives them an affection and desire for greater biblical knowledge, which consequently breeds a desire for greater education. Historical research, grammatical details, language, logic, and rhetoric all find their place within meaningful Bible exposition. This really shouldn't surprise us, but because of unchecked anti-intellectualism in many churches, the word "disciple" has been almost entirely understood to simply mean a "follower" of Christ. And while it is true that the disciples of Jesus followed Him, that is far from its only meaning. A disciple is also a student, pupil, adherent to particular doctrines, and one who embraces a set of teachings.[120] All of this necessarily implies that a Christian is one who is committed to learning. Those who "just aren't into study" are going to have a hard time being a Christian, since growing in knowledge is one aspect that defines a true disciple (cf. 2 Pet. 1:2, 3:18).

Thus, a hallmark characteristic of any good expositor, and disciple in general, is that he loves to study and learn. It simply comes with the territory. To explain the historical background, grammatical nuances, and theological implications of any given passage requires an amount

---

[120] Watson E. Mills and Roger Aubrey Bullard, *Mercer Dictionary of the Bible* (Macon, GA: Mercer U Press, 1990), 215.

of work that only a love of learning could motivate to accomplish. And when you take the opportunity to teach your children at home, you get to portray learning as what it truly is—a blessing from God.

God has graciously given us the capacity to understand and interact with His creation, something that is often overlooked and taken for granted by many students. He has given us minds that can respond and react to stimuli. He has given us the ability to acquire and categorize new information. He has made a way for us to develop, test, and confirm theories about how His laws of nature operate. All of this is a gift, and if you can convey this to your children it will be of great benefit to your expositional ministry. Rather than seeing verse-by-verse teaching as boring, their love of God will result in a love of Scripture. Then, their love of Scripture will result in a love of learning. Digging into the historical background or detailing the grammatical nuances of a passage won't be a dreaded evil, but instead becomes a wonderful opportunity to learn more of the things of God.

Contrast this with public schools. Many kids in public schools do not appreciate education, hate learning, and have a low level of respect for teachers. The sin of intellectual apathy runs rampant. That perspective proves not only to be an obstacle for school subjects, but translates into an equally difficult obstacle for Bible study. Instead of adopting that mentality from classmates, home education gives your children a model of one who appreciates the God-given ability to learn (this all presupposes that *you as a parent* love learning, of course).

With that in mind, a second benefit of home education is that you can incorporate subjects into the curriculum that will support and enhance your expository ministry. Spending time learning about Jewish captivity in Babylon? Tailor your child's history unit for that semester around this ancient civilization. Learning about Paul's use of first-century rhetoric in the book of Romans? Begin teaching your child the basics of the Koine Greek language. In addition to these kinds of specific examples, other school subjects will provide great assistance in helping your child properly understand the Bible.

Consider for example, a subject like language arts. This area of study is critical for properly interpreting the Bible according to the grammatical hermeneutic. Understanding nouns and verbs, pronouns and antecedents, or direct versus indirect objects are foundational building blocks for a proper exegesis of any given passage. Yet, for many students, language arts could not seem any more irrelevant to their lives. However, if you are educating them at home, you can explain how this subject is immediately useful for properly interpreting Scripture, giving them a practical application that will help them understand the significance and necessity of learning it. And if they truly desire to know more about God, this subject will simply be viewed as a stepping stone that provides them with a better knowledge of the Word.

Finally, the opportunity to incorporate the Bible into the curriculum, not only by studying it directly but also by studying great works of theologians from the past, is what sets this kind of education apart. Yes, there is a danger that Bible study could become a sterile, purely intellectual endeavor, rather than a vibrant pursuit of the glories of God found in His Word. But that's unlikely. The greater threat facing most children today is not an over-abundance of biblical instruction that has stripped it of joy, but rather an almost complete malnourishment of biblical instruction that has robbed it of its use. In Mark 8:36, Jesus said, "For what does it profit a man to gain the whole world, and forfeit his soul?" Without being overdramatic, we can make the application that if your child excels in every single school subject but graduates with no Bible knowledge, you've defaulted on your duties as a parent.

Lord of Education

Are there children who become mature Christians despite being educated in secular environments? Certainly. God saves His people out of a variety of backgrounds. But the issue is not "whether our kids can still turn out ok" (pragmatism), nor is it about "doing what fits our family the best" (relativism), nor is it "praying that God would prompt us to make a decision" (mysticism). The real question is, "What does the Bible say God's will is for my child's education?"

After all, if we truly believe that we are stewards of children who belong first and foremost to God, then we must consult Him first and foremost for direction. Our priorities must align with His. For example, we want our kids to become socialized, "fitting in" as members of society. But which society? The world's society? No, Christians are just passing through this world; our citizenship is in Heaven (cf. Phil. 3:20, Heb. 11:13-16). Is that not where we should long for our children to "fit in?" Then surely our means of instructing them must be accordingly (cf. Col. 3:1-2). Often, those who are not being discipled full-time at home are being socialized in ways that would have been unthinkable just a few generations ago. Dr. Al Mohler recounts such a situation:

> I mentioned this just the other day, this is the most chilling thing I've heard in a very long time. I was talking to a man and his wife and they were explaining to me why they'd made a radical change in the education of their children just in the last few days. And it is because they were at dinner and their ten-year-old son heard the mother and father talking about issues related to a headline event with the LGBT complex of issues. And the ten-year-old son said, "That's hate speech, dad."[121]

---

[121] John MacArthur, Ligon Duncan, and Al Mohler, "General Session 8: Q&A" (presentation, Shepherds' Conference 2016, Grace Community Church, Sun Valley, CA, March 11, 2016).

It certainly is commendable that the parents in the aforementioned scenario used the opportunity to re-examine their child's educational situation. They didn't ignore the clear warning signs. Yet, we must also ask, "Is that the standard?" Does a child have to come home articulating an anti-God worldview before the problem becomes clear? After all, for a child to rebuke his father with such a secular perspective means that there has already been a worldview implanted in his heart (cf. Luke 6:45). Surely we must consult a greater standard; otherwise our convictions will only be circumstantial, at best.

To be fair, not every government school system is created equal. There is no doubt that some are little more than juvenile detention centers, while others provide a constructive environment in which teachers are respected and students are relatively attentive. For that reason, you might be tempted to say, "It's ok, trust me. Our public school system is different. There are no blatant attacks on God or Christianity; in fact, there is no mention of God at all!" But wait a minute. Play that back in your mind—*it's ok that God is totally absent from your child's education?* Is that a principle derived from Scripture? No. On the contrary, the Bible explicitly speaks *against* that perspective.

In Romans 1, the Apostle Paul talks about the depravity of man and God's judgment on sinners. He says that God's wrath is being revealed against the wickedness and unrighteousness of men. The result is that such men are abandoned to their lusts, beginning with homosexuality and ending with a litany of other sins (cf. Rom. 1:28-31). And what does Paul say is the reason for God's judgment of them? Is it because sinners shake their fist at God and stomp on the Scriptures in an uncontrollable rage? No—Romans 1:21 says, "For even though they knew God, they did not honor Him as God or give thanks, but they became futile in their speculations and their foolish heart was darkened." God gives men over to their lusts "simply" because they fail to acknowledge Him! This passage is not a description of someone who wages an explicit assault on God; this is a description of someone who knows they have a Creator and decides to suppress that truth in unrighteousness (cf. Rom. 1:18). This is a person who has intentionally left God out of the picture.

If we're being honest, we must confess that this is also the precise description of many secular schools—no mention of God, the Bible, or Christianity, just a "neutral" education. In other words, it's an academic institution which knows God but does not honor Him as God or give thanks. So the reality is that neither a secular public education, nor a secular private education, *nor a secular homeschool education* fits the biblical paradigm. Our job as parents is not to give our kids a values-neutral education (as if such a thing even exists), but rather to give them a Christ-centered education. The standard is godliness, not neutrality.

With that said, the act of homeschooling, by itself, is little more than legalism when viewed as the end-all of godliness, as if homeschooling for the sake of homeschooling is the point. One great temptation is to treat it as the test of sanctification in a person's life, the "Promised Land" that solves all of life's difficulties if only parents would commit to it. Instead, we simply need to recognize that it is just the vehicle that drives all of the training that we want to accomplish in our children's lives. In other words, to homeschool without first having the conviction that it's your duty to raise up mature believers before they leave your home is to forfeit the greatest impetus for why you're doing it in the first place. And without such a conviction it will be difficult to stay the course, particularly when the homeschooling honeymoon period is over and the daily grind is in full swing.

Missionary Paul Washer addresses this potential pitfall:

In our families, doing missions in our families, we must make much about Jesus Christ. We must speak of Christ, glory in Christ—not in our rules, not in our lifestyle, not in all of the things that we think sometimes that are so important. But we must glory in Christ and our children must see that we are passionate about the person of Jesus Christ. Beware of the idolatry of family, the idolatry of intellect, proper manners, and strict living. Calvin said that our hearts are idol factories. He's right. Make sure that your proclamation isn't you, or what you do, but Christ and what He has done. Now let me say this: have no banner over you except Jesus Christ. I honestly know many, many people who are very, very dedicated to raising their children and when you look at them it's very obvious that the banner over them is homeschooling. The banner over them is a godly family. It's what they talk about, it's what they revel in, it's what they desire. And I hear very little about Jesus Christ.[122]

So, why do it? Why invest so much energy in home education? Here's the answer: *to make much of Christ*. We must be driven to homeschool not because it is an end in and of itself, but because it is the means by which we recognize and submit to Christ's Lordship in the area of academics. Colossians 1:18 tells us that Jesus Christ is to "have first place in everything." There is no area of life in which we can legitimately claim to glorify God and yet leave Christ out of the picture. History, Government, Science, Art, Industry—all things belong to Him and exist for Him (cf. Heb. 2:10). All authority in Heaven and earth has been given to Him, thus we must submit to His Lordship even in the area of education. Every mathematical equation, every scientific principle, every historical fact—they all belong to the Lord Jesus Christ, the one in whom are all the riches of wisdom and knowledge

---

[122] Paul Washer, "The Importance of Biblical Family Life for the Spread of the Gospel" (presentation, Sufficiency of Scripture Conference 2009, Northern Kentucky Convention Center, Covington, KY, December 12, 2009).

(cf. Col. 2:3). In fact, because "the fear of the Lord is the *beginning* of wisdom" (Prov. 9:10) those who educate without first acknowledging the Lord Jesus Christ are actually operating on borrowed capital!

Think about it: how do we know that one plus one will equal two tomorrow, just as it does today? Because the Lord Jesus Christ upholds all things, including the relationship between numerical constants (cf. Heb. 1:3). How do we know that Newton's Third Law of Motion is a reliable principle upon which we can base experiments? Because the Lord Jesus Christ holds all things together, including the consistency between opposing forces (cf. Col. 1:17). How do we even know that our minds can properly understand reality around us? Because God made man in His image for the purpose of interacting with His world (cf. Gen. 1:26, 2:15). Our child's schooling must acknowledge that God is the author of rationality.

Theorems, postulates, laws, axioms — we name them after brilliant scientists and mathematicians who discovered them, but it is Jesus who created them. To live as God's creation, among God's creation, studying God's creation, while not acknowledging the God of creation is like hosting a party at a rich neighbor's house and taking credit for how wonderful the accommodations are! And that is exactly how Satan operates. God has created all things, yet Satan roams the earth offering the pleasures of the world as if he owns the place (cf. Matt. 4:8-9, 1 Pet. 5:8). Thus, it is our job as believers to refute this lie and let all people, first and foremost our children, know that every square inch of real estate on this planet actually belongs to Jesus (cf. Psa. 24:1).

For this reason, it is not enough to acknowledge our Lord and Savior only in "religious" matters; we must proclaim His excellencies in every sphere of life (cf. 1 Pet. 2:9). Otherwise, we need to rethink our understanding of Proverbs 3:5-6, which states, "Trust in the Lord with all your heart and do not lean on your own understanding. *In all your ways acknowledge Him,* and He will make your paths straight." One pastor offers the following wisdom:

> We have been desensitized by this world to have a wrong mindset in a certain area. We can view sitting with my children and opening up the Bible in a devotional time as something I as a father have responsibility for, but somehow math and reading and history and science are not, simply because when I open the Bible it's "spiritual" and math is not spiritual. Folks, that simply is not true. Christ is to have preeminence in all things. Do you realize every single thing in this world revolves around the Lord Jesus Christ? Every single thing. If you have some part of your life that He has nothing to do with, get it out of your life, folks. Get it out.[123]

If our expository ministry is to have enough time at its disposal to deliver the full counsel of God, home education is a critical component. If we are to guard our children from influences which will undermine our ministry, homeschooling is the route we must take. If we are to raise up children who love to study the Word, an academic upbringing under the counsel of godly parents fits the need.

There are indeed critical circumstances that hinder parents from discipling their kids full-time at home. If you are in such a situation, rest in God's grace and peace as you struggle mightily in ways many will never understand. But if your main concern is that educating your children at home is simply not something you can afford, pause for a moment and consider if *not* educating your children at home is something you can afford. It's possible that sending your children to a government school could be the costliest thing you ever do.

---

[123] Tim Conway, "Public, Private, or Homeschool? Some Principles to Consider (9 of 12)" (presentation, Sunday Service, Grace Community Church, San Antonio, TX, January 22, 2006).

Timothy's father, being a Greek, was quite likely involved in any number of first-century philosophical and religious systems such as Stoicism, Epicureanism, and worship of the Olympian god Zeus. The fact that Timothy had learned of the one true God and became a believer is truly a testament to the God-honoring commitment of his mother and grandmother. And the fact that Timothy had matured in the faith to become a pastor later in life is truly a testament to the God-honoring commitment of his mentor, Paul. Those experiences set Timothy on a course for spiritual success, which is why he simply needed to continue in what he had learned. Likewise, we need to raise our children in such a way that when they become adults and go out into the world on their own we can legitimately remind them to "continue in what they've learned."

Ultimately, how you educate your children is a decision you must make, but it is not a decision for which the Bible lacks a normative standard. God has not left His people without a conclusive set of principles regarding education. Unfortunately, rather than making an intentional and informed decision, many simply follow cultural customs without evaluating the ramifications. But remember: every education comes with a worldview and every child is being discipled—the only question is, by whom? Jesus is Lord of education; may we honor Him as such.

8
THE LOCAL SHEPHERD

"Preaching is powerful because it is an extension of God's own revelation. Therefore, every believer and member of God's church should not only care about preaching, but have the utmost reverence for this God-ordained act which communicates God's Word to us in a unique way."[124]

–Emilio Ramos

Focus Text: *You therefore, my son, be strong in the grace that is in Christ Jesus. The things which you have heard from me in the presence of many witnesses, entrust these to faithful men who will be able to teach others also. (2 Timothy 2:1-2)*

Expository preaching? Systematic theology? Hermeneutics? The terms start to add up quickly. Who is adequate for these things? Do you basically have to be a seminarian or biblical scholar in order to parent your children the right way? No, of course not. Instead of having a seminary-level education, what if you *knew someone* with a seminary-level education? Someone who could model for you the kind of ministry that you want to implement in your home? Someone who has already demonstrated how to shepherd a flock? Ephesian 4:11-13 tells us that God has indeed provided for that need with "pastors and

---

[124] Emilio Ramos, "What Is Preaching and Why Should You Care?," *Heritage Grace Blog*, accessed March 3, 2017, http://heritagegrace.com/heritage-grace-blog/what-is-preaching-and-why-should-you-care.

teachers, for the equipping of the saints for the work of service, to the building up of the body of Christ; until we all attain to the unity of the faith, and of the knowledge of the Son of God, to a mature man."

Are you in need of a theologian who can equip you for making disciples in your home? God has graciously provided for that need. He has gifted the church with men who possess the skills and abilities not only to bring *us* up in the faith, but to teach us how to bring up *others* in the faith, including our children. Here we see the concept of expository parenting come full circle: expositors in the pulpit demonstrate the pattern of verse-by-verse teaching that parents ought to follow in the home, and parents who seek to teach the Scriptures at home will need to rely on those who exposit the Scriptures from the pulpit. Thus, one of your greatest allies in the work of expository parenting is your local church pastor.

But first, let's take a step back for a moment. Imagine that you have just been saved out of a thoroughly pagan background. Most of the people around you have no biblical knowledge of God. Few people have personal copies of Scripture. And you are marginally literate, at best. How are you going to learn the "full counsel of God?" Moreover, how are you to raise your children based on such limited knowledge of Scripture? The answer is: your local church pastors. And although such a scenario may sound far-fetched, this was precisely the first-century situation in which the Apostle Paul wrote to Timothy.

Without a doubt, estimating literacy rates from long ago has proven to be a difficult task. One scholar puts his estimate of literacy in ancient Rome below thirty percent for males and below ten percent for females. [125] This scholar also goes on to make the excellent point that

---

[125] William V. Harris, *Ancient Literacy* (Cambridge, MA: Harvard UP, 1989), 266-281.

when Jesus rebuked His hearers for not having "read" the Scriptures, it was well-deserved because they were scribes—the select few in Jewish culture whose job it was *to be literate!* What's clear is that illiteracy was much more common than we might realize.

Therefore, without the ability to read, and no personal copies of Scripture, most congregants would be utterly dependent on their pastors to teach them God's Word. Going home to study their own Bible, consult an extensive number of Bible commentaries via computer software, and research passages on the internet, all in the comfort of an air-conditioned room, are luxuries they could never have dreamed would be available. One church historian reminds us that this was also the case well past the first century, stating:

> Certain kinds of behavior can only take place where certain social and economic conditions can be found. And if I were to say to you, "Well, do you read the Bible every day?" You'd say to me, "Of course I read my Bible every day. I go to my room by myself and I take out my Bible and I read it." That immediately tells me something about the culture in which you live. It tells me you have access to cheap print, for a start. It tells me that you have access to private space. And it tells me you can read. And I want to suggest that those three things were not available to most Christians throughout most of church history. [126]

It only makes sense, then, that the overall emphasis of the New Testament is actually on the public proclamation of Scripture, as opposed to its private study.[127] The apostles knew that most believers would come to faith in Christ by literally *hearing* the Word, not reading

---

[126] Carl Trueman, "The Church: Does It work, and, If So, How?," (presentation, Conference 2009—Ecclesiology, Covenant OPC Church, Orland Park, IL, September 26, 2009).
[127] Thomas R. Schreiner, *Galatians* (Grand Rapids, MI: Zondervan, 2010), 372.

it (cf. Rom. 10:17). They recognized that faithful pastors were the sole means by which many Christians could gain access to the Scriptures and grow in their faith.

The problem today is that since we do have our own personal Bibles, and possess the ability to read them, we have largely ignored the fact that pastors are still just as needed for spiritual insight and guidance. In a sense, we have wrongly assumed that owning our own Bible has automatically granted us the ability to rightly handle it. Far too often there is a "just me and the Holy Spirit" mentality when it comes to learning God's Word. And this error comes not only from those in the pew, it is also reinforced by many in the pulpit.

Consider the all-too-common scenario in which a pastor urges his congregation to go home and study Scripture, yet doesn't preach sequentially through the Bible on Sunday mornings. By doing this, he is assuming that his members are able to learn the entire Bible on their own. Logically then, he is also asserting that the mature Christian life is only for the literate. What about those who cannot read? Or are less capable of proper interpretation? Or do not have access to additional resources for assistance? Is it simply "too bad" for them? It ought not be. That is not what Christ intended for His church.

Of course, recognizing that modern believers need help understanding Scripture, many book publishers have produced "simplified" Bible translations and paraphrases that cater to those who are untrained in interpretation. Sadly though, this often ends up obscuring, rather than clarifying, the actual meaning of the text. A simplified translation gives the reader the sense that he can properly interpret the Bible, but it is a sense founded on the fact that the words of Scripture may have been radically altered from their original equivalent. As Pastor John MacArthur says,

People say we need to bring the Bible into modern times. Dead wrong, dead wrong. We need to bring the modern reader into Bible times. You have to take the hearer back and reconstruct the original setting. That's the only way you can understand the meaning of Scripture. And that, in that one statement alone, eliminates all modern, updated, transliterations of the Bible. What you want in a Bible that is in the hands of a believer is the most accurate word-for-word translation of the original text, because that's the purest form of the message.[128]

Thus, rather than producing a "dumbed-down" translation that only loosely follows the actual wording of the original Greek and Hebrew, the real solution is to produce a translation that is as close to the original text as possible, and then allow an expositor to help his congregation understand it correctly. We need fewer Bible studies with chairs facing each other, and more Bible studies with pews facing the front. In the end, whether you are an illiterate, first-century believer without a Bible, a literate, 21st-century believer with your own personal Bible, or somewhere in between, you need to sit under expository preaching in a local church.

Faithful Men Who Will Teach Others

In The Great Commission found in Matthew 28:18-20, the Lord commanded His disciples to teach others to obey His commands. And because The Great Commission itself was a command, the implication is that His disciples were to go and make their own second-generation disciples, who in turn would go and make their own third-generation

---

[128] John MacArthur, "Consequences of Non-Expository Preaching, Part I," *PM 501: Fundamentals of Expository Preaching*, The Master's Seminary Theological Resource Center, accessed September 16, 2016, http://www.theologicalresources.org/the-masters-seminary/24-fundamentals-of-expository-preaching.

disciples, and so on. How long was this pattern to continue? Well, the fact that Jesus promised to be with them "even to the end of the age" gives us the answer—this disciple-making pattern was and is to continue until the end of the Church Age. Consider that Jesus issued this command right before He departed—although He would be with them via the Holy Spirit, His physical presence would be absent until His second coming. Thus, He wanted to make sure that the disciple-making effort would continue even after He was gone. We see this same mentality from the Apostle Paul prior to his departure as well:

> *You therefore, my son, be strong in the grace that is in Christ Jesus. The things which you have heard from me in the presence of many witnesses, entrust these to faithful men who will be able to teach others also.*
> *(2 Timothy 2:1-2)*

In this passage, the "things" which Timothy had heard from Paul refer to the truths of the New Covenant. And Paul made it clear that he had safeguarded the message (cf. 2 Tim. 4:7), being wholly devoted to communicating it in its entirety to his disciple Timothy. On that basis, what we see in 2 Timothy 2:2 is a grace-based, multi-generational, disciple-making pattern very similar to The Great Commission. Just as Christ told His disciples to teach their own disciples, so too did Paul tell Timothy to entrust to others everything he had learned. In fact, this passage represents four generations of Christians: "me" (referring to Paul), "you" (referring to Timothy), "faithful men" (referring to Timothy's disciples), and "others also" (referring to the disciples of Timothy's disciples).

But there is one major difference. When Christ commissioned His disciples, that disciple-making pattern logically extends to all believers; we are all commanded to make disciples. On the other hand, when Paul told Timothy to train up "faithful men," the reference is to church leaders, men trustworthy enough to deliver the full counsel of God just as they received it (cf. 1 Cor. 4:1-2, Titus 1:9).

In other words, Paul did not have in mind a general use of the word "men," but rather, specifically wanted Timothy to make sure to raise up trustworthy, male co-laborers who could pastor a group of believers.[129] For that reason, Paul went on to reiterate the qualifications for elders so that Timothy would remember how to identify such faithful men (cf. 2 Tim. 2:24-26). Paul was thinking not of his own interests as he awaited death, but instead was looking far into the future to make sure that the church would be taken care of after his departure.

So what does any of this have to do with you as a parent? The reality is that the task of biblical exposition is not to be taken lightly. As the Apostle Peter noted, some Scriptures are simply more difficult to understand than others, and the danger is that we might distort them to the detriment of ourselves and our hearers (cf. 2 Pet. 3:16, 2 Tim. 2:14). This ought to serve as a sobering reminder to you as you consider the task of explaining the Bible to your family.

After all, pastors often spend an incredible amount of time and money getting a seminary education so that they might be equipped to rightly handle the Word. And while it is certainly not a biblical requirement that a man attend seminary before shepherding a local church (the Bible certainly makes no mention of it), those who wish to hold the office of pastor are still under obligation to possess the skills and abilities needed to properly interpret and teach the Bible (cf. 1 Tim. 3:2, 2 Tim. 2:2). The amount of meticulous attention to detail, historical

---

[129] George W. Knight, III, *The Pastoral Epistles: A Commentary on the Greek Text.* (Grand Rapids, MI: W.B. Eerdmans, 1992), 391.

knowledge, and training in the original languages required for expositing a passage is certainly not something that anyone is born with, and it is for this reason that many men devote their younger years to obtaining these skills that will guide them for the rest of their lives.

Thus, it would be both foolish and arrogant for us to assume that we possess the inherent ability to teach through the entire Bible without help. Yes, anyone who is indwelt by the Holy Spirit will be able to glean spiritual truths from Scripture (cf. 1 John 2:27). But if you are truly planning on walking your family through the Bible verse by verse, it is virtually guaranteed that you will be desperate for help at some point. Diving past the surface of the text into its rich, theological depths often requires time-tested wisdom and training, which is why men of God who have been spiritually gifted for pastoring and trained in expository preaching serve as one of the most important resources for your family. These are the "faithful men" that Paul told Timothy to train, and for the sake of your family you must do everything within your power to find them.

Identifying a Faithful Shepherd

Although there are numerous passages throughout the Bible that help us identify godly men, three in particular stand out as presenting the necessary characteristics of a faithful pastor: 1 Timothy 3:1-7, 2 Timothy 2:24-26, and Titus 1:6-9. Between these three passages, there are a whopping thirty-eight qualifications (granted, some of them are duplicates). With regards to parenting, the qualification that initially stands out is "one who manages his own household well, keeping his children under control with all dignity" (1 Tim. 3:4). Although every qualification stands as equally necessary, this ability is particularly insightful because it indicates that a man has properly led his own flock at home, making him prepared to expand his influence to an entire church body. To clarify this, the Apostle Paul even posed the rhetorical question, "If a man does not know how to manage his own household, how will he take care of the church of God?" (1 Tim. 3:5). It's clear that a leader's testimony (both to the church and the world) is crippled if his closest disciples are unruly.

Among the other requirements, there is only one other ability listed: he must be able to teach the Word with sound doctrine (cf. 1 Tim. 3:2, 2 Tim. 2:24, Titus 1:9). But if the pastor is to serve as a model parent (albeit an imperfect one, like the rest of us), one would almost think that there should be other skills listed, such as being an "effective counselor" or "able to inspire others." After all, we as parents need help from our church leaders in order to raise our children better. Yet, "able to teach" is the only other skill that is listed, because in reality that is all that is needed. Paralleled only by intercessory prayer, the ability to rightly interpret and explain the Scriptures is the most important tool in any Christian's arsenal. And since Scripture is sufficient for all things pertaining to life and godliness, our greatest desire should be to learn how to effectively explain it to our children— teaching them the Bible equips them for every aspect life. Thus, as pastors preach and teach the Word, they are, in fact, giving you help with your parenting.

If you are to be an expositor for your family, you need to learn from an expositor. Consider the words Jesus spoke in Luke 6:39-40: "A blind man cannot guide a blind man, can he? Will they not both fall into a pit? A pupil is not above his teacher; but everyone, after he has been fully trained, will be like his teacher." Ultimately, our teacher is the Chief Shepherd, the Lord Jesus Christ. Yet at the same time, the Chief Shepherd has appointed under-shepherds to keep watch over His flock. So the reality is that your local pastor serves as a model of how to handle the Bible as he stands in the pulpit each week, which has a major influence on you whether you realize it or not.

The way a pastor prepares for the message, interprets the related passages, explains the text to you, and urges you to submit to God's Word will directly impact how you likewise do those things for your children. Every pastor ought to recognize that his Sunday morning sermon is a major influence on his local church not only by the *content* of the expository sermon, but by the very *act* of expository preaching itself. It's been pointed out that expository preaching is more *caught* than *taught*. Pastor John MacArthur explains:

> What I demonstrate for them on a Sunday is exactly what I want them to do. I want them to read the Scripture, to come to grips with the words, the phrases, the grammar, the definitions. I want them to go to their concordance and other resources and find cross-references that enrich and explain and enhance and embellish. I want them to find passages in Scripture that illustrate this truth. I want them to know that if these are the various options, this is why this one can't be right, and this is why this one is the option of choice. I want them to be in the process because I want them to learn to study the Bible for themselves. If all I ever do is tell stories, and pontificate, and come up with things that are some kind of ingenious expression of my own cleverness, they are completely without an example of what it means to do what they need to be doing, and that is studying the Word of God. The people who sit under exposition will reproduce the approach to Scripture that they see modeled in front of them.[130]

Perhaps you are a new believer or simply don't know your Bible well

---

[130] John MacArthur, "Consequences of Non-Expository Preaching, Part II," *PM 501: Fundamentals of Expository Preaching*, The Master's Seminary Theological Resource Center, accessed August 19, 2016, http://www.theologicalresources.org/the-masters-seminary/24-fundamentals-of-expository-preaching.

enough to feel confident teaching your children. All the various aspects of expository parenting may seem beyond your reach. What should you do? How can you get started? If you don't know where to begin, the best thing to do is listen diligently to your pastor exposit the Word on a Sunday morning, and then turn around and teach your kids that same portion of Scripture the following week, just as you saw it modeled.

Listen for how your pastor interprets the passages, develops his outline, explains theological truths, and draws application from the text. Then study further and explain the passage to your children. Do this for several months (or more, depending on your needs) and you are already well on your way into the joys of expository parenting. Simply follow along with your pastor and then relay the information. Like a snowball rolling down a hill, sitting under an expositional ministry (with the commitment to mimic it within your family) will cause you to grow in the Word in ways you may never have imagined. It will only be a matter of time before you begin a more expanded ministry with your children.

Beyond Sunday mornings, you can take even more advantage of your pastor's wisdom by asking him for specific help with teaching the Bible. And if your pastor has a genuine love for you and your family, he will undoubtedly be thrilled if you were to come to him and ask for assistance ministering the Word to your kids. More than likely, a pastor would be so overjoyed by a member of his congregation being interested in such things as hermeneutics, exegesis, and expository preaching that he would need a minute to gather his composure! Talk with your elders about how they prepare to preach. Ask them for "behind the scenes" advice on what you can do to teach the Bible at home. Once you are set to teach through a book of the Bible, here are examples of the kinds of questions that would be helpful to ask:

How can I preach Christ from this book of the Bible?

How can I use this passage to evangelize my child?

What are some interpretative errors that I need to avoid?

What are the most common objections to this passage?

What study resources would you recommend for this?

What are the key passages that I should emphasize?

What are some age-appropriate applications I can offer?

What major doctrines are developed from this book of the Bible?

Which book of the Bible should I teach through next?

Certainly, pastors are just as busy as the rest of us, so our reliance on them ought to be tempered in such a way that we don't overload them with our own needs at the cost of the congregation's needs. We ought not to bombard a single pastor with a slew of questions, some of which we may be able to answer with a little research on our own. But the point is that as you plan to work your way through the Bible, your local pastors will be a tremendous asset in empowering you for ministry by both demonstrating and explaining how to carry out biblical exposition.

Identifying an Unfaithful Shepherd

Unfortunately, though, the reason many parents don't know the best way to disciple their flocks is because they're not seeing it modeled in the pulpit. We live in a day and age when pastors believe they have the liberty to preach what they want and how they want, as demonstrated by all of the various sermon series that are hand-crafted and tailor-made for the modern ear. In addition, many fall into the error of preaching *reactively* rather than *proactively*.

Consider, for example, the average topical sermon series that a pastor preaches. How did he determine that this was a topic that needed to be addressed? In many cases, the answer will be something along the lines of having "sensed" the felt-needs of the congregation, experiencing a hunch or intuition that helped him with his decision. It is as if he has a spiritual sixth-sense by which he peers into the hearts of his congregation and addresses the particular need of the moment.

The problem with this? Aside from not actually possessing such a sense, this kind of preaching is, by definition, always *reactive.* Using the Bible merely as a response, this type of preaching attempts to diagnose the condition of the hearer and then produce a message for the situation. On other occasions, a pastor may read through the weekly news and craft his sermons in response to what he finds. Is the world becoming too feministic? Then this kind of pastor decides to do a ten-week series on male and female roles within marriage. Is consumerism becoming more rampant each year? Then this kind of pastor decides to pre-empt the Christmas shopping season with a month-long series on covetousness.

Even with good intentions and genuinely biblical topics, such an approach uses the Bible like a drug prescription rather than a fitness plan. The result is a pulpit ministry that is endlessly chasing issues in the church, rather than proactively equipping the church. Yes, the Bible can and should be used to treat our spiritual ailments, but first and foremost it ought to lead us into righteous living as we follow the Savior. Yet, without a pastor building up a local church in sound doctrine and the full counsel of God, parents end up raising their children the same way they see it modeled—using the Bible reactively.

Think about it: as a parent you could spend a lifetime attempting to anticipate all the different aspects of the Christian life that you need to teach your child. And believe it or not, many popular parenting techniques do just that. It is common to hear so-called experts identify the various things that they perceive to be necessary to teach children from the Bible (which, of course, means that they believe there are things in the Bible that are unnecessary to teach). Beyond that, reactive parenting quickly becomes nothing more than a response to each and every one of your child's failures. Many parents are content to take their Bibles off the shelf only when there is a major problem or a "big sin" in their child's life that needs to be addressed. On other occasions, parents try to pre-empt the negative influence of society on their child by overdoing it with biblical instruction on a given topic (just as with many topical sermons in church). But if your parenting strategy is to bounce from topic to topic, trying to build a makeshift theological wall for your child, you can rest assured that temptation and doubt will find their way through the cracks. Instead, a complete and impenetrable wall needs to be erected—a wall made of verse-by-verse expository preaching.

With that said, many parents have the best of intentions to lead their families, yet fail to realize just how negatively impacted they have been by the kind of preaching they hear at church. In fact, many people do not understand the magnificence of God's Word for the simple reason that it has been so extensively misrepresented to them over the course of their lives. Aside from the run-of-the-mill topical sermons that plague many churches, there are all kinds of unhealthy preaching practices that pastors implement that cripple their congregation's understanding of Scripture. And many times it's difficult for well-meaning moms and dads to recognize that they are being misled. After all, if a pastor stands in the pulpit with an open Bible, it's assumed that he is being faithful to the text. Yet, much of modern-day preaching falls woefully short of what could be considered legitimate expository preaching.

As a discerning parent trying to evaluate a pastor's faithfulness to the Bible, it's helpful to make a contrast between quality preaching and foreign substitutes. Pastor Emilio Ramos likewise says,

> Some of the best ways to know whether or not what you are hearing Sunday after Sunday is true preaching is to know what preaching is not. Preaching is not theoretical musings, private speculations made public, talking, personal testimonies, lecturing, or even merely teaching by imparting biblical data. [131]

Obviously, if a pastor rarely refers to the Bible during his message then you know that something is amiss. Yet, just because a pastor has an open Bible and quotes it during his message doesn't mean he is actually performing true expository preaching. The following are common practices that often pass as biblical preaching. Perhaps you recognize some of these, but if not, that's even more reason why you ought to be aware of them:

> *Proof-texting.* If ever there were a "favorite" method of mishandling the Bible, one that works well with any given topical sermon, proof-texting would be it. With this practice, a pastor first decides what principle he wants to teach his congregation and then he searches the Bible for texts that offer "proof" for the principle that he has selected (completely ignoring the original context and purpose of the passage).
>
> During his message, the preacher will then either casually cite the chapter and verse number of the passage, or quickly recite the passage itself, all the while assuming that his hearers are unaware of the passage's original context. In some cases, a pastor may

---

[131] Emilio Ramos, "What Is Preaching and Why Should You Care?," *Heritage Grace Blog*, accessed March 3, 2017, http://heritagegrace.com/heritage-grace-blog/what-is-preaching-and-why-should-you-care.

simply tell a funny personal anecdote and then attach a verse to the end of it to give it a moralistic or "Christianized" slant.

The appeal of this technique is that the pastor can come up with his own personal platitude and then give the impression that the Bible substantiates it by citing verses to go along with it. Thus, he uses the Bible's inherent authority in order to justify his own ideas, even though his selected passages are unrelated and misapplied.

A true expositor will cite contextually-related verses during his sermon in order to explain the book of the Bible he is teaching through, whereas the proof-texting pastor cites contextually-unrelated verses in order to sanction his own message.

Clipboarding.[132] Just as a digital clipboard is used for copying and pasting text on a computer, this practice occurs when a preacher plucks verses from various passages in the Bible and joins them together to form a new sequence. The difference between this practice and proof-texting is that with a proof-text there is no interpretation offered—the verse is simply cited in passing without any connection to anything else (solely for the purpose of justifying the pastor's own point). But with this practice, the individual verses are metaphorically "copy and pasted" together, and then interpreted according to this new sequence, as if it actually represents the original author's stream of thought.

A pastor will quote a verse from one part of the Bible, explain it, and then quote from a completely unrelated passage in the Bible, explain it, and so on, treating this group of verses as if they

---

[132] Frank Viola and George Barna, *Pagan Christianity? Exploring the Roots of Our Church Practices* (Carol Stream, IL: Barna, 2008), 232-233.

are one continuous thought found in Scripture. When a pastor implements this practice, it is never as blatantly obvious as if someone were to physically cut and paste parts of the Bible together. Rather, it happens when a pastor jumps back and forth in and out of various biblical passages. The net effect is an acontextual string of passages that have totally abandoned the original meaning. Often times, this technique is used to avoid saying what the verses actually say, while still giving the appearance of having worked through a large portion of Scripture.

The true expositor is a servant to the Word of God, whereas this practice demonstrates that a pastor is using the Word of God to serve himself.

Luckydipping.[133] Believe it or not, some ministers pride themselves in the fact that they don't prepare to preach a particular passage of Scripture, but instead stand before the congregation and "dip" their finger into their Bibles to a random ("lucky") passage from which to preach. They often claim that it is a more spiritual practice because the Holy Spirit will "lead" them to the right passage each Sunday morning.

In reality, this is little more than treating the Bible like a Magic 8 Ball—but sadly, a Magic 8 Ball is likely more balanced in its results! After all, flopping open the Bible is unlikely to lead a preacher to Genesis 1:1 or Revelation 22:21, let alone the full counsel of God over the course of time. And yet, there are even entire denominations committed to this practice![134] It is true that the effectiveness of a pastor's preaching is entirely dependent on

[133] R.C .Sproul, *Knowing Scripture* (Downers Grove, IL: InterVarsity, 2009), 70-71.
[134] "Who We Are: Church Worship," *Apostolic Christian Church of America,* accessed March 3, 2017, http://www.apostolicchristian.org/page.cfm?p=557.

the Holy Spirit, but that in no way excuses intentional preparation beforehand. On the contrary, the effectiveness of a pastor's preparation is *also* dependent on the Holy Spirit.

A true expositor will show himself approved by being devoted to intentional study and the systematic teaching of the Scriptures. Luckydipping is not a practice that teaches disciples to obey all that Christ commanded, but instead teaches disciples to mishandle and misuse all that Christ commanded.

Cherry-picking.[135] The practice of cherry-picking has really only been made possible because of the overwhelming number of English translations on the market. With this technique, a pastor first chooses certain key words and phrases that he wants to use for his given theme or topic. But because a single translation may not contain those same catchwords, he selects individual verses from a variety of translations in order to craft his message.

Perhaps one verse in his message may come from a word-for-word translation. Another verse in his message may be cited from a thought-for-thought translation. And finally, some verses may be quoted from a paraphrase in order to round out his outline. Throughout the sermon he might use various words and phrases from an assortment of translations in order to make sure that his theme word or phrase is always present.

Rather than telling the congregation what God has said, this practice is a clear sign that a preacher is using the Bible to say what he wants to say. He first determines his own words and then finds the translation that gives him what he wants. And make no

---

[135] David Lang and Michael Lawson, *Macs in the Ministry* (Nashville, TN: Thomas Nelson, 2010), 119.

mistake about it—some high-profile pastors are more than happy to confess this practice, claiming that it's a necessary technique in order to fully explain what the Greek text originally said.[136] It's true that no English translation is perfect, but that is all the more reason not to compound the error by jumping around to additional English translations.

Perhaps the solution to the dilemma is overlooked because of how obvious it is: a true expositor will explain any given English translation by examining the passage in its original language, rather than obscuring it with a handful of cherry-picked English translations.

Leapfrogging.[137] As a pastor leads his congregation through the Bible, he will inevitably come across a passage from time to time that is not as easy to teach as others. What is the tempting course of action at that point? Skip it. With the practice of leapfrogging, a preacher teaches through a biblical passage, skips over a verse or set of verses (either by not reading it, or by reading it but not explaining it), and then continues on his way in the passage.

Perhaps the verses in question are difficult to interpret (like the symbolism in the prophet Daniel's vision), uncomfortable to explain (like the intimate content of the Song of Solomon), contrary to his own denomination's theology (like the doctrine of God's sovereignty over salvation), potentially offensive to the hearer (like Christ's radical demands for discipleship), or perceived to be boring in nature (like a genealogy, census, or benediction). Whatever the case may be, this type of preacher

---

[136] Rick Warren, *The Purpose Driven Life* (Grand Rapids, MI: Zondervan, 2002), 345-346.
[137] Don Wilton, *See You at the Finish Line* (Nashville, TN: Nelson, 2006), 92.

decides that this portion of the Bible is unworthy of his proclamation and unnecessary for his hearers.

In one example, a story is told of a pastor who began teaching verse by verse through the book of Romans from the first chapter all the way through the seventh chapter, but then skipped to the twelfth chapter in order to avoid doctrines such as election and predestination that are plainly set forth in chapters eight through eleven![138]

Of course, this practice functionally denies the Bible's own claim that all Scripture is profitable and necessary for equipping believers (cf. 2 Tim. 3:16-17). After all, to skip over a God-breathed passage is to say that God wasted His breath. But by definition, consecutive exposition means that no verse is passed over. The true expositor recognizes that if the Holy Spirit wrote it, he needs to preach it.

The fact that these examples sound more like carnival games than preaching practices ought to be a dead giveaway that they have no legitimate place in the pulpit. In all honesty, it's sad that these kinds of tactics even exist because each of them is symptomatic of a serious defect in a pastor's perspective of God's Word. It is disappointing, to say the least, that preachers would expend so much energy and go to such great lengths to *avoid* simply preaching the Word. Bear in mind, this is not to say that every pastor who exhibits some or all of these characteristics has a particularly nefarious reason for non-expositional preaching. Something as mundane as laziness could be the culprit. But

---

[138] Voddie Baucham, L. Michael Morales, R.C. Sproul, and R.C. Sproul Jr., "Questions and Answers" (presentation, The Autobiography of God: 2011 Fall Conference at Reformation Bible College, Saint Andrew's Chapel, Sanford, FL, October 15, 2011).

the bottom line is that if you have to poke and prod your pastor to get him to teach the Bible, that is good enough evidence that his driving passion is something *other* than teaching the Bible. And that's a problem.

Besides the Bible's clear requirement for expository preaching, on a very practical level you can be sure that these approaches will inevitably have a detrimental effect on your own Christian walk. Not sure about that? Look at the list again and you'll notice something: *each of these errors is also commonly practiced by the average layman during his own personal Bible study.* Plucking verses out of context, piecing together unrelated passages to form a self-styled theology, opening the Bible to random passages for daily devotions, finding a translation that better fits one's preconceived ideas, and skipping the "hard stuff" are all commonplace practices in the homes of many. And if we're being honest, these approaches to the Bible didn't come naturally; they were learned. After all, when it comes to virtually *any other book*, we intuitively know that it ought to be read from start to finish and interpreted so as to determine the author's intent.

In the end, nothing parallels sitting under the ministry of an expositor and seeing and hearing him handle the Word Sunday after Sunday. As one author put it, "If you're at a healthy church, you should expect expository preaching every week. It's good and right to have high expectations of the preaching in your church. But you need to be ready to hear it; don't forget there are two sides to that equation. There's expository preaching and then there's expository listening."[139] Thus, learning about expository preaching is important, and reading about great expositors of the past is helpful, but hearing expository preaching within the context of your local church is *critical*. Are you a

---

[139] Dan Dumas, *A Guide to Expository Ministry* (Louisville, KY: SBTS, 2012), 65.

member of a healthy church?

Finding a Faithful Church

Unfortunately, finding a church that practices genuine expository preaching is easier said than done. As Pastor Steve Lawson says,

> Tragically, exposition is being replaced with entertainment, doctrine with drama, theology with theatrics, and preaching with performances. What is so desperately needed today is for pastors to return to their highest calling—the divine summons to "preach the word" (2 Tim. 4:1-2).[140]

In the first century, Timothy was tempted to abandon the Word because of the threat of persecution, but today we see pastors abandon the Word for the appeal of innovation. Of course, many would object to this characterization, claiming that such an assessment of modern preaching is unfair, unkind, and unjustified. Ask the average churchman about preaching methodology and he would undoubtedly say that there's nothing wrong with the average topical sermon series and other forms of non-expositional preaching. But rather than justifying the practice, what this actually does is demonstrate just how widespread the error is. In other words, it does not refute the argument, it *proves* it! The utter absence of expository preaching in our modern day has left the average person with the inability to diagnose the problem with topical preaching. Little do they realize that a lack of expository preaching is ultimately to their own detriment. Far too many people have sat under the soul-starving sedative of topical preaching rather than the soul-stirring stimulant of expository

---

[140] Steve Lawson, "Preach the Word," *Tabletalk Magazine*, Ligonier Ministries, January 1, 2010.

preaching. One scholar laments the crisis of sub-biblical preaching as follows:

> Part of me wishes to avoid proving the sordid truth: that preaching today is ordinarily poor. But I have come to recognize that many, many individuals today have never been under a steady diet of competent preaching. As a consequence, they are satisfied with what they hear because they have nothing better with which to compare it. Therefore, for many individuals, the kettle in which they live has always been at the boiling point, and they've simply adjusted to it. As starving children in Manila sift through the landfill for food, Christians in many churches today have never experienced genuinely soul-nourishing preaching, and so they just pick away at what is available to them, trying to find a morsel of spiritual sustenance or helpful counsel here or there.[141]

With that said, if you are in a church where the Word is being taught verse by verse, praise God! A church that is providing expository preaching will have a pronounced effect on your ministry in the home by partnering with you to deliver the full counsel of God to your children. If your goal is for your kids to learn the entire Bible before they leave your home, you can determine which books of the Bible you need to teach them based on which books they've already learned (or will learn) at church.

On the other hand, if you look back through the past several months of Sunday morning sermons at your church and you see cliché message series titles such as "How to Reignite Your Marriage" or "Five Ways to Overcome Stress," rather than series titles such as "Galatians" or "Hebrews," that ought to be a cause for concern. Pastor Mike

---

[141] T. David Gordon, *Why Johnny Can't Preach: The Media Have Shaped the Messengers* (Phillipsburg, NJ: P & R Pub., 2009), 17.

Abendroth provides advice that makes assessing a church simple:

> When you look for a new church (or when you go on vacation), call the church and ask them this question: "What book of the Bible is your pastor preaching through right now?" Their answer will tell you the church's view of the Scripture, expository preaching, and much more. It is rare indeed to find a "seeker-sensitive" church preaching through books sequentially.[142]

Likewise, if your pastor engages in the aforementioned non-expository preaching tactics, you need to determine how long you can justifiably remain at that church. Certainly there are many reasons that people give for leaving a church, and far too often they are trivial—the color of the carpet, the seating in the sanctuary, or the size of the youth group. But preaching the Word is not one of them. As the leader of his family, one of the most important things a man can do is get his wife and children to a biblical church where the pastor will not only feed him on a Sunday morning, but will model it in such a way that he can continue feeding his family throughout the week.

Of course, before leaving a church your first order of business would be to speak with your elders and explain the non-negotiable nature of expository preaching. This is the kind of faithful accountability that is required of any congregant. Legitimate care and concern for your church demands that you respectfully and graciously, yet unwaveringly, speak with your elders and urge them to conform their preaching ministry to what God requires. Perhaps your efforts would be the God-ordained catalyst for correction. Perhaps your elders would repent of their neglect and begin transitioning to the

---

[142] Mike Abendroth, *Jesus Christ: The Prince of Preachers: Learning from the Teaching Ministry of Jesus* (Leominster, England: Day One Pub., 2008), 159.

expository ministry required of them. But, if the end result is anything other than a corrected, expositional preaching ministry, then you need to look for a new church—one that honors God and His Word. Consider the comments of Pastor John MacArthur:

> One of the sad things when you think about our nation today and where Protestant religion has gone is the demise of really faithful, consistent, uncompromising, biblical preaching. And you can lay the blame at the preacher's feet, if you want. It certainly belongs there. But I'm convinced that it belongs not only at the feet of the preacher but at the feet of the people who fail to hold the preacher accountable for what God said he was to be. It's a dual responsibility.[143]

In fact, this kind of accountability is embedded right in Paul's letter to Timothy. Although we may at first assume that the letter of 2 Timothy was a private one, simply from one man to another, the reality is that it (like many others) was actually intended to be read aloud in a group setting. In this case, the setting was the church at Ephesus in which Timothy ministered.

Evidence of this comes from the fact that Paul ended his letter with the plural form of the word "you," when he wrote, "Grace be with you" (cf. 2 Tim. 4:22). Because the English language lacks a plural form for the word "you" (aside from the informal word "y'all"), it's easy to read this concluding remark and miss its significance. But the implication of this grammatical detail is profound: the presence of a plural pronoun indicates that although the letter was directed towards Timothy, it was intended for all to hear—hence the reason Paul

---

[143] John MacArthur, "The Priorities of a Faithful Teacher," *GTY Resources: Study Guides*, Grace to You, accessed September 27, 2016, https://www.gty.org/library/sermons-library/55-20/marks-of-the-faithful-preacher-part-1.

finished by addressing the entire church body.

This means that when Paul told Timothy to join him in suffering for the Gospel (cf. 2 Tim. 2:3), the whole congregation also counted the cost of Christianity. When Paul told Timothy to flee youthful lusts (cf. 2 Tim. 2:22), every churchman's conscience was pricked. And when Paul issued the solemn charge for Timothy to "preach the Word" (cf. 2 Tim. 4:2), it was a public command heard by all so that accountability would be provided by all.

On a practical level, you ought to ask yourself this: how is it that so many churches are quick to distribute Bibles but slow to perform expository preaching? Is it really acceptable for a pastor to hand out a book that he is unwilling to teach? Furthermore, if you can't learn the Bible at your local church *where can you learn it?* Listen to a sermon on a CD? Find one on the internet? All that indicates is that there are faithful men of God in *other* local churches who *are* faithfully teaching their congregations the Bible like God requires. Sadly, there are indeed those who use the faithfulness of other shepherds as an excuse to neglect their own responsibility.[144]

Of course, that is really no excuse at all. Any pastor who does not teach the Bible verse by verse forfeits the right to lament biblical illiteracy among his people. Simply put, the pew will never rise any higher than the pulpit. You as a parent ought to be able to look at your son or daughter and say, "The man in the pulpit who preaches to us is who we need to emulate. Consider the way he handles the Bible and let's follow his lead." Ultimately, if you're forced to *listen* elsewhere in order to hear expository preaching, you need to *attend* elsewhere in

---

[144] Aaron Loy, "5 Really Bad Reasons to Leave Your Church," *God/Church* (blog), Relevant Magazine, January 27, 2014, http://archives.relevantmagazine.com/god/church/5-really-bad-reasons-leave-your-church.

order to hear expository preaching.

Like other elements such as a plurality of qualified elders, proper administration of the ordinances, and church discipline, this is not a minor issue. Expository preaching is foundational, not fringe. The church you attend will be a major influence in the lives of your children, and to that end, you must find a church where your children's hearts will be shepherded accordingly. Don't neglect the souls of your family members for the sake of convenience. Dr. R.C. Sproul elaborates on this point, saying,

> The spiritual nurture of your soul and of your children's souls is so important that if you have to drive two hours for worship and for instruction in the apostolic truth, then that's an obvious decision—you drive two hours. Or move. But it has to be a priority in every Christian family to be somewhere where there is true worship, true Gospel, true doctrine, for the sake of eternity.

In reality, a church with sub-biblical preaching is *not* going to improve. It can't. A church that is not preaching verse by verse has severed itself from the very God-ordained means of correcting its own errors. And beyond taking a laid-back "wait-and-see" approach to determine if change may happen, it would also be inappropriate to stay at an unbiblical church with the intent to become a spiritual insurrectionist, trying to overturn the leadership and "force" them to practice expository preaching. After all, would you really want to be at a church where you've convinced the elders to exposit the Bible *begrudgingly*?

Finally, the Bible nowhere portrays a Christian's calling as that of a "church-missionary," one who stays in an unbiblical church for the purpose of reaching other members with the truth that they need to hear from the pulpit but never will. Not only is that a spiritually dysfunctional situation, it is a spiritually dangerous situation—both for you and your family, all of whom need to be a part of a church where your souls are nourished with biblical instruction (cf. 1 Tim. 4:6). After all, if care for orphans is to be one of the highest priorities of the church (cf. Jas. 1:27), one of the best ways to evaluate a local church is to determine how well it would provide spiritual care to your children in your absence. How does your current church measure up?

Faithfulness Then and Now

Hundreds of years ago, the Protestant Reformers grappled with these same issues, recognizing the need for true preaching in true churches. In fact, the Reformers' commitment was so great that they actually *defined* a biblical church based on whether or not the Word was taught properly. Certainly, a biblical church is defined by more than expository preaching—but not less. Men of the past understood that the way the Bible is handled in the pulpit is a key component for evaluating a church's fidelity to Christ.

For example, the 1560 Scottish Confession of Faith lists "the true preaching of the Word of God" as the *first* characteristic by which the true church is distinguished from the false church.[145] And what exactly constituted the "true preaching" of God's Word in their minds? As the primary author of the confession, Scottish pastor John Knox described it as none other than sequential exposition:

> We think it most expedient that the Scriptures be read in order, that is, that some one book of the Old and the New Testament be begun and orderly read to the end. And the same we judge of preaching, where the minister for the most part remaineth in one place; for this skipping and

---

[145] Douglas Bond, *The Mighty Weakness of John Knox* (Orlando, FL: Reformation Trust Pub., 2011), 126.

divagation from place to place, be it in reading, be it in preaching, we judge not so profitable to edify the Church, as the continual following of one text.[146]

Men of today have carried on a similar perspective as well. The organization *9Marks*, led by Pastor Mark Dever of Capitol Hill Baptist Church, exists to categorize the necessary elements of church life according to Scripture, and to equip local churches to be conformed to these elements. At the top of this organization's list of characteristics is the work of expository preaching. *9Marks* defines it as follows:

A sermon is expositional if its content and intent are *controlled* by the content and intent of a particular passage of Scripture. The preacher says what the passage says, and he intends for his sermon to accomplish in his listeners exactly what God is seeking to accomplish through the chosen passage of his Word.[147]

Both Dever and Knox correctly identify the preaching of the Word as the most important characteristic in distinguishing a biblical church from an unbiblical one. The false church stands over the Word of God, using the Bible for its own purposes; the true church humbly submits to the Word of God, and by extension, to Christ Himself.

Sadly, many churches have ignored the counsel of godly men from the past and present. By and large, the modern church has traded the birthright of expository preaching for a bowl of topical stew. As if the widespread departure weren't bad enough, some church leaders are so out of step with biblical preaching that they have declared

---

[146] William M. Taylor, *John Knox* (New York: A.C. Armstrong & Son, 1885), 151.
[147] Mike Bullmore, "A Biblical Case for Expositional Preaching," *Preaching & Theology* (blog), 9Marks, February 2, 2010, https://9marks.org/article/biblical-case-expositional-preaching.

sequential exposition to be "cheating," simply because of the fact that each week's sermon is a continuation from the previous week's passage![148] By the world's standards, treating every verse with reverence is cheating, but by God's standards it is faithfulness. This faithfulness must characterize the place you call your church home.

Accept No Substitutes

One of the essential traits of any quality church is that its congregation is in the process of learning the entire Bible. That this even needs to be said, or could possibly be disputed, is really just a testament to how dire our situation is. Sure, there are many Sunday-morning CEOs, many vision-casting leaders, and many Christian life-coaches, but where are the pastors who are preaching the Word? Why are we starved for expository preaching? Dr. Al Mohler expresses similar concerns:

> One of the hallmarks of our time is that we face a crisis of preaching. Indeed it would be an exercise in self-delusion if we tried to pretend that nothing is wrong with the preaching that happens in most evangelical churches. Let me ask some honest and difficult questions: If you picked an evangelical church at random and attended a Sunday morning service there, how likely is it that you would hear a faithful expository sermon, one that takes its message and its structure from the biblical text? If you answer that question honestly, you'll admit that your expectation would not be very high. Further, do you believe that as time passes it is becoming more likely or less likely that you would hear an expository

---

[148] Ed Stetzer, "Andy Stanley on Communication (Part 2)," *Interviews: Leadership* (blog), Christianity Today, March 5, 2009, http://www.christianitytoday.com/edstetzer/2009/march/andy-stanley-on-communication-part-2.html.

message in that random church?[149]

Of course, no church is perfect. And no pastor is perfect. But it must be said that the issue of expository preaching is not a matter of perfection versus imperfection; it is a matter of obedience versus disobedience. Any given preacher is unlikely to interpret every verse flawlessly. He may get tripped up in certain passages. He may never be a world-class, internationally-recognized expositor. But the evidence of his faithfulness is that he stands in the pulpit, opens the Bible, and begins reading it, explaining it, and exhorting his people to submit to it—verse by verse, Sunday by Sunday, year by year. That is the kind of ministry that God commends.

So where does this leave you and I? First, if you feel inadequate for the work of teaching your children the Bible, welcome to the club! The task of sequential exposition is an undertaking with eternal ramifications, so it naturally stands as a monumental task. If legitimate discipleship were easy, more parents would probably be doing it!

Second, the good news is that for those parents who truly want help learning and teaching the Bible, God has provided for His people, as He always does. There are pastors who demonstrate expository preaching and equip others to follow suit. These men take seriously their role in 1 Peter 5:3, in which God charges them to "be examples to the flock." When you find yourself in need of encouragement, counsel, and guidance, your local pastor is the God-given resource. Learn from him. Follow him. Latch on to him and don't let go.

Finally, although there is a famine in the land for the hearing of the Word of God, there are still faithful churches out there. Every

---

[149] R. Albert Mohler, *He Is Not Silent: Preaching in a Postmodern World* (Chicago: Moody, 2008), 50.

Sunday you have the incredible opportunity to see biblical exposition in action, and the effect of such a ministry on your family's spiritual well-being simply cannot be overstated. Find a church that exposits the Word sequentially; accept no substitutes. Provided you've been teaching your children the Scriptures at home, they will be all the more understanding if it becomes necessary to exchange the familiarity of an unbiblical church for the faithfulness of a biblical one. Once your family is participating in a local assembly in which the leaders are dogmatically committed to expository preaching, first tell God how thankful you are for them, and then tell them what you told God.

9

MOTIVATION FOR MINISTRY

"Through our life, through our obedience, we are called to solemnly testify of the Gospel of the grace of God in our life to all those that the Lord Jesus Christ gives us the opportunity of speaking. And when you have that as your goal, it will help you to prioritize things."[150]

–James White

Focus Text: *Paul, an apostle of Christ Jesus by the will of God, according to the promise of life in Christ Jesus, to Timothy, my beloved son: Grace, mercy and peace from God the Father and Christ Jesus our Lord. I thank God, whom I serve with a clear conscience the way my forefathers did, as I constantly remember you in my prayers night and day, longing to see you, even as I recall your tears, so that I may be filled with joy. For I am mindful of the sincere faith within you, which first dwelt in your grandmother Lois and your mother Eunice, and I am sure that it is in you as well. For this reason I remind you to kindle afresh the gift of God which is in you through the laying on of my hands. For God has not given us a spirit of timidity, but of power and love and discipline. (2 Timothy 1:1-7)*

Here you are. You recognize the necessity of sequential exposition. You understand the purpose of biblical hermeneutics. You appreciate the importance of systematic

---

[150] James White, "Session 6" (presentation, The Supremacy of Scripture: Yesterday, Today, Forever Conference, Goodwood Baptist Church, Cape Town, South Africa, May 8, 2016).

theology. You affirm the urgency of evangelism. You realize the need for full-time discipleship. You intend to fellowship in a biblical local church. And now you're just overwhelmed.

At this point, perhaps you're thinking, *"There's no way I can accomplish all of this!"* Such a thought is really not out of the ordinary — after all, we are talking about setting out on a course of spiritual development that will impact the rest of your child's life. And although adulthood certainly lends itself to further discipleship, the bulk of your son or daughter's training has to occur within a roughly eighteen-year period. The clock is already ticking and perhaps you have never even studied through the entire Bible yourself, let alone considered teaching through it. The thought of expository parenting seems like nothing more than a pipe dream.

It's obvious that a feeling of defeat right at the outset of a task is often times enough to prevent us from ever beginning in the first place. This happens all the time when it comes to things like exercise routines or financial planning. After all, consider how many people purchase a gym membership, only to put off their first workout session until "next Monday." Or sit down to figure out a budget, but decide that adjusting the finances will have to wait until "next month's paycheck." We often think procrastinating will give us more time to prepare, not realizing that it's just the opposite: procrastination simply gives us more time to solidify the bad habits we already have. In the end, this makes it harder, not easier, to begin.

In light of that temptation, the Bible teaches us that once our conscience is convicted, our obedience must be immediate. Consider the words of James, the brother of Jesus: "Come now, you who say, 'Today or tomorrow we will go to such and such a city, and spend a year there and engage in business and make a profit.' Yet you do not know what your life will be like tomorrow. You are just a vapor that appears for a little while and then vanishes away. Instead, you ought to say, 'If the Lord wills, we will live and also do this or that.' But as it is, you boast in your arrogance; all such boasting is evil. Therefore, to one who knows the right thing to do and does not do it, to him it is sin" (James 4:13-17). Of course there is much that could be said about the passage, but there are two things to contemplate with regards to our obedience.

The first principle is found in James 4:14, in which James reminds us that our lives are but a vapor. We have no idea what tomorrow will bring, or whether there will even be a tomorrow for us here on earth. The very concept of "tomorrow" is a matter that is entirely subject to God's grace. Thus, to intentionally put off until tomorrow what should begin today is actually to presume upon the grace of God. It is, in effect, saying, "God, I assume that you are going to give me another day of life, so I will get around to obeying then."

The truth is that Satan has no problem with such a perspective. Christian obedience is no threat, so long as it doesn't begin until tomorrow. Why? Because tomorrow is always the day that is yet to come. As one theologian said, "Tomorrow is the devil's day, but today is God's. Satan does not care how spiritual your intentions are, or how holy your resolutions, if only they are determined to be done tomorrow."[151] In effect, if your obedience is delayed until another day, your obedience will always be delayed. Instead, we must conform our perspective to that of the Psalmist's: "I hastened and did not delay to keep Your commandments" (Psalm 119:60).

A second application from James that we ought to consider is the final phrase of the passage, which states, "To one who knows the right thing to do and does not do it, to him it is sin." Often in the Christian

---

[151] J.C. Ryle, *Thoughts for Young Men* (Edinburgh, UK: Banner of Truth, 2015), 7.

life we think of sins in terms of the ungodly deeds a person commits—immorality, theft, blasphemy, and others. While it is certainly true that those are wicked deeds, easily identified as such, they only represent sins of *commission*—that is to say, sinning by doing what God forbids.

However, there is a second category of sins, and these are the sins of which James speaks. The second category would be sins of *omission*—that is to say, sinning by neglecting to be or do what God requires. Often, these sins are harder to recognize because by definition, they are not present; evil things done are easier to identify than righteous things left undone. But this particular truth from James adds immense weight to all the rest of Scripture because it reveals to us that what we find required of us in the Bible is not optional, nor suggested, nor offered simply as an opinion to be debated. Instead, we will be held accountable for all of the things that are required of us by Scripture. To willfully neglect the requirements placed upon us by God's Word puts us in a position of sinfulness.

Therefore, believe it or not, James has much to say to us in the way of biblical parenting. As parents, we cannot afford to put off until tomorrow that which must begin today. Your child will transition from diapers to diplomas in the blink of an eye, so don't wait for that perfect opportunity when all the stars align to begin the task of expository parenting. We live in a fallen world and that opportunity will never come. But what if you feel like you've already wasted a number of years? Give thanks to God for the forgiveness found in Jesus Christ and then simply begin today.

With that said, how do we get motivated for this? The world would offer psychological advice such as "practicing positive self-talk" or "deconstructing your fears" in order to become inspired. But expository parenting is a lofty spiritual endeavor, not a shallow life dream or personal goal. A spiritual task like expository parenting needs spiritual motivation for those who are spiritually-minded, and the Bible provides it.

Undoubtedly, the book of 2 Timothy contains a heap of commands that would bury even the ablest saint. But before he issued instructions, Paul actually began his letter with the motivating words needed to encourage Timothy. By extension, these words encourage all believers, and such gracious words could not be more fitting for those entering into the work of expository parenting. Pastor John MacArthur affirms that this letter truly is intended for all of us when he says,

> These very personal comments reflect principles pertinent not only to Paul's discipling of Timothy but also to Christian parents, Sunday school teachers, youth leaders, pastors, counselors, neighbors, and friends—to any believer who is helping another grow toward maturity in Jesus Christ and effectiveness in ministry.[152]

Although Timothy's fears were likely different than you and I face, the five major aspects of Paul's encouragement still serve to motivate us just the same. These aspects are: *the mandate by God, the mercy of God, the memory of godly service, the model of godliness,* and *the mission from God.* They were intended to strengthen Timothy's resolve for the work of shepherding his church, and they also contain tremendous power to ready us for the work of shepherding our families.

The Mandate by God

> *Paul, an apostle of Christ Jesus by the will of God, according to the promise of life in Christ Jesus... (2 Timothy 1:1)*

---

[152] John MacArthur, *The MacArthur New Testament Commentary: 2 Timothy* (Chicago: Moody, 1995), 1.

In this first verse, Paul began with the common introduction by referring to his apostleship from Christ Himself. Like the other apostles, Paul was commissioned directly by the Lord. Although the twelve disciples were commissioned while Christ was still on the earth after His resurrection (cf. Matt. 28:16-20), Paul also encountered Christ directly while on the road to Damascus (cf. Acts 9:1-6). Thus, he possessed the same apostolic credentials as the others. He saw the risen Christ (cf. 1 Cor. 15:3-9), had been commissioned for the role by Christ (cf. Mark 3:14), was able to perform miracles to verify his God-given authority (cf. Heb. 2:3-4), and served as the spiritual foundation of the church (cf. Eph. 2:20-21). Thus, he was not a "second-tier" apostle, nor of any lesser status than the others. Rather, he was fully qualified to issue authoritative and binding commands to believers on behalf of God.

Why was this important to reiterate in a letter to Timothy? After all, Timothy had served alongside Paul for a number of years and was well aware of Paul's credentials. Surely he didn't need to be taught this, right? It was simply because he wanted to make it clear that his letter to Timothy was not on the basis of personal opinion or helpful suggestion, but rather came by way of divine command. It was the equivalent of grabbing Timothy by the shoulders and staring him in the face with divinely-empowered sobriety. Paul had not authored this letter as helpful "hints" for Christian living, but as binding instructions that demanded Timothy's prompt response. Thus, to begin motivating his disciple, Paul deferred to his God-given apostleship right from the start. That, of course, would undoubtedly prove to be a highly-motivating reminder to Timothy—to neglect Paul's commands would be to neglect God's commands.

Likewise, pastors of today have this same mandate. The apostolic authority in this letter, like others in the New Testament, ought to serve as a splash of cold water in the face of those who intend to minister God's Word—it is to be done God's way, without exception. Such a reminder ought to be sufficient on its own to conform every pastor's preaching ministry to the expository standard that God requires. As apologist Dr. James White says,

> God has chosen to use the foolishness of preaching as His means of saving His people. So, preach the word. Do not try to replace the what of preaching. There is only one word, only one message. God is glorified when His word is preached. He is not glorified when someone else's word is preached. The good servant will preach the word out of obedience even when his eyes see nothing but resistance to that message and when it costs him dearly. That is his task, that is his joy, and that is his fulfillment.[153]

Similarly, consider Paul's apostolic authority as you shepherd your family. Let it serve as the first motivating factor for you as it did for Timothy. We often think that when we stand before God we will be accountable only for our own lives. Yet, just as a pastor will give an account to God for his flock (cf. Heb. 13:17), the reality is that while our children are in our home, we are also accountable for that time with them.

Without recognizing this kind of accountability, it's easy to understand why so many parents are passive when it comes to the discipleship of their children. They have forgotten that the birth of their child has also brought about the requirement for discipleship. It may shock our modern sensibilities, but godly elders in the past would have considered implementing church discipline for any father who

---

[153] James R. White, *Pulpit Crimes: The Criminal Mishandling of God's Word* (Birmingham, AL.: Solid Ground Christian, 2006), 35.

neglected to instruct his children in the Word![154] Teaching our children the Bible is not merely one "method" among alternatives; it is the necessary foundation for all biblical parenting.

Thus, if for no other reason, you must engage in the intentional discipling of your children out of sheer obedience. You do not want to stand before God having spiritually starved one of His creatures for close to two decades. Timothy was under divine orders to lead his flock, and so is every parent. Recognize that when the Bible says, "Fathers, do not provoke your children to anger, but bring them up in the discipline and instruction of the Lord" (Eph. 6:4), this also comes to you by way of a mandate from God.

The Mercy of God

To Timothy, my beloved son: Grace, mercy and peace from God the Father and Christ Jesus our Lord. (2 Timothy 1:2)

Referring to Timothy as a son, the Apostle Paul continued his introduction by expressing a genuine desire for Timothy's goodwill. While this was a formal greeting routinely given by Paul, it was anything but routine formalism. Not only did Paul have a genuine love for those under his care, he made sure to remind them of the even greater love that God has for them.

Like every man, Timothy was born under the wrath of God (cf. Eph. 2:3). Yet, like every believer, Timothy was born again, according to God's great love, into a new life of redemptive peace (cf. Eph. 2:4). It is this work of redemption that Paul referred to when he spoke of

---

[154] Jeff Pollard and Scott T. Brown, *A Theology of the Family* (Wake Forest, NC: National Center for Family-Integrated Churches, 2014), 51.

God's grace, mercy, and peace—not only pointing out God's kindness to Timothy in the past, but also God's continued kindness in the present and never-ending kindness into the future.

So we see that the second motivating factor for Timothy's ministry is the same factor that motivates us in every area of life: the Gospel itself. Paul's wish for Timothy included the three aspects of grace, mercy, and peace. The common distinction between grace and mercy is that grace is God's granting of undeserved blessing whereas mercy is God's withholding of well-earned punishment. The third element, peace, is a product of the first two elements, grace and mercy. Those who have experienced the grace of being declared righteous through faith alone, as well as the mercy of being saved from eternal torment, will consequently experience peace—peace with God (cf. Rom. 5:1), peace with others (cf. Rom. 12:18), and even an inner-tranquility that comes from a clean conscience (cf. Heb. 9:14). Paul reminded Timothy of the goodness of God who had given him so much, a goodness that put him forever in His debt to serve, honor, and glorify Him. Faithful ministry is the only logical response to such kindness.

Have you also been a recipient of this amazing grace? Have you experienced the life-saving, sin-forgiving, heart-changing, debt-paying, relationship-restoring, hope-giving effects of the Gospel? If so, you likely have but one question: "Having been given so much by God, what can I do for Him out of a thankful heart?" Even to ask that question is considerable evidence that you've truly experienced divine mercy. It is a good indication that you are ready and willing to respond with grace-based expository parenting. If God went to such great lengths to reach you, surely you'd go to whatever lengths are necessary to be used by Him in reaching your children. The mercy of God was the second aspect of Paul's motivation for Timothy, and continues as motivation for us today.

The Memory of Godly Service

> *I thank God, whom I serve with a clear conscience the way my forefathers did, as I constantly remember you in my prayers night and day, longing to see you, even as I recall your tears, so that I may be filled with joy. (2 Timothy 1:3-4)*

Like two soldiers who spent grueling hours together in a foxhole, Paul went on to reminisce about the endless time he had spent with Timothy laboring for the Gospel. As was common, Paul expressed his thankfulness not to Timothy directly, but to God for empowering Timothy. This serves as an example of God-centered encouragement that provides real and meaningful support to believers.

For someone who was dying in a Roman prison, Paul demonstrated what can only be considered a supernatural ability to express love towards others—going so far as to say he was constantly thinking not of himself, but of Timothy, night and day in his prayers. Knowing that he had faithfully served the Lord, just like believers who came before him, Paul experienced a clear conscience and was confident that he had truly met the demands of his ministry. But it's obvious, based on the testimony of Scripture, that Timothy played an incredible role in helping Paul fulfill his ministry. Thus, Paul's clear conscience was, in part, on account of the loyal service Timothy provided (cf. Phil. 2:22). And Paul thanked God for supplying such an incredible co-laborer.

In 2 Timothy 2:10-11, Paul stated that Timothy followed right along in persecution, and as we look through the account provided in the book of Acts, we see the kind of sacrificial service that Timothy provided—beginning with Timothy's willingness to be circumcised in order to evangelize the Jews better (cf. Acts 16:3). After that, Timothy was right alongside Paul, accompanying him as he was beaten with rods (cf. Acts 16:22), thrown in jail (cf. Acts 16:23), pursued by mobs (cf. Acts 17:13), and vilified by Jews (cf. Acts 18:12). Timothy had devoted his life to ministering with Paul, which was undoubtedly a memory that Paul looked back on with nothing but appreciation. Thus, Paul reminded Timothy that he was praying for him and remembering their times together.

Apparently, these times not only included those of joy, but those of grief. Paul said that he thought of Timothy *even while recalling his tears*. These "tears" most likely refer to the last time Paul had seen Timothy, since Paul associated the tears with a longing to see him once again. In fact, Paul had a similar experience when he left the Ephesian elders years prior—that too was a time filled with tears and grief (cf. Acts 20:36-38).[155] Surely he missed his young disciple, and wanted to make sure it was known because of the tremendous encouragement it would provide.

This often happens in our own lives as well. When we learn that others are praying for us, it encourages us all the more because we realize the deep impact that the Gospel has had on our personal relationships. Not only that, but as we look back on our lives, we begin to understand when and where God has providentially orchestrated the direction of our lives. Knowing that the course of our life is an answer to the prayers of fellow Christians, we become filled not only with joy, but a greater resolve to serve the Lord.

With that said, know this: if you are considering the work of expository parenting, you have been prayed for—not necessarily by name, but as a co-laborer in the great task of raising children to know

---

[155] John MacArthur, *The MacArthur New Testament Commentary: 2 Timothy* (Chicago: Moody, 1995), 7.

and love the Lord. There are few things in life that parallel the joy of ministering the Word at home—the unity of parents laboring in the Word together, the responsiveness of children in learning the Bible, the peace of mind in parenting with a purpose, and the knowledge that God is working in and through our efforts. Think of those that love you and are praying for your family, and let that serve as motivating encouragement for you to carry out this task.

The Model of Godliness

For I am mindful of the sincere faith within you, which first dwelt in your grandmother Lois and your mother Eunice, and I am sure that it is in you as well. (2 Timothy 1:5)

As previously mentioned, Timothy was already a well-respected Christian by the time Paul met him (cf. Acts 16:2). We know that God sovereignly saved Timothy, granting him a new heart and faith in Jesus Christ. But we also know, as Paul did, that God used the models of godliness found in Timothy's mother and grandmother as the means of bringing Timothy to salvation. Timothy had been taught the Old Testament Scriptures from a young age (cf. 2 Tim. 3:15). Based on this, we recognize that his mother and grandmother were dedicated to the task of raising him according to God's Word, and they served as immeasurably important models of godliness.

Sadly, it would appear that Timothy did not have much of a godly influence from his father, who was a Greek (cf. Acts 16:1). Apparently his mother and grandmother, surrounded by other supporters, took on the task of educating Timothy in the Scriptures. Yet, despite this difficult situation, those godly examples were used to bring Timothy to spiritual maturity, proving just how important such an example is in the life of a young child.

It may well be that you find yourself in a similar situation. Perhaps, for a number of reasons, you have the burden of single-handedly raising your children to know Christ. If so, you ought to draw on this example that Paul cited, resting in the fact that God can and will use your faithfulness to shape the lives of your children, regardless of the other parent's influence (or lack thereof). Does this legitimize absentee fathers or mothers? Of course not. But what it demonstrates is the grace of God powerfully working amidst our fallen situations.

Single or not, as you raise your children in the Scriptures, remember that you are not alone. Not only do you have other parents right alongside you, but perhaps by God's grace you have older generations of Christians within your own family. Even more, you have believers of all ages in your local church body. Let these people encourage you and remind you of the legacy of faith that you are building. Rely on them for encouragement, refer to them for wisdom, and recognize the models of godliness they provide for you and your children. There truly is great joy to be found in knowing that you are serving within a community of believers who are committed to helping you teach the Scriptures at home. A multigenerational group of believers committed to the work of exposition provides an inspiring picture of the Bible's enduring ability to escort us through every stage of life.

Finally, don't forget that you also serve as that model of godliness for your fellow brothers and sisters in Christ. They, too, need just as much encouragement. Be an example of a parent who is so committed to Scripture that others can see you working day in and day out to teach your children the full counsel of God. You can be certain that your zeal for the truth will be contagious.

With that said, maybe you don't find yourself surrounded with as much support as you'd like. The amount of effort required to teach the full counsel of God is not something that everyone will embrace. Maybe you're one of only a few who embarks on the journey of expository parenting. Or perhaps members in your own extended family are antagonistic towards Christianity. Allow that to be all the more motivation you need to begin a pattern of biblical discipleship in your family. The enthusiasm to work through the Bible verse by verse with your children may simply need to begin with you. Find God-given inspiration for expository parenting not only by relying on other models of godliness, but by knowing that in the future you will be serving as that model of godliness for the next generation.

The Mission from God

> *For this reason I remind you to kindle afresh the gift of God which is in you through the laying on of my hands. For God has not given us a spirit of timidity, but of power and love and discipline. (2 Timothy 1:6-7)*

After those introductory remarks in the letter, Paul began to transition into his reason for writing. Timothy had begun to fall prey to the kind of fear of man that so often plagues us as believers. Not only had Emperor Nero's persecution of Christians led to increased hostility, but Timothy was still facing heresy and false teachers within the church. As if hostility from unbelievers wasn't enough, Timothy had to deal with spiritual imposters who were spreading heresy like a disease and upsetting the faith of those in his congregation (cf. 2 Tim. 2:16-18). Like a soldier encircled by the enemy, Timothy had nowhere to go for safety. Ultimately, this was the occasion for writing, yet the presence of these threats did not surprise Paul in the least.

He understood why Timothy had become timid. He understood how the fear of man could cripple a minister of the Gospel. Paul himself faced opposition from those who sought to undermine the Gospel and he rightly predicted that others would face the same opposition (cf. Gal. 1:6-10). It didn't shock Paul that Timothy was fighting insecurity and uncertainty. Thus, to reassure him, Paul pointed Timothy's eyes upward—to the God who had not only ordained him for service, but had granted him the spiritual gifts to succeed.

When Paul wrote to Timothy, he referred to the "gift of God" given through the laying on of hands. Just as all believers receive a spiritual gift upon conversion, so too had Timothy received his spiritual gift. In his case, Timothy was appointed to be a pastor through a prophecy given about him, and commissioned by a group of elders, which included Paul (cf. 1 Tim. 4:14). Based on that, Timothy's gifting for ministry was no small issue. God Himself had granted divine revelation to prophetically appoint Timothy to the role of pastor, and godly men affirmed him for the position. Clearly God intended for Timothy to fulfill this role.

Although Timothy was feeling nervous and timid about the situation he found himself in, Paul referred back to Timothy's ordination as a reminder that Timothy had a mission from God that had to be accomplished. Paul had gritted his teeth, coming to the end of the ministry that God had planned for him, and he expected Timothy to follow suit. In order to be a good servant who was faithful with what he had been given, aborting the mission was simply not an option for Timothy. This was a non-negotiable assignment.

But God's gift to Timothy didn't end there. If God had thrust upon Timothy the task of pastoring a church, battling against false teachers, and enduring persecution from Rome without any additional resources, it would be understandable for Timothy to buckle under the weight. That would be like trying to scuba-dive without an oxygen tank, or ride a bicycle on a flat tire. But God was so much more gracious to him. Yes, Timothy was given the mission to pastor a church. Yes, it was difficult, costly, and frightening at times. But God also equipped him to handle it. He didn't simply bury Timothy under a pile of responsibilities without any means of accomplishing them.

So after reminding Timothy of his ordination, Paul went on to say, in 2 Timothy 1:7, that God had *not* given Timothy a spirit of timidity, but rather of "power, love, and discipline." Timothy obviously would have had the spiritual ability to teach (since that stands as a requirement for all elders), but Paul also reminded him that God had provided three other elements for success.

The first element Paul listed for Timothy is "power," coming from the Greek word *dunamis.* This word means "the ability to perform marvelous deeds," and, when speaking of Christians, it refers not to the *believer's* innate ability to accomplish things for the Lord, but rather to *God's* ability, working in and through the believer, to accomplish His purposes.[156] An example of this is found in Luke 1:49, in which Mary, the mother of Jesus, calls God the "Mighty" One when she was told that she would give birth to the Son of God. Using a form of the word *dunamis,* she realized that only a miracle could have led to conception for a virgin such as herself. In fact, this term is used regularly throughout Scripture (120 times in the New Testament!), ultimately because *everything* a believer accomplishes for the Gospel is empowered by God.

The second element Paul pointed out as part of Timothy's gifting

---

[156] John MacArthur, *The MacArthur New Testament Commentary: 2 Timothy* (Chicago: Moody, 1995), 18.

is "love," coming from the Greek word *agapé*. This type of love is not the emotional love of *philia*, nor is it the sensual love of *eros*. Instead, it is a love of the will—a love that puts others first and seeks the interest of others.[157] This love is listed among the fruit of the Spirit found in Galatians 5:22, allowing believers to carry out the same self-sacrificing service that our Savior Jesus Christ did. The Apostle John used the verb form of this love in 1 John 4:19 when he explained that we love because Christ first loved us. Thus, Paul reminded Timothy that part of his gifting included this crucial factor that would compel him to have compassion for others.

The final element Paul mentioned is "discipline," coming from the Greek word *sóphronismos*. Although this Greek word is a hapax legomenon (appearing only once in the entire New Testament), related forms of the word appear in verses such as Acts 26:25 and 1 Timothy 3:2, referring to prudence and self-control. Essentially, this word carries the idea of being able to determine the best course of action in a situation—discretion leading to wise behavior.[158]

Think back on the first two characteristics, "power" and "love," that were listed by Paul: on the one hand, a wrong understanding of power could have caused Timothy to behave in a prideful, domineering manner. On the other hand, a misguided grasp of love could have caused Timothy to be undiscerning and spineless. Many of us know of the kind of pastor who leads a heavy-handed ministry, running roughshod over helpless congregants, and we also know of the kind of pastor who is tolerant to a fault, leading a non-confrontational ministry of chaos. How could Timothy balance power

---

[157] John MacArthur, *The MacArthur New Testament Commentary: 2 Timothy* (Chicago: Moody, 1995), 18.
[158] George W. Knight, III, *The Pastoral Epistles: A Commentary on the Greek Text.* (Grand Rapids, MI: W.B. Eerdmans, 1992), 372.

and love in such a way that he would avoid either of these extremes? *Discipline.* This third characteristic is the element that determines how a person responds, based on an appropriate knowledge of the situation. Therefore, this characteristic enabled Timothy to apply the other two attributes in their proper amounts, so that he would be neither overbearing nor over-tolerant.[159] Thus, discipline was the final factor that would be critical for the stability of Timothy's ministry.

With these three elements of Timothy's gift, Paul highlighted the fact that God had adequately equipped Timothy for the mission. God hadn't simply dropped Timothy behind enemy lines without equipment and supplies—Paul clearly stated that God had *not* given Timothy a spirit of timidity. Instead, God equipped Timothy with power to carry out the task, love to have compassion for others, and discipline to maintain a balanced ministry.

But notice that when Paul reminded Timothy of these characteristics, he actually said, "God has not given *us* a spirit of timidity." The three elements of power, love, and discipline were not limited merely to Timothy, nor only to Timothy and Paul, but instead are granted to every believer in Jesus Christ. To be sure, Timothy's ordination to the role of pastor in the church was certainly specific to him—not all of us are granted that role. But the other characteristics (power, love, and discipline) are, in fact, given to each and every one of us.

This means that if you are a believer in Jesus Christ you are equipped for ministry with these same characteristics! When your human weakness becomes a discouragement to your ministry in the home, trust God to continue exercising His power through your frailty

---

[159] Verlyn D. Verbrugge, *The NIV Theological Dictionary of New Testament Words: An Abridgment of New International Dictionary of New Testament Theology* (Grand Rapids, MI: Zondervan Publishing House, 2000), 554.

(cf. 2 Cor. 12:9). On days when your patience is wearing thin with your kids, consider and reproduce the sacrificial love God has shown you (cf. John 13:34). And as you seek to balance expository parenting with all of the other duties in life, ask God for the discipline to help you stay on track without embittering your children (cf. Col. 3:21).

Simply put, you can carry out this task! More importantly, you *must* carry out this task. If you plan on outsourcing the development of your child's spiritual life, you are mistaken. There is much to be said for men and women who courageously evangelize on college campuses, in prisons, and near shopping centers. After all, the Bible indicates that disciples are primarily made by going out to meet lost people where they are. But make no mistake about it: if you're a parent, The Great Commission has come to you—in a bassinet, a booster seat, or a bunk-bed. We are all commanded to participate in The Great Commission, and a great deal of that participation occurs within the walls of our own homes.

As you pursue this endeavor, take time to truly understand this reality: *you are equipped.* You have been granted salvation (cf. Phil. 1:29). You have been granted all things pertaining to life and godliness (cf. 2 Pet. 1:3). You have been granted faithful pastors to lead you (cf. Eph. 4:11-13). And finally, when it comes to this unquestionably challenging work, you have not been given a spirit of timidity. Instead, you have been granted power, love, and discipline to accomplish this great mission from God.

10
SHEPHERDS UNTIL THE END

"In an emotional moment, I think: when I'm on my deathbed and my kids are all gathered around, I hope they remember those days. I hope they remember those days where they had a sinful, frail, fallible dad, but that dad was pointing them to the Lord Jesus Christ who never compromised."[160]

–Mike Abendroth

Focus Text: *For I am already being poured out as a drink offering, and the time of my departure has come. I have fought the good fight, I have finished the course, I have kept the faith; in the future there is laid up for me the crown of righteousness, which the Lord, the righteous Judge, will award to me on that day; and not only to me, but also to all who have loved His appearing.* (2 Timothy 4:6-8)

The year was 1517. A German professor had written a scholarly document questioning many of the practices found within the Roman Catholic Church. His knowledge of Catholic beliefs (such as the selling of indulgences and the idea of Purgatory) simply could not be reconciled with what he found in the Bible. Thus, he posted a list of objections to the door of the local university chapel. Although he was merely seeking to open up a theological discussion about these issues, the list was instead taken to print for duplication by

---

[160] Mike Abendroth, "No Compromise Radio: Family Worship" (online video clip), YouTube, February 25, 2014, https://www.youtube.com/watch?v=8ijXXtmcqTw.

students at the university, distributed throughout the area (with widespread acceptance), and ultimately became perceived as a full-blown attack on the Roman Catholic Church.[161] As it turned out, the fumes of the Protestant Reformation that had been building over the fifteenth-century were finally ignited by the spark of this sixteenth-century document.

The professor responsible for this was, of course, the Protestant Reformer Martin Luther, and his document is known as the *95 Theses*. With the catalyst of the *95 Theses*, the Reformation was officially underway and Luther would be known as the man responsible for it. The common people began to learn about the Bible's true teachings—that salvation is by grace alone through faith alone, that Purgatory is a manmade invention, and that all believers are part of a holy priesthood—contrary to what the Roman Catholic Church taught. And just like toothpaste when it's squeezed out of a tube, there was no going back. The average layman learned the true message of the Gospel; the religious bondage and spiritual chains were gone.

In 1518, Luther's writings were officially condemned as heretical. In 1520, Luther was commanded to recant his beliefs. And in 1521, Luther was formally excommunicated from the Roman Catholic Church, having defied the Pope himself, and declared to be a heretic and outlaw. [162] Thus began Luther's renegade-like ministry which pulled back the curtains of spiritual darkness in Germany and the surrounding countries. Centuries later, his life remains a blessing and inspiration to many.

But how exactly was one man capable of so much? What was

---

[161] Steven J. Lawson, *The Heroic Boldness of Martin Luther* (Orlando, FL: Reformation Trust Pub., 2013), 10.
[162] Bruce L. Shelley, *Church History in Plain Language, 4th ed.* (Nashville: Thomas Nelson, 2013), 253.

SHEPHERDS UNTIL THE END

ultimately the secret to his success? Undoubtedly, Luther was a bold intellectual. Certainly, he was a fearless leader. Clearly, he was a zealous pioneer. But the greatest revival in the history of Christianity (since the time of the apostles) was not brought about by these things. Like many of the other Reformers, we might be tempted to think that Luther's contributions to the cause were primarily those of a theologian or academic. And while he certainly fulfilled those roles, he served in an even greater capacity: as a preacher.

From 1510 until his death in 1546, Luther is known to have preached a whopping 7,000 sermons (an average of four per week).[163] Preaching sequentially through over thirty books of the Bible, in an average of three to five verse increments, Luther's chief aim was obvious: to deliver the divine mail.[164] He recognized that God's Word, which had been all but veiled and obscured by the Roman Catholic Church, was the key to spiritual freedom for his fellow countrymen. Implementing the practice of *lectio continua*, Luther dealt blow after blow (verse after verse!) to the Pope and his false religion through relentless preaching. The impact of Luther's work in this way can hardly be calculated. Yet, it wasn't Luther himself that made the Reformation a success. His own words disclose the true secret to what was accomplished:

> Take myself as an example. I have opposed the indulgences and all the papists, but never by force. I simply taught, preached, wrote God's Word; otherwise I did nothing. And then while I slept... the Word so greatly weakened the papacy, that never a prince or emperor inflicted such damage upon it. I did nothing. The Word did it all. Had I desired to

---

[163] Steven J. Lawson, *The Heroic Boldness of Martin Luther* (Orlando, FL: Reformation Trust Pub., 2013), 3.
[164] Steven J. Lawson, *The Heroic Boldness of Martin Luther.* Orlando, FL: Reformation Trust Pub., 2013), 68.

foment trouble, I could have brought great bloodshed upon Germany. Yea, I could have started such a little game at Worms that even the emperor would not have been safe. But what would it have been? A fool's play. I did nothing; I left it to the Word.[165]

Luther knew full well that if it had been up to him to conjure up persuasive arguments, the Reformation may have been nothing more than a religious flare up quickly extinguished by the state religion. Sure, it's possible that he could have started an uprising against the Pope using his own worldly ambition. Or perhaps there was enough despair among the common people that Luther could have leveraged their discontentment to begin a physical conflict. But Luther's great aim was to engage in *spiritual* warfare—knocking down any and all arguments that set themselves up against the true Gospel of salvation by grace alone, through faith alone, in Christ alone (cf. 2 Cor. 10:5).

Undoubtedly, he knew that a superficial strategy would only provide superficial change. Thus, he unleashed the Word of God and rested in the comfort of knowing that the Holy Spirit would use this double-edged sword to pierce the hearts of his hearers (cf. Heb. 4:12). Looking back on what had been accomplished, he had to admit that he did nothing; the Word did it all.

As you look to disciple your children in the knowledge of the Lord Jesus Christ, you too ought to rely on the Word with Luther's level of commitment. If the Word of God was powerful enough to rescue an entire continent from spiritual darkness in the sixteenth and seventeenth centuries, it can surely work wonders in the lives of your children. As Pastor Steve Lawson says, "Every season of reformation

---

[165] John S. Oyer, *Lutheran Reformers Against Anabaptists: Luther, Melanchthon, and Menius, and the Anabaptists of Central Germany* (The Hague: M. Nijhoff, 1964), 33.

and every hour of spiritual awakening has been ushered in by a recovery of biblical preaching."[166] Such an awakening is desperately needed in the modern family. Will you carry the Reformation from the church to the couch? Deliver the full counsel of God to your children, and you can trust that it will produce the same spiritual refreshment for your family that is has for saints of past generations. God's Word will give your children a balanced faith, a united faith, and a mature faith.

A Balanced Faith

One of the pitfalls of a preaching ministry that doesn't teach the Bible verse by verse is its susceptibility to imbalance. Because topics and themes are selected by the pastor, there is a great danger in portraying a lopsided version of Christianity. Too much wrath? Not enough grace? Too much Heaven? Not enough Hell? How can the topical pastor know that he is accurately representing the various aspects of the faith in the appropriate amounts? He can't.

Thus, in most cases there is simply an ongoing and unaddressed disparity in what comes out of the pulpit. Scores of churches are characterized by a "love-only" version of Christianity—not simply the God who is love (as 1 John 4:8 teaches), but a god who is *only* love. On the other hand, there are also a number of "hate-only" churches—teaching not only of the God who is angry with the wicked every day (as Psalm 7:11 says), but a god who is *only* angry. These examples represent the radical ends of the non-expository spectrum.

But what about churches that haven't fallen into one of these two theological ditches? In many cases, the balance is simply left up to the

---

[166] Steve Lawson "Preach the Word," *Tabletalk Magazine*, Ligonier Ministries, January 1, 2010.

pastor's discretion; he attempts to "discern" what his church needs to hear, and responds accordingly. And while this may sound spiritual, what it actually resembles is a car that has hit a patch of ice on the road—swerving one way causes the driver to overcorrect and swerve back the other way, which then causes the driver to counter back to the other side of the road, and on it goes. As he looks over the coming months, this kind of pastor prepares his sermon series in such a way that after preaching about a "negative" topic like sin, the lake of fire, or Satan, he makes sure to plug in a series (or two) about "positive" things like grace, unity, and friendship. He maintains a sense of balance by swerving back and forth to make sure that each topical angle offsets the other. In some cases, pastors even determine their topics based on the frequency with which they believe certain issues should be taught—making sure to address "fan-favorite" topics such as marriage, finances, and leadership every so many months or years.

But this kind of topical tightrope was never meant to be walked by pastors. Rather than trying to maintain self-determined balance, the pastor that performs verse-by-verse preaching will find rest in the balance Scripture provides. Sequential exposition aligns the preacher with the same proportions of topics and themes found in Scripture. God's Word dictates how much time to commit to each and every aspect of the faith by virtue of the amount of Scripture that has been written about it.

Similarly, how do we as parents know that we are properly representing Christianity to our kids? What can we do to make sure we speak enough about the various topics and doctrines of the faith? We must first come to realize that such a decision was never ours to make.

One pitfall that we are liable to make as we raise our kids is to try to overcorrect for the religious imbalances of our own upbringing.

Think about it: those who grew up in a harsh, and perhaps legalistic, Christian home may find themselves trying to avoid that error with their own kids by downplaying Christian obedience, overstating God's patience, or outright denying essential elements of organized religion such as church attendance. On the other hand, those who grew up in an unrestrained, and perhaps licentious, home may notice a tendency to understate Christian freedom, deemphasize God's love, or portray their own manmade rules as biblical law.

How do we avoid these errors? How do we remove our own bias, as much as is humanly possible, as we disciple our children? By letting God's Word speak for God. As we commit to expository parenting, our ministry in the home will find the correct theological balance on its own, because each passage will address topics in the God-ordained amount. And as we complete the task of delivering the entire Bible to our kids, the result will be a well-rounded faith that recognizes the multi-faceted aspects of Christianity.

For example, one of the greatest areas of concern for Christian parents, and rightly so, is the area of sexual purity. Because of how serious an issue this is, it is perhaps one of the most difficult to address in a balanced and biblical fashion. On the one hand, a great number of parents are much too laidback in their approach to this issue. They speak lightly on the subject, conveying no tone of seriousness regarding the great temptation of sexual sin. In some cases, they may avoid the issue altogether, feeling uncomfortable or ill-equipped to tackle the subject with their children. The common outcome of this is a child who has little to no spiritual compass in the area of sexuality, leaving him or her susceptible to deviancy of every kind—ultimately becoming a follower of whatever society portrays as acceptable.

On the other hand, a number of parents strongly oppose sexual sin, but do so in such a heavy-handed way that they portray sex itself as inherently bad or "filthy." This type of parent presents sex as an evil that is to be avoided at all costs, creating a culture of condemnation and guilt for children who would dare to have any sexual thought cross their minds. Often times, the outcome of this end of the spectrum is a child who has a very skewed and unhealthy view of sex itself, making it difficult to find godly joy when he or she gets married and is free to engage in sexual activity. Prior to marriage, a teenage boy in such a home is often left with the unbearable burden of trying to artificially suppress even the idea of sexual development in his life.

What do both of these ends of the spectrum lack? *Balance.* Godly balance. Where can we find the corrective? Exposition of the Bible. By teaching the full counsel of God, you can rest assured that you are treating this area of the Christian life not from a particular perspective that you believe to be adequate, but with the perspective that God Himself has determined to be adequate.

Faithfully exposit the Scriptures verse by verse and you will address the area of sexuality according to God's intended proportion. You will preach the seriousness of sexual offenses as they are listed, described, and condemned throughout Scripture. As you work your way through the Bible, your child will see the unintended consequences of polygamy. They will learn of the Seventh Commandment given to Moses on Mt. Sinai. They will see the devastating effects of King David's sin with Bathsheba. They will hear of Jesus' teaching about lust in the Sermon on the Mount. They will be exposed to Paul's reminder that homosexuality is a form of God's judgment. They will understand the spiritual significance of the harlot in the book of Revelation. The wickedness of sexual sin will come across resoundingly clear through verse-by-verse exposition of the Scriptures.

But you will also preach the beauty of marital intimacy as it is found, described, and exalted throughout Scripture. Your children will learn of the origins of the one-man, one-woman union created in the Garden. They will hear Proverbs that describe the blessing that comes from the wife of one's youth. They will learn, in quite vivid detail, of the joys of intimacy found in Song of Solomon. They will be taught by Paul that marriage is God's gracious provision and protection for those with sexual desires. And most of all, they will discover that the faithful intimacy of a man and his wife represents the glorious Gospel of Jesus Christ, the Savior who came from Heaven to redeem His bride, the church.

God's Word will do the balancing for you. It will do the convicting for you. It will do the exalting for you. It will do all of the heavy lifting in every single area of the Christian life, if you simply commit to teaching it.

A United Faith

Undoubtedly, one of the most critical aspects of the local church is unity. In fact, much of the New Testament was written to help believers stand united (cf. 1 Cor. 1:10, Rom. 15:5-7). One of the greatest examples of this unity is found in Acts 2:42-47, which speaks of those in the early church as having "all things in common," sharing their possessions "as anyone might have need," and eating meals "together with gladness." This paradigm for local church life provides an immense amount of instruction for us today. The Holy Spirit was obviously working in powerful ways to bring about a sense of oneness to these Christians, many of whom had come from other nations to celebrate the Passover Feast (cf. Acts 2:5-11). How then was there was such immediate unity?

Ask the average churchman today how to bring about this kind of unity, and you are likely to get an answer that essentially says, "Don't nitpick doctrine. Just love God and love others." There is a great desire in many churches to have the kind of unity seen in the early church, but the means and purposes of obtaining that unity are often misguided.

Truth be told, a number of churches today are looking to unite simply for the sake of unity, fellowship for the sake of fellowship, and be in community for the sake of community. Interpersonal relationships are the number one priority to be pursued, no matter the cost. A church such as this becomes a type of spiritual country club in which success is measured solely by how well people get along and how many new members are added to the club each month.

But when relationships become priority number one, what ultimately must go by the wayside? Doctrine. Biblical teaching. Theology. Why? Because in order to create an offenseless environment, a place in which all perspectives are welcome and relationships thrive without friction, sound teaching must be downplayed. Some churches would even go so far as to neglect biblical and doctrinal teaching *intentionally* for the purpose of providing so-called "unity." We see this mentality articulated in phrases like "doctrine divides" or "deeds, not creeds." In effect, this mindset believes that fellowship is enhanced when theology is softened.

And what facilitates such a perspective? Topical and other non-expository forms of preaching. When doctrinal depth is nothing but an obstacle to be overcome, hand-picked verses from the Bible provide the solution. Skipping the contentious parts of Scripture allows superficial unity to continue uninterrupted.

But the reality is that God's Word *is* inherently divisive (cf. Matt. 10:34, 2 Tim. 4:3). Truth, by its very nature, cannot coexist with error. Theological perspectives do have the potential to create gaps in relationships. And as God's Word is taught there will be non-negotiable truths presented. But what is often forgotten is that God's

SHEPHERDS UNTIL THE END

Word is also inherently *unifying*. Doctrine is actually the most critical factor for uniting believers (cf. John 17:17-21). And in fact, apart from sound doctrine, the best one can hope for is simply a form of shallow sentimentalism.

Revisiting the account of the local church found in Acts 2:42 shows us the true secret to biblical unity: "They were continually devoting themselves to the apostles' teaching and to fellowship, to the breaking of bread and to prayer." What is the first thing in the list that caused believers to join together in harmony? *The apostles' teaching.* Some who were present on the day of Pentecost were native to Jerusalem, while others were foreigners from surrounding nations, and it was sound doctrine that bridged whatever cultural or social gaps that may have been present. The apostles' teaching is what provided the renewing of their minds in order to bring about unity, because it led them all to learn the same things about reality, believe the same things about Jesus, and respond to the same truths in their lives. Thus, as they continued together in their newfound faith, it was God's Word (not emotional sentimentality) that formed the unbreakable bond.

The harmonious nature of the early church can also characterize your home. We often think that preaching is the act of pouring God's Word into the mind of the hearer, and certainly that is true. But have you also considered just the opposite? That the hearer's mind is actually being poured into God's Word? Just as liquid metal is cast into a mold to shape it into the finished product, so too is the believer's mind cast into the mold of God's Word to form him into Christlikeness. In fact, in Romans 6:17 Paul even refers to God's Word as a type of "pattern" or "mold" to which believers are conformed once they are saved from sin. Thus, when the Bible is taught in its entirety, it causes believers to be conformed into one mind, bringing about spiritual unity and common purpose. This same deep and abiding unity also occurs when you teach your children "the apostles' doctrine" at home. Your children will learn biblical truths from you that will form them into the same doctrinal pattern.

Furthermore, unity is not only caused by the doctrine that is produced by sequential exposition, but also in the very effort of sequential exposition itself. Think about the united purpose that would develop if you, your spouse, your parents, your friends, and your local church all came together in a joint effort: teaching the full counsel of God to your children. Such an effort (which is simply the outworking of The Great Commission) puts all involved parties into a common cause together. The coordinated effort is unifying. You and your spouse are teaching the Bible and catechizing your children daily, your pastor is leading your children through the Bible each Sunday, and your friends are being encouraged to do the same in the lives of their own children. Pouring God's Word into the lives of disciples becomes the common cause, as it should be.

As you take the initiative in expository parenting, seeking the help of others in that endeavor, you have the opportunity to experience precisely the kind of unity that is presented in Scripture. You will be of one mind, pursuing one goal. Fellowship will be real, deep, and meaningful. And the result, according to God's grace, is that your kids will be brought up in a faith that is not only aligned with yours, but more importantly, aligned with the truth of God's Word. Expository parenting requires a united purpose, relying on united minds, resulting in a united faith.

A Mature Faith

Finally, one major effect of sequential exposition is that it forces us to learn, study, consider, and obey the portions of our Bible that we either have not known about, or that we might not necessarily find appealing—which ultimately matures us. Because the text is simply taught and explained in order, we become confronted with truths that would have otherwise been avoided.

In a moment of honesty, many of us would have to admit that there are cobwebs in certain corners of our Bibles—passages that have been long neglected. When it comes to these passages, not only have we never ventured to study them, but many pastors have never ventured to teach them to us. As a result, our spiritual growth has been stunted. Like a child eating candy for dinner instead of vegetables, we might survive and look healthy on the outside for a time, but inwardly we are malnourished and wasting away.

Living in a day and age characterized by triviality, we find many churches avoiding issues like death, coming judgment, persecution, and other topics of a serious nature. The Bible says that eternity is set in the heart of man (cf. Ecc. 3:11) and yet man does everything in his power to suppress the notion that anything other than the here and now is relevant to his existence. Phrases like "You Only Live Once" fuel the secularist's juvenile and reckless behavior, and although many churches would adamantly reject such a perspective, the overall childishness of culture has had an undeniable effect on church ministry.

Clearly, there are many church leaders whose thinking and behavior is just as sophomoric as what is seen in culture at large. But even among the more dignified, there has been a noticeable drift to cater preaching to those with an immature appetite and unsophisticated palette for biblical truth. Man-centered preaching that focuses on the congregations wants and desires, rather than God-centered preaching that focuses on His wants and desires, constitutes much of what passes as biblical instruction. Of course, from the hearer's perspective there is nothing wrong—a church that mentions the name of Jesus, claims to love people, and at least opens the Bible on Sunday mornings is considered to be more than faithful.

Yet, at its heart, leading a congregation month after month with topical messages does little more than affirm that natural bent in our hearts to neglect the more difficult elements of the faith. And for some who preach, that is precisely the intent of using the Bible in such a fashion. After all, if a pastor's mentality is to "give the people what they want," you can be sure that what the people *don't* want is preaching that touches on issues like the universal depravity of man, the thousand-year reign of Christ, or the sovereignty of God in salvation. Those topics are not likely to be considered relevant or exciting to the average churchgoer who's looking for a quick fix to his marriage problems, career stresses, or financial woes. And yet, a faith that has been matured by verse-by-verse exposition is *precisely* what is needed for such issues.

The ability to see beyond the here and now, to "set your mind on things above, not on the things that are on earth" (Col. 3:2), is exactly what the struggling believer needs for daily life. Why? Because a believer that has been taught through each book of the Bible has received a God-centered perspective of the situations he faces in life. This kind of person is able to view a difficulty in life more according to the way God sees it (as but one moment in His grand redemptive plan), rather than in the way man sees it (as an inescapable situation with no hope in sight). An immature faith, on the other hand, is less capable of withstanding the worrisome aspects of life in a God-glorifying manner—aspects such as grieving to the glory of God, being persecuted to the glory of God, suffering to the glory of God, and so on.

Yet, the apostles leave us with an example to follow—they didn't turn to Greek philosophy (the secular psychology of their day) in order to deal with difficulties, but instead continued "looking for the blessed hope and the appearing of the glory of our great God and Savior, Christ Jesus" (Titus 2:13). When you have never been led to examine the far-reaches of God's Word you are left only to focus on things here and now, and the strength of your faith ultimately becomes a product of circumstance rather than Scripture. But by being taught the entire Bible verse by verse, a believer's heart and mind are exposed to passages that force them to reorient their thinking and conform it more to God's thinking, preparing their minds to respond to troubles with an eternal perspective.

Sequential exposition takes its hearers to eternity past, when God chose to redeem us. Sequential exposition takes its hearers to eternity future, when Jesus will create a new Heaven and new earth for us. And sequential exposition takes its hearers to the foot of the cross, the centerpiece of history, in which our redemption was accomplished.

With that said, expository parenting will give your children this deep knowledge of life, God, man, and salvation, among other things. And when God's Word becomes implanted in their hearts and minds, they can rely upon it during difficult times. Their faith becomes matured by Scripture, ready to be tested by trials.

A.W. Pink, in his momentous work on God's sovereignty, likewise affirms that our ability to glorify God is intricately linked with our eternal perspective:

> Here is the fundamental difference between the man of faith and the man of unbelief. The unbeliever is "of the world," judges everything by worldly standards, views life from the standpoint of time and sense, and weighs everything in the balances of his own carnal making. But the man of faith brings in God, looks at everything from His standpoint, estimates values by spiritual standards, and views life in the light of eternity. Doing

this, he receives whatever comes as from the hand of God. Doing this, his heart is calm in the midst of the storm. Doing this, he rejoices in hope of the glory of God.[167]

Paul's preaching was intended to present every man complete in Christ (Col. 1:28), and we must strive to present our children accordingly. The eternal perspective that is characteristic of mature saints comes only by way of the Word of God (cf. 1 Pet. 2:2, John 17:17). Just as making your child eat green beans (even though he wants candy) keeps him healthy and matures his palette, so too will expository parenting keep him spiritually healthy and develop his love for the Bible. When it comes to physical growth, it's impossible to see the impact that proper nutrition immediately provides. Likewise, it may not be possible to see the day-to-day spiritual growth that expository parenting provides. But time will vindicate its great necessity.

Until the Chief Shepherd Appears

So how did the story end for Paul and Timothy? Like any man on his death bed, the Apostle Paul had his own mortality on his mind throughout this second letter. Unlike his first imprisonment years prior, Paul knew that there would be no release this time around. But he was able to face the end with confidence, joy, and hope. He knew that he had faithfully passed on the entire New Covenant message to Timothy; he had completed the course of ministry that was ordained for him by God.

When departing from the Ephesian church earlier in his ministry, his conscience was clear because he had faithfully declared the whole

---

[167] A.W. Pink, *The Sovereignty of God & The Attributes of God* (Louisville, KY: GLH, 2014), 81.

purpose of God to them (cf. Acts 20:26-27). His final words to Timothy in this letter reflect that same settled disposition:

> For I am already being poured out as a drink offering, and the time of my departure has come. I have fought the good fight, I have finished the course, I have kept the faith; in the future there is laid up for me the crown of righteousness, which the Lord, the righteous Judge, will award to me on that day; and not only to me, but also to all who have loved His appearing. (2 Timothy 4:6-8)

In writing this letter, Paul gave Timothy a number of instructions to remind and encourage him to be a faithful messenger of God's Word. But perhaps the greatest influence on Timothy was Paul's own life; Paul served as a model of the very letter he sent, even to the very end. By saying that he was "being poured out as a drink offering," Paul indicated not only that he knew he was at the end of his life, but that he considered even those final moments to be an act of worship to the God he loved and served (cf. Rom. 12:1).[168] Although Paul's death is not recorded in the Bible, church history tells us that Paul was beheaded in Rome shortly after writing this final letter. In a strange irony, he lost his head to gain a crown—and gain it he undoubtedly did.

Certainly, Paul was just like us in that he was born a sinner in need of saving grace (cf. 1 Tim. 1:15). He was not a perfect man. Yet the message he had for Timothy came across just as clear as it had to the Corinthian church: "Be imitators of me, just as I also am of Christ" (1 Cor. 11:1). Since pastors are to serve as examples to the flock, knowing

---

[168] Tremper Longman, III and David E. Garland, *The Expositor's Bible Commentary. Vol. 12, Ephesians–Philemon* (Grand Rapids, MI: Zondervan, 2006), 594.

that they will receive a crown of glory when the Chief Shepherd appears (cf. 1 Pet. 5:1-4), it is no surprise that God mightily used the Apostle Paul as a trophy of grace that Timothy could look to as an example of a biblical, God-honoring minister.

In fact, his spiritual son Timothy did carry on the legacy to the extent that he suffered persecution for it. This is attested to at the end of the book of Hebrews, in which we read, "Take notice that our brother Timothy has been released, with whom, if he comes soon, I will see you" (Heb. 13:23). Apparently, Paul's example left such an impact on Timothy that he was willing to go to prison for the sake of the Word. Timothy knew that despite his own imprisonment, the Word of God could never be imprisoned, just as his mentor said (cf. 2 Tim. 2:9). Timothy was committed to the Word regardless of the cost, just as his mentor commanded (cf. 2 Tim. 4:2). And Timothy overcame the timidity that was stifling his ministry, just as his mentor desired (cf. 2 Tim. 1:6-7). Ultimately, he lived up to his own theophoric name, "Timothy," which means "one who honors God."

Know this: if Timothy was able to draw on Paul's letter for guidance, you can too. Do not be discouraged or intimidated by expository parenting; you can carry out the task. Unlike Paul, this may not cost you your life, yet you are still encouraged to spend it. No one may take your life for expository parenting, yet you are still encouraged to give it. Like Paul and Timothy, you too must use your life to minister the Word. You too must shepherd your children verse by verse until the Chief Shepherd appears, looking forward to that glorious day when we are united with Him and awarded crowns of righteousness.

The time you have at home with your children will go faster than you can imagine. May you be able to enter into eternity having delivered all of God's Word to them while they were young, leaving a legacy of expository parenting for them to follow. Dad, you will not say at the end of your life, "I wish I would have spent more time out on the golf course, instead of studying and teaching the Bible to my family." Instead, you will greatly rejoice in a wise son who is following the Lord (cf. Prov. 23:24). Mom, you will not say at the end of your life, "I wish I would have pursued a professional career, rather than stayed at home teaching my children." Instead, you will be filled with gladness when they thank you for all of your godly counsel (cf. Prov. 31:28). More than anything, though, you will be able to face the time of your own departure like Paul—with the joy of having lived out a Spirit-empowered, God-glorifying ministry that prepared the next generation of believers for The Great Commission.

After all, the work of expository parenting must be completed by every generation. One generation's faithfulness will provide a tremendous benefit to subsequent generations, but the struggle to teach the full counsel of God is one that will need to be fought repeatedly. Once you finish your leg of the race in the lives of your children, they will need to pick up the baton and run their leg with their own children. Ultimately, they must adopt the mentality that Pastor John MacArthur articulates:

> We who love the Lord and His church must not sit by while the church gains momentum on the down-grade of worldliness and compromise. Men and women before us have paid with their blood to deliver the faith intact to us. Now it is our turn to guard the truth. It is a task that calls for courage, not compromise. And it is a responsibility that demands unwavering devotion to a very narrow purpose.[169]

---

[169] John MacArthur, *Ashamed of the Gospel: When the Church Becomes Like the World* (Wheaton, IL: Crossway, 1993), 55.

At the same time, the reality is that once your children have left your home, that doesn't mean your shepherding days are over. Just as the Bible nowhere portrays a pastor retiring from ministry, neither should parents consider their work done once they have an empty nest.

On the contrary, Paul was committed to ministry until his dying moments, just like the other apostles (cf. 2 Pet. 1:14-15). Sure, your work of shepherding in your child's adult life will differ from their time in childhood. Your relationship with them will look more like that of co-laborers (which is actually a good indication that your efforts truly bore fruit). But the fact is, the concept of multi-generational discipleship also extends to grandchildren (cf. Deut. 4:9, 6:2). Even more, there are multitudes of "spiritual children" within the church who would undoubtedly benefit from the guidance of someone who has taught through the entire Bible (cf. 3 John 1:4, 1 Thess. 2:11-12). Will you continue the work as long as God gives you breath?

In the end, we have to recognize that we've been entrusted with an incredible treasure to deliver. The Bible, like a 66-sided jewel, demonstrates the glory of God in the salvation of sinners through the Gospel of Jesus Christ. So, rather than exhausting ourselves chasing the endless barrage of parenting "techniques" and "tricks" (which ultimately fail), we as parents must return to the simple but effective means God has given for raising up disciples. We must devote ourselves to "prayer and the ministry of the word" (Acts 6:4). Anything less represents, at best, an ungrateful spirit towards the God who has graciously saved us and granted us His Word to deliver. So deliver it, we must.

To those men and women who love Jesus Christ, love the Word of God, love their families, love their local church, and love the lost, expository parenting is the way forward—not because it is one new method among many, but because it is the God-honoring application of pastoral principles written long ago.

So, do you want to lead your children to saving faith? Preach the Word! And the Law of Moses in Exodus will thunder down on their natural self-righteousness. Do you want to instill in your young ones a strong work ethic? Preach the Word! And King Solomon's wisdom in Proverbs will address their sluggish tendencies. Do you want to cultivate harmony among your children? Preach the Word! And the incarnational humility of Christ in the book of Philippians will provide the template. Do you want to prepare your son to love his future wife? Preach the Word! And the Apostle Paul's letter to the Ephesians will plumb the depths of Christ's sacrificial love for His bride, the church. Do you want to equip your kids with principles of discernment? Preach the Word! And Jude's characterization of spiritual impostors will prepare their minds and sober their spirits. Do you want to comfort your daughter when her faith is under attack? Preach the Word! And the spiritual balm of the Apostle Peter's first letter will provide the divine comfort. Do you want to explain to your children the pitfalls of a post-modern worldview? Preach the Word! And the writer of Judges will describe the ensuing moral chaos when every man does what seems right in his own eyes. Do you want to inspire your children to evangelize their peers? Preach the Word! And Luke's historical precision in the book of Acts will motivate their feet to spread the good news.

Although we are incapable, in our own power, to change the hearts and minds of our children, God has given us His authoritative, trustworthy, effective, clear, and sufficient Word. And in the end, when it comes to expository parenting, you do nothing—the Word does it all.

Made in United States
North Haven, CT
22 July 2025

70912549R00167